DEVOTIONS™

January

Eileen H. Wilmoth, editor
photo by Ward Patterson
Volume 42

© 1998 The STANDARD PUBLISHING Co., 8121 Hamilton Avenue, Cincinnati, Ohio, 45231, a division of STANDEX INTERNATIONAL Corp. Topics based on Home Daily Bible Readings, International Sunday School lessons, © 1995 by the Lesson Committee. Printed in U.S.A.

GOOD CITIZENS

SCRIPTURE: Romans 13:1-10

VERSE FOR TODAY: Seek the peace of the city where I have caused you to be carried away captive, and pray to the Lord for it; for in its peace you will have peace (Jeremiah 29:7, *New King James Version*).

HYMN FOR TODAY: "God of Our Fathers"

Have you ever noticed a parent who guides a child with his eyes? The child obeys, and they have love and respect for one another. The child knows that the rules are for his own good.

God has delegated His authority to parents, teachers, employers, and governments. Christians are to demonstrate responsible behavior, living to glorify God and enrich society. Civil government is a provision of God to uphold right and overthrow wrong. Love provides the motive to cooperate and encourage good government.

Jeremiah encouraged people to pray for peace. We who believe that God hears and answers prayer have a wonderful opportunity to support our leaders. In 2 Timothy 2:1, Paul encouraged young Timothy to make intercession and give thanks for all those in authority. We, too, can lift our leaders up to God in prayer.

Christians have been instructed to be salt and light in their communities. Salt gives flavor and holds back corruption, and light shines forth to keep people on the right path.

PRAYER THOUGHTS: Father, we ask for Your wisdom and guidance for government leaders. Teach us all to overcome evil with good. For Thine is the kingdom and the power and the glory, amen.

January 1-3. **Dorothy N. Snyder** lives with her husband, Wilbert, in Boulder, Colorado. She is a retired business woman and writes a monthly column for her church newsletter.

LOVE BUILDS TRUST

SCRIPTURE: 1 Corinthians 8:1-6

VERSE FOR TODAY: There is no fear in love; but perfect love casts out fear, because fear involves torment. But he who fears has not been made perfect in love (1 John 4:18, *New King James Version*).

HYMN FOR TODAY: "Love Lifted Me"

A man had just buried his wife. His little daughter had lost her mother. Their hearts seemed to be breaking, and loneliness engulfed them as they came into an empty house. At bedtime the father placed the little girl's bed near his own. Then he turned out the light and lay down. After a while, through the darkness, came the little girl's voice, "Daddy, are you there?"

And he answered, "Yes, Dear, I'm here. Now you go to sleep."

After a period of silence, the little voice came again, "Daddy, are you still there?

Once again he answered patiently, "Yes, Dear, I'm still here. Now you go to sleep."

After a long period of silence her voice came again, this time more confident, "Daddy, I can't see you, but I know you're there."

Social pressures brought calamity to the Israelites when they disregarded God's laws and forgot His abiding presence. We, too, live in a world where many gods compete for our loyalty. Yet, even though we seem trapped by our fears, let us never forget the security of God's love.

PRAYER THOUGHTS: Father, we thank You for Your abiding presence. Deliver us from the pride that would undermine the faith of another. Teach us to love as Jesus loved. Amen.

THE GREATEST GIFT

SCRIPTURE: 1 John 4:7-12

VERSE FOR TODAY: And now abide faith, hope, love, these three; but the greatest of these is love (1 Corinthians 13:13, *New King James Version*).

HYMN FOR TODAY: "Why Should He Love Me So?"

A person knelt as he washed the gangrenous sores on the swollen, inflamed body of a soldier in battle. A passerby turned away and said, "I wouldn't do that for a million dollars."

The other replied, "Neither would I."

Only the love of God can inspire and motivate us to bring our noblest love to man's gravest needs. God's love, when channeled through us, can heal many of the hurts of the world.

A forgiving and selfless love is the natural response of a life surrendered to God and in whom His Spirit dwells. It differs from the love of things and the cheap attachment people sometimes display in the news media. The love that God wants to see in His people is not possessive, anxious to impress, inflated with its own importance, touchy, or such that gloats over the wickedness of other people.

Humankind is hungering for a demonstration of a love that knows no end of its endurance. What a challenge to older or housebound persons who can demonstrate love through prayer!

What a privilege to join Jesus in prayer for the hurting and needy people far and wide who all need His aroma of love!

PRAYER THOUGHTS: Our Father in Heaven, open our eyes to see You as we've never seen You before. Open our ears to hear Your Spirit speaking. Open our hearts to embrace the world in Your love. In Jesus' name, amen.

RICH TOWARD GOD

SCRIPTURE: Luke 12:13-21

VERSE FOR TODAY: Then he said to them, "Watch out! Be on your guard against all kinds of greed; a man's life does not consist in the abundance of his possessions" (Luke 12:15, *New International Version*).

HYMN FOR TODAY: "O Perfect Love"

Today's Scripture reading contains a parable of a man who did not have his priorities straight. The story was prompted by a person in the crowd listening to the teaching of Jesus. We can guess that a dispute over inheritance arose between two brothers and one of the men, seeing Jesus as a fair man, sought to have Jesus settle the case. A lesson followed on what is really important in one's life.

The rich fool looked at his full barns and concluded that he had sufficiently provided for himself. All that remained for him was a lifetime of enjoyment. The rich man was a fool. At the end of the day he died. This man was not rich toward God.

Life requires decisions with eternal consequences. We can be so earthbound that we are unable to see the eternal picture. The only way to see the "big picture" is to use God's vision of His creation. God has purpose and meaning for our lives that reach into eternity. When we realize this purpose and meaning in Christ, we become rich toward God and in harmony with God's will for our lives.

PRAYER THOUGHTS: God, give us the courage to see our lives in the light of eternity; to release the temporal and hold fast to all that is good. Lord, we are thankful for Your blessings and provisions. We acknowledge that it all comes from You and Your grace. Amen.

January 4-10. **Dr. Willard Walls** and his wife, Ruth, are church planters in Great Britian where they conduct family seminars and a counseling ministry.

NO WORRY, NO FEAR

SCRIPTURE: Luke 12:22-34

VERSE FOR TODAY: But seek his kingdom, and these things will be given to you as well (Luke 12:31, *New International Version*).

HYMN FOR TODAY: "I Heard the Voice of Jesus Say"

"Not to worry" is a common expression among the British when they want you to understand that something is not all that important. Someone who is constantly anxious about things is sometimes call a worrywart. Few people have worry-free lives. Nonetheless, Jesus emphatically tells us not to worry. It is not a suggestion, it is a commandment. We miss what life is all about when we let worry dominate our thoughts. Worry offers no positive change in anything we do. It degrades our quality of life. Jesus provides all that we need.

Why do we worry? Jesus hints as to the reason we worry—lack of faith and fear. Look around at God's creation. The flowers and birds are provided for by God. We, too, are God's creation and He will provide for us.

Jesus knows us well: "O you of little faith!" The disciples sleeping in the boat awakened to a fierce storm and feared for their lives: "O you of little faith!" Peter walking on the water took his eyes off Jesus. Jesus said to Peter, "O you of little faith." Again He said these words to the disciples in Luke 12:28. Place your faith in Jesus; trust in His words. Jesus is in control.

PRAYER THOUGHTS: Heavenly Father, forgive the times when we lack faith and confidence that You are in control. In our hearts we know that You will provide for our every need. Help us through the Spirit to live His truth out in our daily lives. Amen.

AMBUSHED BY GREED

SCRIPTURE: Proverbs 1:8-19

VERSE FOR TODAY: But among you there must not be even a hint of sexual immorality, or of any kind of impurity, or of greed, because these are improper for God's holy people (Ephesians 5:3, *New International Version*).

HYMN FOR TODAY: "Cleanse Me"

Monkey trappers in North Africa have a method of catching their prey. Gourds are filled with nuts and firmly fastened to a branch of a tree. Each has a hole large enough for the unwary monkey to stick his forepaw into it. When the hungry animal discovers this, he quickly grasps a handful of nuts, but the hole is too small for him to withdraw his clenched fist. The monkey doesn't have enough sense to open up his hand and let go in order to escape, so he is easily taken captive.

The daily papers regularly report consequences of crimes that result from greed. When in court the defendant will often blame his crime on the influence of others in his or her life. We are influenced by others. We can become victims very easily. Today's text warns us to choose our associates carefully and fastidiously avoid those that attempt to involve us in greedy ambitions.

Parents have a grave responsibility in guiding and instructing their children in the way of the Lord. That responsibility includes helping the children find the right friends; those that share the same godly values and goals as your family.

PRAYER THOUGHTS: Lord, thank You for Your wise counsel and guidance from the Scripture. We pray that You will bring into our lives wise mentors and companions that will help us walk in Your will. Forgive us for our vain ambitions and creed. Create in us hearts that are content with what You provide for our physical and spiritual well-being. Amen.

NEVER SATISFIED

SCRIPTURE: Ecclesiastes 5:1-10

VERSE FOR TODAY: Whoever loves money never has money enough; whoever loves wealth is never satisfied with his income. This too is meaningless (Ecclesiastes 5:10, *New International Version*).

HYMN FOR TODAY: "Through All the Changing Scenes of Life"

There's a true story that comes from the sinking of the *Titanic*. A frightened woman found her place in a lifeboat that was about to be lowered into the raging North Atlantic. She suddenly thought of something she needed, so she asked permission to return to her stateroom before they cast off.

She ran across the deck that was already slanted at a dangerous angle. She raced through the gambling room with all the money that had rolled to one side, ankle deep. She came to her stateroom and quickly pushed aside her diamond rings and costly items as she reached to the shelf above her bed and grabbed three small oranges.

Now that seems incredible because thirty minutes earlier she would not have chosen a crate of oranges over even the smallest diamond. But death had boarded the *Titanic*. One blast of its awful breath had transformed all values. Instantaneously, priceless things had become worthless. Worthless things had become priceless. And in that moment she preferred three small oranges to a crate of diamonds.

The writer of Ecclesiastes writes, "The lover of money will not be satisfied with money; nor the lover of wealth, with gain" (Ecclesiastes 5:10, *New Revised Standard Version*).

PRAYER THOUGHTS: Heavenly Father, we find true satisfaction only in You. Help us choose those things in life that bring pleasure to You. Place in our lives the ability to discern what has eternal value. In Jesus' name, we pray, amen.

TRUST IN THE LORD

SCRIPTURE: Jeremiah 17:5-11

VERSE FOR TODAY: But blessed is the man who trusts in the LORD, whose confidence is in him (Jeremiah 17:7, *New International Version*).

HYMN FOR TODAY: "Thou Art Worthy"

A missionary in Africa had been witnessing faithfully to a certain individual. Following their conversation one day, the unconverted man placed a small statue and a silver coin on the table before him. Then he took two slips of paper and wrote something on each. Putting one beside the image and the other with the money, he turned to the Christian worker and said, "Please read this." On the note by the idol were written the words, "Heathen god." The sheet next to the coin bore the inscription, "Christian god." From what that needy soul had observed in the lives of the merchants from so-called "Christian" nations, he concluded that money was their god and the object of their devotion!

Don't put your trust in anything but the true and living God. Trust placed elsewhere is misguided and fruitless. One who fails to rely completely in God's grace will find that he lives in a wasteland. The prophet Jeremiah tells us that trusting in the Lord is like having an unending supply of life-giving nourishment. It is a tree planted by the water where its roots have found the stream and the tree is secure and productive.

PRAYER THOUGHTS: Lord, we want our lives to be as the tree planted by the water, near Your life-sustaining nourishment. May our lives be secure in You and productive in the ways of Your Kingdom. Grant in us a desire to be honest and upright in all our dealings so that Your name is honored. In the name of Jesus, we pray. Amen.

January 9

YOU SHALL NOT COVET

SCRIPTURE: Micah 2:1-5

VERSE FOR TODAY: Rather, we have renounced secret and shameful ways; we do not use deception, nor do we distort the word of God. On the contrary, by setting forth the truth plainly we commend ourselves to every man's conscience in the sight of God (2 Corinthians 4:2, *New International Version*).

HYMN FOR TODAY: "He Is Exalted"

A man was out walking in the desert when a voice said to him, "Pick up some pebbles and put them in your pocket, and tomorrow you will be both sorry and glad."

The man obeyed. He stooped down and picked up a handful of pebbles and put them in his pocket. The next morning he reached into his pocket and found diamonds and rubies and emeralds. And he was both glad and sorry. Glad that he had taken some—sorry that he hadn't taken more. And so it is with God's Word. The Word of God can bring satisfaction to life above anything that we can hope to gain.

The prophet Micah has some harsh words for people who plan evil ways of amassing wealth at the expense of others. Micah portrays a person that stays awake at night planning schemes for taking what is not rightfully his. God's holy Word is rejected as having no value. His greedy motivation is driven by covetousness.

A decisive choice must be made. Will you choose that which is of great, everlasting value—the Word of God—or the wealth of this world that perishes? Choose wisely.

PRAYER THOUGHTS: Father, create in us clean hearts that seek to be honest. Forgive our covetousness and greed for things that do not belong to us. By Your Spirit form in us a sense of contentment that allows us to be free from the entanglements of things that are temporal. Amen.

RIGHTFUL DUE

SCRIPTURE: James 5:1-6

VERSE FOR TODAY: Do nothing out of selfish ambition or vain conceit, but in humility consider others better than yourselves (Philippians 2:3, *New International Version*).

HYMN FOR TODAY: "My Life, My Love, I Give to Thee"

James follows the thoughts of yesterday's text from Micah. God's judgment is upon those that gain their wealth unjustly. James' description is a lifestyle of self-indulgence, luxury, and extravagance gained at the cost of depriving others of what is rightfully theirs. In particular, he addresses those that are guilty of avarice. They have withheld the pay from the laborers. This sin is so dreadful that their cries have been heard by the Lord and judgment and justice will follow.

The greedy can also deprive by taking the extreme opposite of self-indulgence through miserly living. For many years, Hetty Green was called America's greatest miser. When she died in 1916, she left an estate valued at $100 million, a vast fortune for that day. But she was so miserly that she ate cold oatmeal in order to save the expense of heating the water.

When Mrs. Green's son had a severe leg injury, she took so long trying to find a free clinic that his leg had to be amputated because of advanced infection. People say that she hastened her own death because she did not eat properly.

Either extreme does not honor God. Let us seek balance in our lives by maintaining integrity in the management of our material possessions.

PRAYER THOUGHTS: Father in Heaven, we honor You today for Your grace and for providing for our daily needs. There are times when we doubt that what we have is sufficient. Forgive us for our faithlessness and let us rest on the surety of Your promises. Amen.

LESSONS WE LEARN FROM CHILDREN

SCRIPTURE: Matthew 18:1-4

VERSE FOR TODAY: Jesus said, "Let the little children come to me, and do not hinder them, for the kingdom of heaven belongs to such as these" (Matthew 19:14, *New International Version*).

HYMN FOR TODAY: "Jesus Loves Me"

There are times when we do not know what to do. In those moments, we want to trust God, but it's often difficult to actually step out by faith and trust Him.

During World War II, the King of England ordered an evacuation of children from the bomb-torn areas in London. Since many of the youngsters had never been away from home, they were upset. A mother and father put their young son and daughter aboard a crowded train and said goodby. The little girl began to cry. She told her brother she was scared because she didn't know where they were going. Brushing his tears away, he put his arm around her to comfort her. "I don't know where we're going either," he said, "but the king knows!"

Many of us feel alone and uprooted. But though we may not always understand where God is taking us, we are assured that He knows!

We must hang on to God and let Him show us the way. As a child loves and trusts his parents, so we must love and trust our God.

PRAYER THOUGHTS: Heavenly Father, thank You for sending Your Son to become our Savior. We love You and are grateful that You love us. Help us learn to trust You more. In Jesus' name. Amen.

January 11-17. **Kenneth Meade** has ministered to the Church of Christ at Manor Woods in Rockville, Maryland, for 43 years. He and his wife, Jan, have two children and four grandchildren.

USEFUL FOR THE LORD

SCRIPTURE: Matthew 20:17-28

VERSE FOR TODAY: "Here is my servant, whom I uphold, my chosen one in whom I delight; (Isaiah 42:1, *New International Version*).

HYMN FOR TODAY: "Make Me a Servant"

An issue of *Forbes* magazine gives an interesting suggestion. A Citizens Advisory Committee urged that the unused railroad tracks crisscrossing our country be cleared to provide paths for walking, biking, jogging, horseback riding, cross-country skiing, and backpacking. The roadbeds traverse a variety of landscapes and many are scenic routes . . . needing only the removal of ties and rails, followed by the laying of a suitable surface. That sounds worthwhile—converting unused land into nature trails that will delight and benefit the public.

The potential of many people lies unused because they are thinking in terms of what others can do for them rather than how useful they can be to others.

We are created in the image of God. He gives each of us a purpose on earth in preparation for spending eternity with Him. Let's make it easy for people to love us because we have "a servant's heart."

There is tremendous joy in giving. As we make life more meaningful and enjoyable for others, we find a deeper joy and satisfaction in our lives. We serve an awesome God who is always involved in serving us.

PRAYER THOUGHTS: O Lord, forgive us when we become demanding and want people to do things for us. Help us find joy in doing things for others. Give us patience and strength to be kind and not to criticize others. You have done much for us and we want to show our love for You by helping other people in any way we can. To Your glory in Jesus. Amen.

DOING WHAT JESUS DID

SCRIPTURE: John 13:1-15

VERSE FOR TODAY: Set an example for the believers in speech, in life, in love, in faith and in purity (1 Timothy 4:12, *New International Version*).

HYMN FOR TODAY: "I Would Be Like Jesus"

We all need a role model. Jesus is the best role model we can find. He set high standards for us to follow.

The following story contains a lesson. A newly hired salesman stunned his superiors with his first written report, for it clearly revealed that he was nearly illiterate. He wrote: "I seen this outfit who ain't never bought a dimes worth of nothin from us an sole them some goods. I am now going to Chicawgo." But before he could be fired, a second letter arrived. It read: "I came to Chicawgo an sole them haff a millyon." Hesitant to dismiss the man, yet afraid of what would happen if he didn't, the manager gave the report to the President. The next day the staff was amazed to see those two reports on the bulletin board with this memo: "We ben spendin two much tim tryin to spel insted of tryin to sel. I want everybody should read these letters from Gooch, who is doin a grate job, and you should go out and **do like he done!"**

God expects our best. But sometimes we get so preoccupied with appearances that we lose sight of our primary purpose.

The disciples were surprised when Jesus washed their feet. He was teaching them about doing what is right rather than talking about it.

Time is passing by and we must do our best today.

PRAYER THOUGHTS: Jesus, the more we learn about You, the more we realize how important it is for us to let You be our role model. We love You, Jesus! Amen.

FINDING JOY IN HELPING OTHERS

SCRIPTURE: Romans 15:1-6

VERSE FOR TODAY: We urge you, brothers, warn those who are idle, encourage the timid, help the weak, be patient with everyone (1 Thessalonians 5:14, *New International Version***).**

HYMN FOR TODAY: "Make Me a Blessing"

One of the most difficult things in life is to be patient. There may be many reasons why this happens. The Word of God says, "We who are strong ought to bear with the failings of the weak" (Romans 15:1, *New International Version*).

A minister tells of a man who was taking a driving lesson out in the country. Within an hour he had learned to start the car, go forward and backward, and steer reasonably well. He concluded that driving was easy, so his instructor suggested that he practice on a nearby throughway. After a few minutes in the roaring traffic, the man pulled off on a side road and stopped. Mopping his brow, he said, "If it weren't for those other people, it would be simple."

Yes, there are times when those "other people" become a source of irritation to us. As Christians, we can't live selfishly or in isolation.

God's Word challenges us to be grateful for what God has done and to be caring people. Do you know anyone who could use your help today? God surrounds us with opportunities to help others and to give words of encouragement. We find real joy when we help others.

PRAYER THOUGHTS: Dear God, help us to see ways in which we can be an encouragement to others and work with them that together we might do a better job for You. In the name of Jesus, we pray. Amen.

RECEIVING BLESSINGS WE CANNOT EARN

SCRIPTURE: Genesis 32:3-12

VERSE FOR TODAY: In a loud voice they sang: "Worthy is the Lamb, who was slain, to receive power and wealth and wisdom and strength and honor and glory and praise!" (Revelation 5:12, *New International Version*).

HYMN FOR TODAY: "Thou Art Worthy"

Jacob wanted to have peace and love with his brother Esau. Because of how Jacob had treated Esau, he wasn't sure Esau would accept him. "Esau ran to meet Jacob and embraced him; . . . " (Genesis 33:4, *New International Version*). Doesn't that make you feel good inside?

During the Civil War, Abraham Lincoln often visited the wounded. Once he saw a young man near death. "Is there anything I can do for you?" asked the president. "Please write a letter to my mother." Unrecognized by the soldier, the chief executive sat down and wrote as the youth dictated: "My dearest Mother, I was badly hurt while on duty, and I won't recover. Don't sorrow too much for me. May God bless you and Father. Kiss Mary and John for me." Lincoln signed the letter for him and then added this postscript: "Written for your son by Abraham Lincoln."

Asking to see the note, the soldier was astonished to discover who had shown such kindness. "Are you really our president?" he asked. "Yes," was the quiet answer. "And now, is there anything else I can do?" The lad replied, "Will you hold my hand? I think it would help to see me through to the end."

Jesus alone is worthy. When we humble ourselves in obedience to Him, He provides for our needs—He holds our hand.

PRAYER THOUGHTS: Thank You, God, for Jesus and all He's done for us. We don't deserve it but we're grateful to You. In Jesus' name. Amen.

HONOR IS GIVEN TO THE HUMBLE

SCRIPTURE: Proverbs 15:25-33

VERSE FOR TODAY: The fear of the LORD teaches a man wisdom, and humility comes before honor (Proverbs 15:33, *New International Version***).**

HYMN FOR TODAY: "Humble Thyself in the Sight of the Lord"

Have you ever heard the expression, "It's hard to be humble when you're perfect like me?" It might be humorous if we didn't see people who seem to live by that principle. In the Scripture, Philippians 3:3 challenges us, "Do nothing out of selfish ambition or vain conceit, but in humility consider others better than yourselves" (*New International Version*).

Few people are like the man who was referred to as "Mr. Anonymous." Every six weeks he drove to nursing homes in an unmarked van and delivered one or two suit boxes full of roses. Then he left. He sought no recognition; he simply wanted to bring joy. I like to think of "Mr. Anonymous" as a Christian who has taken the words of the Savior to heart: "But when you give to the needy, do not let your left hand know what your right hand is doing, so that your giving may be in secret. Then your Father, who sees what is done in secret, will reward you" (Matthew 6:3, 4, *New International Version*).

We realize that we are not perfect, but we serve a perfect God. Honor is not something we demand. Honor is given to us by others when we humbly serve in a manner that glorifies God. Let's be found faithful to Him when He returns.

PRAYER THOUGHTS: Father, we are grateful that You loved us enough to provide for our salvation. May we find joy in serving others. We love serving You and giving You all the honor and glory. In Jesus' name. Amen.

I WANT GOD

SCRIPTURE: Isaiah 57:15-21

VERSE FOR TODAY: The LORD is close to the brokenhearted and saves those who are crushed in spirit (Psalm 34:18, *New International Version*).

HYMN FOR TODAY: "He Is Lord"

I want God! Our God is holy and mighty. As Creator of the universe and judge of eternity, He holds all power. Yet, His greatest desire is to provide for us. He wants to dwell within us and prepare us to spend eternity with Him.

A small crippled boy was hurrying to catch a commuter train. Carrying some gift packages under his arm, he was experiencing great difficulty in manipulating his crutches. As the people rushed by, someone accidentally bumped into him knocking the brightly wrapped parcels in all directions. The man who caused the mishap stopped only long enough to scold the youngster for being so clumsy and getting in his way. Another gentleman, seeing the boy's distress, went to his aid. He quickly picked up the scattered gifts and slipped a dollar bill into the youngster's pocket, saying, "I'm sorry, Sonny! I hope this makes up a little for your trouble." With a smile he went on his way. The child, who had seldom been shown such kindness, called after him in gratitude, "Mister—please, Sir, are you **Jesus?**" "No," replied his new-found friend, "but I am one of His followers."

Let us humble ourselves and let God work through us. May our example create a desire in others to know more about Jesus. The greatest thing in all the world is knowing Him. Let us live in a manner that will cause people to want God.

PRAYER THOUGHTS: Almighty God, thank You for creating us. May those around us see You in our lives. In Jesus' name. Amen.

WATCH FOR THE CHILDREN

SCRIPTURE: Matthew 18:6-14

VERSE FOR TODAY: But if anyone causes one of these little ones who believe in me to sin, it would be better for him to have a large millstone hung around his neck and to be drowned in the depths of the sea (Matthew 18:6, *New International Version***).**

HYMN FOR TODAY: "Cleanse Me"

Two church leaders who confessed to inappropriate behavior were dismissed by the eldership from leadership responsibilities. Some in the church were shocked and angry.

The leadership dealt with the situation, so the impact on new and weak believers was minimal. The elders were firm in their decisions and Christian in their attitude. One family joined the fellowship saying, "We want to be a part of a church that will confront moral issues in an honest and loving way."

Believers, individually and as a fellowship, must always be sensitive to how our actions impact others. Moreover, we dare not ignore the warning of Jesus about causing others to fall into sin.

We are not responsible if one rejects Christ's offer of forgiveness, but we'll stand before God to answer an obligation not to be a stumbling block to the Christian growth of a brother or sister.

May we never forget what a serious matter it is to impede another's relationship with Christ.

PRAYER THOUGHTS: Heavenly Father, help us to be lights to lead rather than dark places that confuse. In the name of Jesus, we pray. Amen.

January 18-24. **E. Ray Jones** is a retired minister and now is active in leading seminars for churches around the United States. He and his wife, Betsy, reside in Clearwater, Florida.

CONFRONTING IN LOVE

SCRIPTURE: Matthew 18:15-20

VERSE FOR TODAY: "If your brother sins against you, go and show him his fault, just between the two of you. If he listens to you, you have won your brother over" (Matthew 18:15, *New International Version*).

HYMN FOR TODAY: "I Love Thy Kingdom, Lord"

The study of Conflict Management began at the University of Michigan. The course began as Conflict Resolution. Soon the author realized that there is no resolution so it became Conflict Management.

Jesus gave his community guidelines by which they could resolve conflict enough to restore relationships. If you have a conflict with a brother, Jesus said, try to keep it a private matter between the two of you. If you and your brother can resolve your disagreement, you can become closer friends. However, if that attempt fails, you then can bring others into the situation to help resolve the conflict.

It is unfortunate that we often reverse that process. When differences arise we tell our side of the issue to everyone who will listen. Sometimes we will select someone to attack our adversary. Only then do we approach the person with whom we have a conflict.

Is there anyone with whom we have a conflict today? Have we applied the conflict management that the Word of God teaches? Have we gone privately to the one with whom we have a disagreement?

PRAYER THOUGHTS: Father, give us the courage to confront the individual or group with whom we may be in conflict. Only then will the church become the fellowship of love. We pray for Your guidance today. In the name of Jesus, amen.

FORGIVENESS THAT KEEPS ON GOING

SCRIPTURE: Matthew 18:21-35

VERSE FOR TODAY: Then Peter came to Jesus and asked, "Lord, how many times shall I forgive my brother when he sins against me? Up to seven times?" (Matthew 18:21, *New International Version*).

HYMN FOR TODAY: "When We All Get to Heaven"

In the first-century world, one was said to have a happy death if he had avenged himself of all his enemies. In his play, *Ajax,* Sophocles has a hero insult the corpse of his enemy and laugh at a soldier for expressing pity for the one who died.

Jesus spoke to this world with a revolutionary message. Hate must give way to love and revenge must be replaced with mercy and forgiveness.

Jesus loves, and has taught us how to forgive. He answered the question of "seven times seven" with, "I tell you, seven times seventy."

However, actions that take place because of hate, envy, strife, and unforgiveness can't be overlooked. Christians who watch as fellow believers are hurt by other believers want first to retaliate. But Jesus commands that we forgive and the Father will judge on judgment day.

It helps to keep forgiving when we realize what forgiveness does to us and remember how many times we have needed to be forgiven. Moreover, in the light of eternity, the things we find hard to forgive will seem trivial.

PRAYER THOUGHTS: Heavenly Father, give us the strength to keep on forgiving. Remind us of the great love that sent Your Son to earth and finally to death on the cross that our sins might be forgiven. Help us to keep on forgiving. In His holy name, we pray. Amen.

WE CAN BE RESTORED

SCRIPTURE: Galatians 6:1-5

VERSE FOR TODAY: Brothers, if someone is caught in a sin, you who are spiritual should restore him gently. But watch yourself, or you also may be tempted (Galatians 6:1, *New International Version*).

HYMN FOR TODAY: "Softly and Tenderly"

Jesus told a story of a young man who left home for a far off place. He was happy to take his inheritance and leave his father's house. He looked forward to enjoying his freedom. Later he found himself not free but in virtual slavery. The young man had the moral stamina to confront both where he was and what had put him there. He said, "I will go to my father and ask to be one of his servants." But when he returned home, his Father ran to meet him, embraced him, and rejoiced.

We must not overlook the truths about our restoration. Being restored to God does not mean the removal of the earthly consequence of our actions. We do not recover the time, the body, the money, or the negative impact that our sinful life has had on others. But thanks be unto God, when we return to Him and ask for His forgiveness, the Lord restores us to His kingdom and forgives us of our sins.

When we are restored to righteous living once again, we do not glorify the sin. We are receiving God's mercy. Once again we experience the compassion and love our heavenly Father has for us. The gentleness of our brethren will help to assist the restoration process.

PRAYER THOUGHTS: Help us, Father, to be firm, but gentle with those who have fallen into sin. Keep us mindful that none of us is immune to the wiles of the devil. Let us, this day, show the forgiveness to others that You show to us when we seek Your forgiveness. In the name of Jesus, our Savior, we pray. Amen.

KIND AND TENDER FORGIVENESS

SCRIPTURE: Ephesians 4:25-32

VERSE FOR TODAY: Be kind and compassionate to one another, forgiving each other, just as in Christ God forgave you (Ephesians 4:32, *New International Version*).

HYMN FOR TODAY: "Thou Art Worthy"

A cartoon character says, "A lot of people don't have principles, but I do. I am a highly principled person. I have one principle and I live according to that one principle and I never deviate from it." When asked, "What is your principle?" he replied, "Look out for number one!"

Self-centeredness seems to be increasingly taking over the social mentality. The prevailing attitude is, "If I don't take care of myself, no one will." "Use whatever power is available or what's the use of power?" "Put self first!"

To forgive others demands that we give up the power that we believe we have over them because of their guilt over their failures. Often it is difficult to forgive in a tender and compassionate way.

Forgiveness is more than smiles and sweet talk. It means we are sensitive to the need for forgiveness of our wrong doings. We do not forgive in a rude, irritable, or resentful way. We listen carefully to know what needs to be forgiven and what we are being asked to forgive.

Sometimes a forgiving spirit does not change others. But being kind and forgiving changes us. We are richer when we hold no hate in our heart.

PRAYER THOUGHTS: Teach us, O God, not only to be forgiving, but to do so in a kind and gentle way. Help us to see that forgiveness from a cold heart is not so easily accepted. Through Christ we pray. Amen.

HAVE I REALLY FORGIVEN?

SCRIPTURE: Psalm 103:6-14

VERSE FOR TODAY: The Lord is compassionate . . . He will not always accuse, nor will he harbor his anger forever; . . . For as high as the heavens are above the earth, so great is his love for those who fear him; (Psalm 103: 8, 9, 11, *New International Version*).

HYMN FOR TODAY: "Wonderful Grace of Jesus"

Many years ago, a trusted friend of mine betrayed my trust. I was very hurt. Finally, I came to the point of forgiveness—or so I thought.

Recently I had contact with this person, and to my astonishment I reacted in an angry way. I then realized that I had not forgiven the individual. I had buried my resentment only to have it surface years later.

The psalmist tells us that our Father is compassionate and gracious. He is slow to anger and abounds in love. For us, forgiveness can be hard work. It means expressing God's love. It means I not only wish the person who harmed me well ,but that I will do all I can to see that good comes to that person. It requires that I let loose of any desire to retaliate. I will turn that power over to God. I will ask God's Holy Spirit for strength not to revert to an unforgiving attitude.

PRAYER THOUGHTS: Our heavenly Father, search our hearts for hidden hate. Call to our minds any lack of forgiveness. Help us to show abounding love to one another. We know that there is no place for a forgiving Father in a heart filled with hate. Teach us to forgive others as You have forgiven us. Give us a pure, compassionate and loving heart. "Forgive us our debts, as we forgive our debtors," (Matthew 6:12). We pray this in the name of Your Son and our Savior, Jesus Christ. Amen.

GOD'S SUPREME COMMUNICATION

SCRIPTURE: Hebrews 10:11-25

VERSE FOR TODAY: But when this priest had offered for all time one sacrifice for sins, he sat down at the right hand of God (Hebrews 10:12, *New International Version*).

HYMN FOR TODAY: "In the Cross of Christ I Glory"

Laurel and Hardy, a comedy team of years ago, were personal friends. The wife of Mr. Hardy tells of a tender moment when the quality of their friendship was expressed. Hardy had a stroke and was unable to speak. Laurel went to visit and was taken to the room where Hardy was sitting. Mrs. Hardy realized that there was no sound coming from the room. Entering she realized that both men, masters of pantomime, were using their skills to communicate. Stan Laurel was sharing his thoughts and Hardy was able to keep his dignity!

God communicated the quality of His love for us in Jesus Christ of Nazareth. Part of that communication included the words He spoke to those around Him. However, the ultimate expression of love is seen in the acts of Jesus. His supreme communication of love to us was expressed as He took our sins upon Himself at the cross.

It is at the cross that we see Jesus, our High Priest, offering Himself for the forgiveness of our sins. Here He takes on Himself the iniquity of us all. Through His death our sins disappear in the sea of His forgetfulness.

PRAYER THOUGHTS: Thank You, Father, for the demonstration of Your love at Calvary. Thank You that You continue to express love to us in our every day experiences. The cross communicates to us Your love. Let us communicate Your love to others with our words and with our actions. In Thy name, we pray. Amen.

IN TUNE WITH GOD

SCRIPTURE: Acts 10:1-8

VERSE FOR TODAY: The Lord is near to all who call on him, to all who call on him in truth (Psalm 145:18, *New International Version*).

HYMN FOR TODAY: "Break Thou the Bread of Life"

God had a vital role for Cornelius to play in His plan for introducing the Gentile world to Christ. His conversion would break down a historic social wall between Jewish and Gentile people, making it possible for both to serve the same Lord in the same spiritual body. God chose Cornelius to be the first Gentile Christian because he was already on the right wavelength. He and his family were "devout and God-fearing." They were generous with the poor and "prayed to God regularly." When the angel appeared to Cornelius in a dream, he understood the voice and followed the command without hesitation. Because Cornelius was open to God's voice, he was used to facilitate a cultural revolution.

We will find our full potential in God's service when we concentrate on our relationship with Him and strive to comprehend His leading. The time we spend in His Word and in prayer will make us sensitive to His voice and bring us in line with His will. Today, let's be prepared to meet a spiritual challenge and, in so doing, claim a unique place in God's plan.

PRAYER THOUGHTS: Dear God, thank You for guiding us. Challenge us to put our faith into action by using the gifts You have given us. Help us to understand Your specific will for our lives and lead us to invest our time in ways that build up Your kingdom on earth. Amen.

January 25, 29. **Larry Ray Jones** is the Senior Minister of the Northside Church of Christ in Newport News, Virginia. He and his wife, Jane, have two children, Nathan and Laura.

CONFRONTING PREJUDICE

SCRIPTURE: Acts 10:9-16

VERSE FOR TODAY: And the voice spake unto him again the second time, What God hath cleansed, that call not thou common (Acts 10: 15).

HYMN FOR TODAY: "Open My Eyes, That I May See"

James I of England once said, "He was a bold man who first swallowed an oyster." Who would have ever thought to eat an oyster? Thanks to the person who *did* first swallow an oyster, this "repulsive" shellfish is now an epicurean delicacy and a cash cow in many American coastal cities.

In today's lesson, Peter is in the same predicament as the person who swallowed the first oyster. While he is meditating, a blanket of unclean animals is lowered before him. God commands Peter to "kill and eat," knowing full well that Peter is forbidden by Levitical law to do so.

God was not concerned with Peter's dietary habits. Rather, He was challenging Peter to confront his cultural prejudices. God needed a missionary to the Gentiles, and this task required an open-minded servant. God asked Peter to "swallow the first oyster."

There are countless prejudices we must address today. Some people are prejudiced against certain ethnic groups. Some are prejudiced against certain social classes. We must remember that God is not a respecter of persons. He wants His gospel heard by all peoples.

PRAYER THOUGHTS: Father, forgive our prejudices. Help us to see past our biases, so we can better serve You. Help us to consider all people as we minister, and not to deny anyone Your Word. Amen.

January 26-28, 30, 31. **Steve Simpson** is a Christian journalist from Pittsburgh, Pennsylvania.

WELCOMING THE UNWELCOME!

SCRIPTURE: Acts 10:17-23

VERSE FOR TODAY: Then called he them in, and lodged them (Acts 10:23).

HYMN FOR TODAY: "There's Room at the Cross for You"

Hospitality is challenging. Bilbo Baggins of J.R.R. Tolkien's *The Hobbit* finds this to be true. Bilbo is a simple hobbit with a simple life. He loves his mealtimes (there are six in one day) and he loves entertaining company. When thirteen dwarfs show at his door unannounced, however, he finds his simple life turned inside out. The dwarfs are demanding and have table manners that shame all hobbitkind. Though Bilbo bites his tongue several times, he tolerates his guests; and the adventure on which he embarks thereafter bedazzles his simple lifestyle.

God asked much of Peter when He told him to welcome Cornelius' messengers. Gentiles were not welcome in Jewish households. Peter was a simple Jew who ordinarily would have been turned off by Gentile guests. Nonetheless, Peter welcomed them. Peter knew God had an adventure for him. And Peter knew better than to doubt his Lord.

We have no way of knowing what God has in mind for us. We must be willing to go where He leads. We will encounter situations we'd rather avoid. But we must trust God's will for our lives. Who knows what adventures He has in store for us?

PRAYER THOUGHTS: Father, we want to know how we can better obey Your will. Grant us patience when entertaining strangers. Grant us patience in times of trial. Hold us true to You. Together, we can embark on amazing adventures! Amen.

IT'S ALL PERSPECTIVE

SCRIPTURE: Acts 10:24-33

VERSE FOR TODAY: And he said unto them, Ye know how that it is an unlawful thing for . . . a Jew to . . . come unto one of another nation; but God hath showed me that I shall not call any man common or unclean (Acts 10:28).

HYMN FOR TODAY: "Pass Me Not, O Gentle Savior"

In 1997, the London Science Museum purchased a piece of mold from an auction for $25,300. Why would anyone pay that much money for something we clean out of our refrigerators? This particular piece of mold was used by Alexander Fleming in 1928 to create the powerful antibiotic, penicillin.

We wrinkle our noses in disgust when we think of mold. Fleming focused on the positive aspects of mold, and his discovery has healed millions. Mold is as much a part of God's creation as we are. Whether one appreciates its value is a matter of perspective.

In Peter's day, the Jews regarded Gentiles as unclean. Perhaps this prejudice stemmed from Old Testament times when God forbade Jews to marry Gentiles. In any case, God did not make Gentiles unclean. Gentiles were human beings made in God's image, just like anyone else. And just like anyone else, they were entitled to God's love.

Perhaps there are people today with whom we refuse to share God's Word, simply because we consider them "not worth our time." Perhaps what we need is a change of perspective. Rather than dubbing such people "dirty," we should consider them part of God's wonderful creation.

PRAYER THOUGHTS: God, change our perspective on life. Forgive us when we snub others. Help us to appreciate Your creation and consider everyone and everything part of Your creation. Amen.

IN ALL FAIRNESS

SCRIPTURE: Acts 10:34-48

VERSE FOR TODAY: This mystery is that through the gospel the Gentiles are heirs together with Israel, members together of one body, and sharers together in the promise in Christ Jesus (Ephesians 3:6, *New International Version*).

HYMN FOR TODAY: "'Whosoever Will"

Fairness and equality are watchwords of the nineties.

God has always practiced equality. To satisfy His perfect system of justice He condemns us all for our sins. Fortunately, God also exercises equality in responding to our sinful condition with great compassion. Because He loves us, He gave His Son as a sacrifice to pay our debt of sin and set us free.

The spiritual experience of Cornelius was God's way of teaching the church the inclusive nature of His grace. Jesus died for the whole world, and His forgiveness was available for all who accepted Him. In God's kingdom there are no class distinctions between Jews and Gentiles, men and women, or masters and slaves. All are equally redeemed through the precious blood of Christ.

The message of Cornelius is that all people matter to God. Regardless of background or status in life, God still cares. We mattered enough to cost His Son His life on the cross of Calvary. What greater example is there of God's love and compassion for all creation?

PRAYER THOUGHTS: Heavenly Father, You have given us a place equal to all others in Your church. Thank You for offering us forgiveness and salvation through the sacrifice of Your Son, Jesus Christ. Guard our hearts against class distinctions as we reach out to others with Your message of hope and love. Amen.

SALVATION FOR ALL GOD'S CREATURES

SCRIPTURE: Romans 1:8-17

VERSE FOR TODAY: For I am not ashamed of the gospel of Christ: for it is the power of God unto salvation to every one that believeth; to the Jew first, and also to the Greek (Romans 1:16).

HYMN FOR TODAY: "All Creatures of Our God and King"

It started as one man's dream of a de-segregated America. It always starts as a dream. But what exploded from this dream is more than Dr. King—or anyone—could have imagined. America is technically de-segregated, but racial tensions have a hair-trigger tendency to erupt. Though Americans have united in form, they have not yet united in spirit.

An Asian friend of mine believes the church is not exempt from racial segregation. "Sunday is the most segregated day of the week," he said. "It's the day everyone puts on his happy face and attends the church he feels ethnically comfortable in."

Romans 1:16 emphasizes that the gospel is for all men who believe. We have no color in God's eyes. Our souls have no cultural distinction. This was a difficult concept for the Jews in Paul's day to comprehend, and it is a difficult concept for many Christians today.

Are we honest in how we minister inter-racially? Would a member of another race feel comfortable sitting in your church? These are questions we must all ask ourselves.

Perhaps one day, Dr. King's dream will come true, and all God's creatures will join hands and sing, "Free at Last!"

"Free at Last!"

PRAYER THOUGHTS: Father, help us join together. Help us forget racial divisions and love every man, regardless of his ethnic background. Help our churches to reach out to those people it might have overlooked in the past. Amen.

OUR GOD REIGNS!

SCRIPTURE: Acts 17:16-34

VERSE FOR TODAY: And the times of this ignorance God winked at; but now commandeth all men everywhere to repent (Acts 17:30).

HYMN FOR TODAY: "Our God Reigns"

G.C. Lichtenberg once said, "God created man in His own image. . . . Philosophers reverse the process: they create God in theirs." To many, God is a box of Legos: one can build Him any way he wants. Many desire a spiritual relationship with God but do not want to feel guilty of their sins. So each man creates a god who is not troubled by sin.

Paul faced a similar crowd in Athens. His audience had spoiled itself with a salad bar of gods displayed throughout the city. Prominent philosophers debated the "essence of God," but had little desire to know Him. It took much courage for Paul to preach the resurrection to the skeptical Athenians. It took greater courage still to ask each one to repent of his sins.

In our society, each man constructs the god of his choice. Man adopts such phrases as, "We all know God, but by different names." There is no guilt. There is no sin. No one questions another man's god. It is paradise found for the existentialist. But it is unrealistic.

There is one God of the universe, and this God calls all men, regardless of race, to repent of their sins and follow Him. God calls us to be His servants. Like Paul, we should boldly declare, "our God reigns."

PRAYER THOUGHTS: Father, we repent of the sins we have committed. Humble us so we may see the wisdom of Your ways. Help us to minister boldly to others and show to others the love You have shown us. Amen.

DEVOTIONS™

February

photo by Dr. Ward Patterson

TRAIN YOUR TASTE

SCRIPTURE: Romans 12:9-21

VERSE FOR TODAY: Abhor that which is evil; cleave to that which is good (Romans 12:9).

HYMN FOR TODAY: "More Like the Master"

"Eat your spinach," the old preacher said. No one else heard him, for we were guests at a noisy family reunion.

"I don't like it," I objected.

"Eat it anyway. You can *learn* to like it. You can train yourself to like whatever wholesome thing a hostess serves."

He was right. Later I could eat my spinach without even frowning.

Paul wants us to train our taste for other things besides food; to learn to like what God approves and to abhor what He doesn't approve.

Abhor! Ab means away from. *Hor* is from *horrere*, which means shudder. Shudder away from lying and stealing; yes, and away from making a hostess feel badly by rejecting her carefully prepared spinach.

Cleave is one of two words that look and sound alike. The other one means split apart, as you do with a cleaver.

This one means just the opposite: stick or cling inseparably. That's what you do with faith and truth and kindness—with everything good.

PRAYER THOUGHTS: Praise God because He is good and always does good. If you have done something bad, or thought something bad, today or yesterday, ask God to forgive you. Promise to train your taste to like what is good and abhor what is bad. Ask God to help you.

February 1, 2, 4-7. **Orrin Root** is a former editor at Standard Publishing Company. He resides in Cincinnati, Ohio, where he enjoys gardening and writing.

GOD'S MINISTERS

SCRIPTURE: Romans 13:1-7

VERSE FOR TODAY: Render therefore to all their dues: (Romans 13:7).

HYMN FOR TODAY: "In the Service of the King"

How many ministers of God do you know? There's the minister of your congregation and maybe it has an assistant minister, a youth minister, or a minister of music. Some churches have visitation ministers, ministers of senior citizens, and various other specialists.

How about the policeman on the beat? Did you know he is God's minister too? So is your representative in the state legislature, your congressman, your president, the judge in his courtroom, and your king or queen if your country has a king or queen. Some of these people may not know they are God's ministers, but they are. God has decreed that we have government to keep people from robbing and killing each other, and the officials of government serve Him when they do that. Of course, some officials don't always do what God wants them to do, but who does? Not even you!

While you're listing God's ministers, put your own name on the list. The word *minister* means a servant. You are God's servant too, aren't you? One way of serving Him is to study His Word and do what it says. Another way is to obey the law, to respect God's servants in government, and to pay our taxes. Let's all be good ministers of God.

PRAYER THOUGHTS: Thank God for giving us government with laws to guide us in doing right. Thank Him for His servants in the government. Ask Him to help them do their work well. Promise to obey the laws of our country and to live by God's training in the Bible.

WHAT LOVE CAN'T DO

SCRIPTURE: Romans 13:8-14

VERSE FOR TODAY: Love does no harm to its neighbor. Therefore love is the fulfillment of the law (Romans 13:10, *New International Version*).

HYMN FOR TODAY: "Freely, Freely"

Through the ages, the world has sung love's miracles, sometimes even counting the ways it reveals itself. However, in God's economy it's not always what love can do that's as significant as what it cannot do. God's unique love is characterized by don't's as much as do's in its behavior.

After my second child was born through Caesarean section, I was not recovering as quickly as I had hoped. One morning while I slept, after another long, newborn night, a dear friend from church dropped by. My husband welcomed her into the chaotic shambles that was our home. She could have criticized and belittled the disorderliness or told the neighborhood that at 10:00 a.m. I was still in bed. But because God's heart rested within her own, she could not be so unkind. Rather, she cleaned my house and then went home to cook our dinner.

As the fulfillment of the law, Jesus did not curse the weak, poor, and afflicted for their sins or bad judgment but brought healing and encouragement. Neither did He hold our debts against us but paid them with His own blood.

PRAYER THOUGHTS: Precious Father, in acts of love, help us to remember to allow the fulfillment of the law to act through us. Your heart within ours desires to harm no one, so help us to understand and agonize over what love does and does not do.

February 3. **Lisa C. Sharpe,** a pastor's wife from Fayetteville, North Carolina, serves the church by mentoring women through teaching. She and her husband, Ben, have three daughters, Rebekah, Kathleen, and Elizabeth, whom Lisa teaches at home.

CLEAN HANDS AND A PURE HEART

SCRIPTURE: Psalm 15:1-5

VERSE FOR TODAY: Who shall ascend into the hill of the LORD? . . . He that hath clean hands, and a pure heart; (Psalm 24:3, 4).

HYMN FOR TODAY: "Whiter Than Snow"

In ancient times, God's holy hill was the hill in Jerusalem where the temple stood. People who worshiped there ought to do right and speak right and think right. Nowadays we don't need to go to Jerusalem to worship, but we do need to be right in all we do and say and think.

But you and I have done wrong, like everybody else (Romans 3:23). At least we have had some wrong thoughts or wishes. Does that mean we can't worship God? No; it means we need to be forgiven, to have our sins taken away. We can't do that for ourselves, but God can do it for us.

People who are not Christians sometimes do wrong. They need to turn to God, ask for forgivness and follow His ways. People who are Christians should not do wrong, but sometimes they do. They need to confess their wrongdoing to God and ask Him to forgive them (1 John 1:9).

Our Scripture for today is a little song that tells some things we ought to do and some we ought not to do. Of course we're trying our best to do only what is right, aren't we? But when we fail, let's be honest about it. Let's tell God all about it and ask Him to forgive us. And let's promise to do better from now on.

PRAYER THOUGHTS: Thank God that He is able and willing to forgive us. Tell Him honestly about any wrong you have done, anything untruthful or unkind you have said, any wrong thought or wish that has entered your mind. Ask Him to forgive you. Promise to do better.

LET'S DO RIGHT

SCRIPTURE: 1 Peter 2:11-17

VERSE FOR TODAY: The eyes of the Lord are over the righteous, and his ears are open unto their prayers: (1 Peter 3:12).

HYMN FOR TODAY: "Higher Ground"

Long years ago, before we had interstate highways, many northern motorists learned of a speed trap on the road to Florida. The sign was plain: 25 mph. But the road was clear, and local motorists were zipping along at 50. However, if a Michigan license plate just moved with the traffic, the driver went to court and paid a heavy fine.

Christians are out-of-state motorists on earth. Peter calls us "strangers and sojourners." It's not surprising that people of the world are setting speed traps and hoping to catch us saying or doing something wrong as we are just passing through on our way to our home in Heaven.

Around us, non-Christian people are speeding, using obscene language, lying, acting selfishly. That's expected; no one thinks anything of it. But if a Christian is caught doing anything wrong, that's front-page news!

So what can we do? Shall we agitate for a law forbidding discrimination against Christians? Peter suggests a different idea. Just don't speed; don't use obscene language; don't lie; don't act selfishly. Just live so well that the most critical anti-Christian can't find any fault with you.

Can anyone think of a better idea than that?

PRAYER THOUGHTS: Thank God for the privilege of having a home in Heaven. Thank Him for His help and guidance in our journey on earth. Thank Him for the opportunity to meet worldly people and help them find the way to Heaven. Promise to live by the rules of His kingdom.

BE AN ADDING MACHINE

SCRIPTURE: 2 Peter 1:2-11

VERSE FOR TODAY: If ye do these things, ye shall never fall: (2 Peter 1:10).

HYMN FOR TODAY: "I Am Resolved"

It was hard to make a living when prices were higher every week and our children were getting older and more expensive. My wife was the family bookkeeper. She added our income, added our expenses, and decided what we had to do without. That was before computers, but we got an adding machine. It not only added faster, it got the right answer every time.

To balance your spiritual budget, you need to be an adding machine. Peter lists some things to add. **Faith** is believing in Jesus, trusting Him, depending on Him, and doing what He says to do. **Virtue** comes from the Latin **vir**, man. Virtue is manliness: strength and courage and persistence. **Knowledge** is knowing. You need to know what God's Word says. **Temperance** is sometimes translated **self-control**. You need to keep yourself in line with what you learn from the Bible. **Patience** is endurance, staying with it. **Godliness** is reverence: respecting God and obeying Him. **Brotherly kindness** is the attitude of brothers who really love each other. **Charity** is often translated **love**, the kind of love that does good for others.

When all your adding is done, what's the total you get? It's living victoriously in Christ Jesus. So let's get on with our adding.

PRAYER THOUGHTS: Thank the Lord for Heaven, the glorious total when all the adding is done. Admit that all your adding could never earn it; praise God's grace and goodness that prove it anyway. Promise to keep on adding till you reach that total.

METAMORPHOSIS

SCRIPTURE: Romans 12:1-8

VERSE FOR TODAY: Be ye transformed by the renewing of your mind, that ye may prove what is that good, and acceptable, and perfect will of God (Romans 12:2).

HYMN FOR TODAY: "I Would Be Like Jesus"

When I was a boy on the farm, some of the pests we disliked most were the hordes of crawling caterpillars. I suppose a colorful fuzzy caterpillar may be pretty to a disinterested observer, but to us the little brutes were ugly because they were busily devouring the very growing plants on which we also depended for our living.

On the other hand, our farm had few sights more beautiful than a field of alfalfa in full bloom, with the blue flowers half hidden by millions of bright golden butterflies.

How does an ugly crawling worm become a butterfly, flitting in airy lowliness among the blossoms? Borrowing a word from the Greek, scientists say he is *metamorphosed*—and that is the very Greek word that Paul uses in our Scripture to urge us to be transformed.

If we are conformed to this godless world, we are like crawling worms, ugly and destructive. Paul calls us to be metamorphosed: to be transformed into the beautiful characters described in the latter part of our Scripture for today. How can that be done? It starts with the renewing of our minds. We stop our selfish thinking about what we want, and start thinking of sacrificing our selfish interests for the good of all.

PRAYER THOUGHTS: Thank God for Jesus, who gave the example of a life of matchless beauty. Thank Him for the possibility of renewing our selfish minds and being transformed into people more like Jesus. Let's promise to sacrifice our selfish interests for the good of all. Amen.

COMMUNION MEANS "TOGETHER"

SCRIPTURE: 1 Corinthians 11:17-22

VERSE FOR TODAY: Therefore, if you are offering your gift at the altar and there remember that your brother has something against you, leave your gift there in front of the altar. First go and be reconciled to your brother; then come and offer your gift (Matthew 5:23, 24, *New International Version*).

HYMN FOR TODAY: "The Family of God"

In the congregation at Corinth there were some tense times at the fellowship meals. The church was made up of people very different from each other. Some were rich and some were poor. When the rich folks came to the combination pot-luck and communion service, they ate heartily of what they and their friends had brought. When the workers showed up later, with less food, they felt left out. They had been left out. Then the communion service was held. You can imagine that not much "communing" happened. Paul suggested that if they couldn't show Christian fellowship they should forget the pot-luck and eat at home.

Communion means together. Yes, it is with Christ, in remembrance of His matchless gift. But it is done as His body.

If I look down the row and simmer with hatred or laugh in derision or raise a haughty nose in superiority to the person I see there, there is repair work to be done before I bring a proper offering or worship around the Lord's table.

PRAYER THOUGHTS: Loving Father, please forgive us when we have attempted to address You in worship, but have been selfish and insensitive to our family or to our church family Teach us to be like You. Amen.

February 8-14. **Marshall Hayden** serves the Worthington Christian Church in Worthington, Ohio. He and his wife, Judy, have two sons, Eric and Ryan.

"REMEMBRANCE—THE WORTHY MANNER"

SCRIPTURE: 1 Corinthians 11:23, 24

VERSE FOR TODAY: This is my body, which is for you; do this in remembrance of me (1 Corinthians 11:24, *New International Version*).

HYMN FOR TODAY: "My Jesus, I Love Thee"

There's no way that I am worthy to be in the presence of Jesus at His communion table. Often, when we are reading the Bible with someone and we get a few verses past the ones in this text, very often one will say something like, "Ah! That's a tough requirement." And certainly we can understand. Not one of us has ever drunk the cup and thought, "I'm worthy of this." It's scary even to write a phrase like that. I personally like it when the juice is not so sweet; when it makes me pucker a little bit as I swallow it. That sour taste reminds me of the bitterness of sin and the wonder of Christ's sacrifice. I am not worthy.

We must, however, celebrate this wonderful privilege (which is filled with an incomparable hope) in a worthy manner. We pay attention to what is happening. We remember Calvary. We salute His body, the fellowship of the saints. We speak with God in grateful prayer. We hum along with the organ and run the words of "My Jesus, I Love Thee" through our minds. We forget thinking about lunch, or the afternoon football game, or even the Sunday evening plans for the church. We are "all there" with Him, just as He was and is "all there" for us.

PRAYER THOUGHTS: Thank You, glorious Father, for the soothing, satisfying, assuring, painful remembrance that we rehearse each Sunday around the Lord's table. Help us to visualize Your compassion for us as You went to the cross for our sins. We will meet You there wholeheartedly at Your table. Amen.

THE GLORY OF A SPOTLESS LAMB

SCRIPTURE: Exodus 12:1-13

VERSE FOR TODAY: The next day John saw Jesus coming toward him and said, "Look, the Lamb of God, who takes away the sin of the world!" (John 1:29, *New International Version***).**

HYMN FOR TODAY: "Worthy is the Lamb"

In the account of this introduction of the Passover celebration it is easy to see parallels in the church: an exciting, enjoyable, thought-provoking, and uncertain time.

There was sharing to be done. Smaller families got together to eat the roasted lamb. People who lived near each other were guided to act like neighbors.

There was preparation to be made. Proper animals were made ready.

There were instructions to be followed. In the first family, Cain learned that God is honored when we obey, not when we decide that our way is just fine.

The people of God were to be ready—ready to move out of that place to the promised place. They ate the meal with their shoes on. "Yes, Father," would be the proper answer when God said, "Go."

And the lamb, God's lamb—what an astonishing gift! The everlasting Christ is so powerful that He was the hands used by God to make the world. He is so filled with light that in Heaven we won't need any other. But, in order to erase the penalty for our sins, God sent Him as the meekest, most helpless of animals.

PRAYER THOUGHTS: Mighty and loving God! We are in awe, but thrilled with Your gift, Your lamb, who opened not His mouth, but who, for us, opened up Heaven. As we worship the Lamb this week, we will listen for Your instructions, that it be a good feast. Amen.

THE SERIOUSNESS OF OBEDIENCE

SCRIPTURE: Exodus 12:14-28

VERSE FOR TODAY: Therefore everyone who hears these words of mine and puts them into practice is like a wise man who built his house upon the rock (Matthew 7:24, *New International Version*).

HYMN FOR TODAY: "Trust and Obey"

Have you ever played an old game called *Gossip*? A group of people form a circle and someone whispers a sentence to his neighbor. When the message has been passed around the whole circle, the last person announces what was heard. I've always expected that one day it will end up just as it started. But in the games I've played that hasn't happened.

When God has given instructions, it is serious. And the way that God's instructions have been handled by some churches and by some Christians is much worse than an innocent game of "gossip." Not only have things been passed by careless speakers to inattentive listeners, God's "sentences" have been changed because what He has said does not resonate with modern thinking or with what people want to hear.

"I know that God hates divorce, but I want to be divorced. He'll get used to it!"

"Yes, I know that Jesus said 'Love your neighbor, bless them that curse you, do good to them that hate you,' but I don't see why I need to do that!"

And "James said that if I control what I say I can keep my whole self in check. But I just can't do it!"

When we hear the words of Jesus and put them into practice, we build a house that the storms can't blow down.

PRAYER THOUGHTS: We confess, Father, that at times we are very poor listeners, and that sometimes we have blocked our ears on purpose. Please forgive us. We desire to trust and obey. Amen.

IT'S FOR THE FAMILY

SCRIPTURE: Exodus 12:43-51

VERSE FOR TODAY: The LORD said to Moses and Aaron, "These are the regulations for the Passover: "No foreigner is to eat of it . . . " (Exodus 12:43, *New International Version*).

HYMN FOR TODAY: "Leaning on the Everlasting Arms"

In what ways is the church like Israel at this Passover meal? And in what ways are the two different?

We can see the wisdom of a closed experience. Even fraternal organizations and clubs have their private rites and their closed-door sessions. They are committed to some things that are not shared by everyone. In the case of the chosen people of God, there was a serious bond to which each side of the covenant was committed. The memorial meal was for a people in a covenant relationship with almighty God.

In the church we *are* like that, but *not* like that. Our memorial meal (the Lord's Supper), our examination of the Bible and our lives, and our worship of God, are serious. They carry far, far more significance to those who *have* acknowledged God's Son Jesus as Lord, than those who have *not*. The church is His body. It's a family gathering. But in the church we are anxious to have those who are not Christians listen in. It is our great hope that they will hear, believe, respond, and join the family.

To turn off or seem to close out seekers and strangers is not to be the church of Jesus. Nor is it His church if we seem to suggest that God's kingdom is available without an all-your-heart commitment to Jesus Christ as Lord.

PRAYER THOUGHTS: Guide us, Father, as we offer the matchless promise and share the great fellowship in the body of your Son. Amen.

THE BEST DESERVES THE BEST

SCRIPTURE: Exodus 13:1-16

VERSE FOR TODAY: On that day tell your son, "I do this because of what the LORD did for me when I came out of Egypt" (Exodus 13:8, *New International Version*).

HYMN FOR TODAY: "Give of Your Best to the Master"

Kids don't always listen to what their parents say. And preachers' kids don't always listen to what their fathers preach. I must confess to fitting in both of those categories. But there was one thing that my dad used to preach and to say to me personally that I have always remembered.

The first few times I heard it I was irritated by it. Then I tired of listening to it. When I became a man I understood it, believed it to be right, and began shaping my life by it. More recently I have been anxious to pass it on to my sons.

Dad said, "When you are walking near the edge of a cliff, why would anyone see how close he could get without falling? Why wouldn't you stay as far away from the edge as possible?"

A teen-ager knew what he meant. Why flirt with a dangerous lifestyle? Why test God's patience? Why choose something that "might not be OK" with God, when you could choose something that would please God? Why press the boundaries of God's grace?

The people were taught by Moses to consecrate their first-born to God. After all He brought them out of a bad place to a good place. He deserved the best. He still does!

PRAYER THOUGHTS: Forgive us, Father, when we have been tempted to give You less than our best. We pray for Your Spirit's help in discovering exciting ways to give You our best. Amen.

I NEED YOU!

SCRIPTURE: 1 Corinthians 12:14-27

VERSE FOR TODAY: If the whole body were an eye, where would the sense of hearing be? If the whole body were an ear, where would the sense of smell be? (1 Corinthians 12:17, *New International Version*).

HYMN FOR TODAY: "In the Service of the King"

Valentine's Day! It's a good time to remind husbands and wives that "I need you" is a very important thing to say. We know that "the two shall become one flesh," but we tend to take that for granted. Sweet candies would be fine today, but sweet, sincere, and grateful words will be better.

The same words would be very much in order in the church. In Corinth, the Christians had a little problem with pride and competitiveness. Some folks saw their own gifts as very special and the gifts of others as a good deal less special. Somehow they missed the fact that the only reason for having such gifts was that when put together, the body of Christ might be full and strong. "I need you," we'll say. We do need each other. That's the way God planned it.

I may be able to stand up front of an audience without experiencing the number one fear of the American people, public speaking. But if I suggest to you that I am superior to you (the mercy-giver, or the money-maker and giver, the helping hand, or the careful teacher) I am acting like the eye that categorizes the ear as an inferior body part.

PRAYER THOUGHTS: We need You, our great and loving God. In the church (Your Son's body), we confess that we need each other. We recognize that You want and need us (not just me, but us). Thank You for Your promise, for Your plan, and for Your trust. Amen.

FOR WHOM DO YOU LIVE?

SCRIPTURE: 2 Corinthians 5:11-15

VERSE FOR TODAY: And he died for all, that those who live should no longer live for themselves but for him who died for them and was raised again (2 Corinthians 5:15, *New International Version*).

HYMN FOR TODAY: "I'd Rather Have Jesus"

In his book, *The Jesus Style*, Gayle D. Erwin writes that one Christmas, the founder of the Salvation Army, William Booth, wanted to send a greeting of encouragement to all the Salvation Army centers. Finances were short and an aide told him that he could send a message to every center in the world, but it could be one word only. Booth went apart to pray, then came back with his one word of encouragement: "Others!"

It is certainly commendable to live for others, and there are many Scriptures that encourage us to do this. Countless people have laid down their lives to benefit those in need. But Paul, in his letter to the Corinthians, urges Christians to an even higher loyalty. He urges Christians to live for Christ who died for them and was raised from the dead. It was Christ's love that compelled Paul to share the good news of Jesus with others.

How can we live for Christ in our home today? In our school? In our job? In our community? This is the challenge of the Christian life. Even our love for others springs from our love for Him.

PRAYER THOUGHTS: Father, it is so easy to live only for ourselves. Sometimes we are even successful in living for others. But, Father, help us to live for Christ. He died for us and we are His. Amen.

February 15, 16, 18-21. **Dr. Ward Patterson** is Professor of Speech and Ministries at Cincinnati Bible College in Cincinnati, Ohio.

CHRIST'S AMBASSADORS

SCRIPTURE: 2 Corinthians 5:16-21

VERSE FOR TODAY: We are therefore Christ's ambassadors, as though God were making his appeal through us. We implore you on Christ's behalf: Be reconciled to God (2 Corinthians 5:20, *New International Version*).

HYMN FOR TODAY: "I'll Go Where You Want Me to Go"

The government of the United States has embassies in every major capital of the world. An embassy is a representative of our national interests abroad. It flies the American flag, is protected by U.S. Marines as well as local guards, and is considered as American soil. It looks out for the needs of American travelers, expresses American views to the local government, and is an ear on local political matters for the American government. An ambassador is a highly respected representative of our government and its interests.

Paul wrote that Christians are ambassadors of Christ. As ambassadors, we proclaim a message of peace and reconciliation; that God was reconciling the world to himself through Christ. We Christians are a new creation. Christ has taken upon Himself our sin and made it possible for us who are united with Him to be clothed in goodness, the very goodness of God.

We have a marvelous message as we speak to others on God's behalf. God makes His appeal to the world through us.

PRAYER THOUGHTS: O God, thank You for being very near to us, for allowing us to play a part in Your work of reconciliation and peace. May we represent You with our deeds and our words. We thank You for newness in Christ, for the forgiveness of our sins, and for a joyous message to share with others. Amen.

BALANCING ACT

SCRIPTURE: Romans 5:18–6:4

VERSE FOR TODAY: Consequently, just as the result of one trespass was condemnation for all men, so also the result of one act of righteousness was justification that brings life for all men (Romans 5:18, *New International Version*).

HYMN FOR TODAY: "Praise My Soul, the King of Heaven"

In my grandmother's dining room was an antique balance which had weighed ingredients for probably hundreds of pound cakes and barrels of jelly. My cousins and I loved shifting the weights, attempting to achieve perfect balance. Though old, the scale was as accurate as when it was first purchased. No matter which weight we added to one pan, the requirement for an even match in the other pan was the same. To balance anything, the scale made the same demand—equal weight on each side.

Likewise, God's demand—the weight of His righteousness and justice—has always required absolute, precision balancing. The Father knew that all our righteousness could never carry enough weight to equal it. So, "the one man," Jesus, was sent to tip the scale in our favor with "one act of righteousness." Though all our purity is worthless, Jesus standing on the scale on our side perfectly answers God's demand. The joy in His justice is that, no matter who stands beside Him or what one's sin, the balance is unshaken. His standards and grace remain the same for all humanity. We are all justified and found equal to one another in Christ.

PRAYER THOUGHTS: Dear Father, thank You for providing Jesus' atoning death and resurrection for us. Amen.

February 17. **Lisa C. Sharpe**, lives in Fayetteville, North Carolina. She and her husband, Ben, have three daughters, Rebekah, Kathleen, and Elizabeth.

DEAD TO SIN AND ALIVE TO GOD

SCRIPTURE: Romans 6:5-11

VERSE FOR TODAY: In the same way, count yourselves dead to sin but alive to God in Christ Jesus (Romans 6:11, *New International Version*).

HYMN FOR TODAY: "I Surrender All"

I have crawled into the depths of Egyptian tombs and climbed to the top of the Great Pyramid. I'm intrigued by the tomb carvings and the efforts the ancient Egyptians made to assure a pleasant life in the hereafter. Death seemed to be very much in the minds of the ancient pharaohs and their nobility.

Americans, to the contrary, seem very uncomfortable with death. We use euphemisms: "she passed on," "he departed," or "she has gone to her rest." We almost seem to feel that if we avoid death, it will avoid us.

Paul, however, wrote of death and life with frankness and beauty. He saw Christian baptism as a time when believers were united with Christ's death. Further, it pictured their being united with him in resurrection. Believers, in their unity with Christ, are new creatures with an eternal destiny already in place.

I must admit that for me, February is not a favorite month. In the cold clime where I live, February is drab and dreary and a time for hanging on until the first signs of spring break through the white crusted earth. But I know that February will not last forever and something better is soon to come. I know that, also, so far as my life is concerned. I can't wait to experience what lies ahead, living with Christ for eternity.

PRAYER THOUGHTS: Eternal Father, sometimes we feel that we are not really so different from those who do not acknowledge You in their lives. But Your Word reminds us that we are united with Christ. Help us to live in His victory. Amen.

ETERNAL LIFE, THE GIFT OF GOD

SCRIPTURE: Romans 6:12-23

VERSE FOR TODAY: But now that you have been set free from sin and have become slaves to God, the benefit you reap leads to holiness, and the result is eternal life. For the wages of sin is death, but the gift of God is eternal life in Christ Jesus our Lord (Romans 6:22, 23, *New International Version*).

HYMN FOR TODAY: "Wonderful Peace"

Who or what controls you? Do you let sin control? Or does God control?

Paul urges Christians to be dead to sin and alive to God. He calls on us to offer ourselves to God as instruments of righteousness. He entreats us to be slaves of God. This, in turn, leads to holiness and eternal life.

Ted Davisson was a pilot on the Mississippi River and was at the helm of *Bright Field* when the huge freighter smashed into the waterfront shopping mall in New Orleans. The out-of-control ship injured 116 people and heavily damaged stores and hotels at the edge of the New Orleans French Quarter. In testimony before the National Transportation Safety Board, Davisson said that the Chinese captain and crew seemed not to understand his orders.

A communication breakdown can be dangerous on a large ship in a constricted area. It can also be disastrous in an individual life when there is confusion about who is in control. Let us resolve to allow God to be in control of our thoughts and our actions.

PRAYER THOUGHTS: Father, sometimes we value our freedom so highly that we ignore Your will for our lives. We don't realize that when we give ourselves to disobedience, we become slaves to sin. Help us, O Father, to be Your obedient servants. Amen.

BEARING FRUIT TO GOD

SCRIPTURE: Romans 7:1-13

VERSE FOR TODAY: So, my brothers, you also died to the law through the body of Christ, that you might belong to another, to him who was raised from the dead, in order that we might bear fruit to God (Romans 7:4, *New International Version*).

HYMN FOR TODAY: "God of Grace and God of Glory"

A professor once commented that sidewalks for a university should never be planned by an architect. He believed that only grass should be planted around new buildings. Then later, sidewalks could be poured along the paths that students established as they walked to their classes.

It seemed to make sense. Where I teach we have fine sidewalks connecting our college buildings, but students invariably cut across the grass. I've often wondered if it would help to put up "Keep Off the Grass" signs, but I've concluded that that would probably make it worse. There is something about a prohibition that almost invites us to defy it.

In Romans 7 Paul pondered the relationship between the Old Testament law, obedience, and sin. The law was essential to the understanding of what was sinful, so it was holy, righteous, and good. But by its very nature it made sin more evident and visible.

When we belong to Christ, goodness becomes more than the keeping of a useful code of conduct; it becomes a love and loyalty to the One who was raised from the dead. All of this inspires us to bear fruit to God.

PRAYER THOUGHTS: Dear God, help us to be obedient to Your commandments not out of grudging necessity but because our hearts have been given over to doing Your will. Amen.

THE WAR WITHIN

SCRIPTURE: Romans 7:14-25

VERSE FOR TODAY: So then, I myself in my mind am a slave to God's law, but in the sinful nature a slave to the law of sin (Romans 7:25, *New International Version*).

HYMN FOR TODAY: "A Shelter in the Time of Storm"

Several years ago, a Union Pacific Railroad train barreled across the tracks in western Nebraska. The train had two engines, one in the front and another in the rear, operated by remote control from the front engine. Apparently a motorist became upset because the train was blocking traffic so he uncoupled the train. When it moved out, the engineer was unaware of what had happened. As the train rolled along, it separated until there was nearly twelve miles between the sections of the moving train. For nearly fifty miles the divided train moved through crossings and passed other trains. Finally, another train's engineer spotted the problem and notified the railroad. It was fortunate that no one was injured by the runaway cars—operating without lights, whistle, or an engineer.

Do you ever feel like a divided train? Do you ever feel as if a part of you is out of control? Do you ever find yourself doing things you really know you ought not to do and not doing things you know you really ought to do?

Paul was keenly aware of this conflict. He wanted to do good, but sin seemed to wage war against what he knew to be right. Almost in desperation he cried out, "Who will rescue me from this body of death?" He knew, of course, that there was only one answer to this question of the divided self, "Thanks be to God through Jesus Christ our Lord."

PRAYER THOUGHTS: O God, unite us in heart, mind, and body under Your loving control. Amen.

THE POWER OF A VITAL HOPE

SCRIPTURE: Titus 2:11-14

VERSE FOR TODAY: We have this hope as an anchor for the soul, firm and secure (Hebrews 6:19, *New International Version*).

HYMN FOR TODAY: "The Solid Rock"

Hope is a great motivating force. The Pilgrims who came to the shores of a new land in the seventeenth century envisioned a better life in the freedom of the new world. The pioneers who pressed westward to open new lands were driven by their hopes for a better tomorrow. Great achievements are often realized because heroic efforts have been inspired by powerful hope.

God has given us a wonderful hope; hope based on a divine promise that Christians have a tomorrow that is certain. Even death cannot endanger the Christian's assured future. Paul could write confidently, "We wait for the blessed hope—the glorious appearing of our great God and Savior, Jesus Christ" (Titus 2:13, *New International Version*). One day we shall see Him!

Hope can endure sacrifice and hardships. The pioneers lived under the harsh conditions in their quest for a better tomorrow. In like manner, Christ's people turn aside from the "ungodliness and worldly passions, and to live self-controlled, upright and godly lives in this present age, while we wait for the blessed hope—" (verses 12, 13), the victory we have over evil in this world, and our triumph over death itself.

PRAYER THOUGHTS: Heavenly Father, we thank You for the hope we have in Christ. May this hope ever be strong in our thinking and in our hearts. Amen.

February 22-28. **Dr. Henry Webb** is a minister and retired college professor. He and his wife, Emerald, reside in Johnson City, Tennessee, where they continue in service to Christ and His church.

THE CHANGELESS IN THE MIDST OF CHANGE

SCRIPTURE: Hebrews 12:18-29

VERSE FOR TODAY: Therefore, since we are receiving a kingdom that cannot be shaken, let us be thankful, and so worship God acceptably with reverence and awe (Hebrews 12:28, *New International Version*).

HYMN FOR TODAY: "Abide with Me"

"The only thing that does not change is change itself" is a common saying. There are times when we wish we could slow the pace of change. We look back on our lives and wonder where the years went.

A line in a favorite hymn states: "Change and decay in all around I see; O Thou who changest not, abide with me!" As we live in the midst of constant change, we long for more stability and a slower pace. We ask: "Is anything permanent?"

Nothing of a material nature is enduring. All that is material is subject to the laws of disintegration. But God, the creator of all things, is eternal. He is above change for He is spirit. In the same manner, the spiritual component in human beings is also beyond the changes that are inevitable in physical/material creation. God has made provision for the eternal survival of our spiritual nature after our flesh returns to the elements of earth. We will live in the kingdom that cannot be shaken, which is not subject to the laws of physical change. This eternal kingdom of God is our ultimate hope. It is promised to us by Christ. We believe that what the Lord promised, He will surely deliver. We will not be disappointed in this promise!

PRAYER THOUGHTS: Great eternal God, we thank and praise You for the fact that You are unchanged throughout all human time and experience. You are the constant reality that we all so desperately need. Abide with us, we pray! Amen.

FEAR IS OVERCOME BY LOVE

SCRIPTURE: Revelation 1:12-20

VERSE FOR TODAY: There is no fear in love. But perfect love drives out fear, because fear has to do with punishment. The one who fears is not made perfect in love (1 John 4:18, *New International Version*).

HYMN FOR TODAY: "Face To Face with Christ, My Savior"

Fear is one of life's most unwelcome experiences. We tend to fear the unknown, the unmanageable, and the unfamiliar. When the angel appeared to Mary to announce the conception of Jesus, Mary was afraid, and when an angel appeared at the tomb to announce the resurrection of Jesus, the women were afraid. In both cases the angel said, "Do not be afraid." God, our heavenly Father, does not want us to be afraid when we are in His presence.

Some day we shall experience God directly when we see Jesus face-to-face as John did in the text in Revelation. It will be an experience that exhausts our ability to describe. The language John uses stretches our capacity to visualize the vast power and beauty of the risen and reigning Christ. The important thing for us to remember is that we will really see Him, exalted and glorious beyond description.

Will we be filled with fear when we see Him on that day? Perhaps we will be overcome with awe because of His majesty. But if we know Him, if He is a long-time companion, we will rejoice to be in His presence. And when we sense the love which He has for His people, fear will evaporate, even as John wrote, "Perfect love drives out fear" (1 John 4:18, *New International Version*).

PRAYER THOUGHTS: Heavenly Father, You are majestic and powerful and worthy of praise. Most of all, You are LOVE, and because of this, we look to the future with confidence and hope. Amen.

JESUS CHRIST—OUR ETERNAL SOVEREIGN

SCRIPTURE: Revelation 11:15-19

VERSE FOR TODAY: The kingdom of the world has become the kingdom of our Lord and of his Christ, and he will reign for ever and ever (Revelation 11:15, *New International Version*).

HYMN FOR TODAY: "Hallelujah"

Every athlete knows that the score at the end of the third quarter of the game really doesn't matter; it's the score at the end of the final quarter that counts. The eighth inning score doesn't win ball games; it's the score at the end of the ninth that counts.

History will have its final period when all human events come to their final settlement. The outcome is not in doubt. George Frederick Handel has caused the words of verse 15 of our text to be firmly fixed in the mind of all who have heard the "Hallelujah" of his great oratorio, *The Messiah*. The thrilling sense of the ultimate triumph of Christ and His kingdom of righteousness over the forces of evil that have beset His faithful people is caught up in the magnificent cadences of this unmatched choral composition. This is no accident. God is ultimately in charge of His creation and the victory of good over evil. The final triumph of Christ over Satan and his vicious ways is not in doubt. This is a profound truth that we, as Christians, should keep uppermost in our thinking, especially when we become discouraged or are tempted to give up. Evil cannot win! Christ will finally triumph and will reign forever and ever! No doubt about it!

PRAYER THOUGHTS: Thou, O God, are sovereign over all creation. Help us to understand that the evil we see all around us can never triumph over good. You have decreed that it will be the Lord Jesus Christ who will finally reign for eternity. Amen.

REALITY AND HOPE

SCRIPTURE: 1 Peter 1:3-9

VERSE FOR TODAY: We wait for the blessed hope——the glorious appearing of our great God and Savior, Jesus Christ, (Titus 2:13, *New International Version*).

HYMN FOR TODAY: "He Lives"

Hope is vital to living. It is the antidote to despair. Hope always refers to the future. Christians have a great future.

Hope should never be confused with wishful thinking or fanciful illusion. Hope deals with reality. Christians are people who live with a very real hope——an expectation of future events that give meaning and purpose to life itself.

Some years ago a friend of mine was stricken with a fatal illness. As I approached his room in the hospital, I wondered what I could say to encourage him as he faced the uncertain days ahead. I had no need for concern, for he encouraged me. So real was his hope in entering a richer and more joyous life with Christ that it was he who gave me a new sense of reality. My friend wasn't looking for consolation; he was looking forward to what Peter describes in our text for today as "an inexpressible and glorious joy." He made it clear to me that he was anticipating "the goal of [his] faith, the salvation of [his] soul" (1 Peter 1:8, 9, *New International Version*). What a way to face what for all of us is inevitable! Just as God summoned Christ from the grave and caused Him who died to live again, so we believe that He will summon us to life after we have yielded to that last enemy of mankind: death.

PRAYER THOUGHTS: Heavenly Father, we are grateful for the hope You have provided. We face the future unafraid. Help us to treasure this hope and its meaning for our daily life. Amen.

OUR UNSEEN BUT VERY REAL HOPE

SCRIPTURE: Ephesians 1:15-23

VERSE FOR TODAY: I pray also that the eyes of your heart may be enlightened in order that you may know the hope to which he has called you, the riches of his glorious inheritance in the saints, (Ephesians 1:18, *New International Version*).

HYMN FOR TODAY: "Open My Eyes, That I May See"

We were born with two eyes so we may be aware of the things around us. But our eyes don't see spiritual realities, except as they are evident through visible realities. We can't see love, but we can see the evidence of love. We don't see trust, but we can see the consequences of trust. This is why Paul speaks of "the eyes of your heart" (Ephesians 1:18, *New International Version*). The heart becomes aware of spiritual realities like faith, hope, and love.

I have a friend who was born without the gift of eyesight. He has never witnessed a glorious sunset or the delicate beauty of a rose. But he is spiritually sensitive and aware of reality that few sighted persons perceive. Physical blindness is serious but spiritual blindness is an eternal problem. How tragic for any person to be unaware of the blessing of faith, to be oblivious to the experiences of love, or to miss the joy that hope brings.

God, who richly blesses the human family with a world of material abundance, has also provided profuse spiritual blessings. Let's cultivate sensitivity to spiritual truth. It will bless us greatly.

PRAYER THOUGHTS: Heavenly Father, open the eyes of our hearts that we may see more clearly the wonderful spiritual realities that You have provided. Help us to be forever grateful for the richness of Your provision in these blessings. Amen.

CONFIDENCE FOR A JOYOUS FUTURE

SCRIPTURE: Revelation 21:1-8

VERSE FOR TODAY: Just as we have borne the likeness of the earthly man, so shall we bear the likeness of the man from heaven (1 Corinthians 15:49, *New International Version*).

HYMN FOR TODAY: "Sweet By and By"

Hope is a vital part of everyday life. Each new morning finds us anticipating the events of the day. In the long-range flow of life, these daily events are usually of minor significance. However, there are some very big and important events that comprise the hopes of most people: graduation, marriage, and the arrival of a baby. But our ultimate hope relates to the question of life beyond this life. Will we who experience the joys of life in this world, lose it all to what we call death?

Our faith in Christ answers this question with a resounding, "No!" The whole purpose in Christ's coming to earth was to provide us with a hope for eternal life. John has given us a glimpse of this new life as recorded in the final book of Scripture. There will be a *new* heaven and earth. This is a beacon that beckons us ever forward. Here God will dwell with His people. No tears or sorrow will cast a blight on that life; no evil or wrong will ever interrupt its joy.

The hope of a new life in Heaven has sustained believers through the trials, persecutions, and cares of life. Many saints advancing in years and declining in health can look forward to a new life in a new environment free from pain and fear. God says, "Behold, I make all things new" (Revelation 21:5).

PRAYER THOUGHTS: Gracious Father in Heaven, we thank and praise You because You have blessed us with a wonderful hope. When weariness with the burdens of this world weigh heavily upon us, help us to anticipate our future with You. Amen.

THE LORD IS MY LIGHT

The LORD is my light and my salvation;
   whom shall I fear?
The LORD is the strength of my life;
of whom shall I be afraid?
When the wicked, even mine enemies
   and my foes,
came upon me to eat up my flesh,
they stumbled and fell.
Though a host should encamp against
   me,
my heart shall not fear:
though war should rise against me,
in this will I be confident.
One thing have I desired of the LORD,
that will I seek after;
that I may dwell in the house of the LORD
all the days of my life,
to behold the beauty of the LORD,
and to inquire in his temple.

                —Psalm 27:1-4

My Prayer Notes

My Prayer Notes

_____

_____

_____

_____

_____

_____

_____

_____

_____

_____

_____

_____

_____

_____

_____

_____

_____

DEVOTIONS™

March

photo by Dr. Ward Patterson

AND GOD CAME DOWN

SCRIPTURE: John 1:1-5

VERSE FOR TODAY: The people walking in darkness have seen a great light; on those living in the land of the shadow of death a light has dawned (Isaiah 9:2, *New International Version*).

HYMN FOR TODAY: "How Great Thou Art"

It was one of those exhilarating moments. The weather had followed a consistent pattern of sun and rain. As I looked out our window and saw rain glinting with sunshine, I dashed out to find the most perfect, dazzling rainbow I had ever seen. Running from one end of the yard to the other to catch a better look, I shouted to my family and neighbors, "Did you see the rainbow? . . . Guys, you *have* to come see this!"

Finally, I just stopped and soaked in the glow—filled with the realization that only a perfect God could create such a perfect gift and—even more wonderful—that very same God came down to this earth to die for me. The Creator of the universe saw us in our darkened world and, through Jesus Christ, brought us light and new life.

Look at the brilliance of the sun, or the masterwork of the stars in the heavens. Climb a high pinnacle and gaze at the world below, or tenderly caress a newborn baby's hand. Catch the awe of a perfect Creator who loves us so much that He gave up everything so that we might know Him as He is.

Praise God today, for through Jesus Christ, the Word, He has revealed Himself.

PRAYER THOUGHTS: Heavenly Father, thank You for creating us and the world in which we live. Thank You most of all for making Yourself known to us so that we might see You face to face. Amen.

March 1-7. **Pam Coffey** is a minister's wife and mother to twin sons. She lives in Arcadia, Indiana.

JESUS IS OUR LIGHT

SCRIPTURE: John 1:6-9

VERSE FOR TODAY: When Jesus spoke again to the people, he said, "I am the light of the world. Whoever follows me will never walk in darkness, but will have the light of life" (John 8:12, *New International Version).*

HYMN FOR TODAY: "Shine, Jesus, Shine"

Our first worship service on Sunday morning is early. As we walk into the building (especially during the winter months) we must turn on the lights, for we are surrounded by darkness. But on a clear day during the summer season, something wonderful happens. As the sun rises, it shines through the eastern windows of our church building and focuses directly on the cross in the front of the sanctuary. As we bask in the sun's warm glow, our minds are more fully awakened, our spirits are lifted, and we are reminded that the One who gives light to all is present among us.

Jesus Christ is our light. His very presence expels the darkness that Satan casts on the world. If we walk in His light, we will receive life as well. And, as John the Baptist, we must bear witness to that light. As we do, we may receive a variety of reactions. Some people may react to the message with pain or apathy, but others will accept it with joy. No matter how it is received, the message is still the same—Jesus Christ is our light and our only source of life.

Let that be your message to the world today.

PRAYER THOUGHTS: Thank You, dear Father, for Your Son, Lord Jesus, and for bringing light into our lives. May we allow You to shine to the world as we reflect Your love to others today. We pray in Your holy name, amen.

THE MAIN MESSAGE

SCRIPTURE: Mark 1:1-11

VERSE FOR TODAY: As Jesus was coming up out of the water, he saw heaven being torn open and the Spirit descending on him like a dove. And a voice came from heaven: "You are my Son, whom I love; with you I am well pleased" (Mark 1:10, 11, *New International Version*).

HYMN FOR TODAY: "All Hail the Power of Jesus' Name"

It must have been a captivating scene. Here was a man who was definitely not part of the inner religious circle. He was a "PK" (priest's kid) who appeared to have rebelled against the conformed practices of the day, and he was preaching a new and strange message.

Scary . . . some may have thought—and probably he was. A wardrobe of camel's hair and a diet of locusts and wild honey? . . . Well, he's just a little too weird for me.

But crowds were flocking to him and responding to his strange message. How would he handle all this attention? Would it go to his head just like so many others? Would the fallacy of it all show up and just die away?

It didn't. Why? The message remained pure. John, probably against strong temptation, kept the focus of his message on the main thing—proclaiming to the world, Jesus Christ—the Son of God and Savior of all.

When John's disciples were complaining that everyone was going to Jesus, John's response was, "He must increase but I must decrease" (John 3:26). He knew who Jesus was and his message remained pure. *Jesus* is the One.

What is our main message? Are we saying to our world, "*Jesus* is the One?"

PRAYER THOUGHTS: Father, Jesus is the main message to the world. He is our only hope. May we always keep our focus on Him. Amen.

A CHILD OF THE KING

SCRIPTURE: John 1:10-13

VERSE FOR TODAY: Yet to all who received him, to those who believed in his name, he gave the right to become children of God—children born not of natural descent, nor of human decision or a husband's will, but born of God (John 1:12, 13, *New International Version*).

HYMN FOR TODAY: "A Child of the King"

There is no higher position on earth. You may be the king of the richest country in the world. You may be the leader of a mighty world power. You may be the most popular star in Hollywood or the highest paid athlete in all of sportsdom. You may be a supermodel for decades or have the highest IQ in the history of mankind, but these titles don't even come close to the totally awesome position of being named a child of the living God.

You can't earn this position, but it's yours for the taking. The adoption papers have already been filled out through the blood of Jesus Christ. He has made it possible through His own pain for you to stand before the God of all creation and call Him Father. He wants to reach down with His loving arms and draw you close to Him. He longs to pour out His perfect love on you and teach you to love others as He does. He wants you to share the gift He has given you, for He has more than enough love to go around.

Have you accepted God's gift to you? If you have, then you're a child of the King.

PRAYER THOUGHTS: That You would call us Your children, heavenly Father, is a thought too wonderful to conceive. Thank You for making such a wonderful gift possible. Help us to live with the confidence that comes from being Your child. We truly love You. In the name of Jesus, we pray. Amen.

JOY FROM THE LIGHT

SCRIPTURE: Acts 16:25-34

VERSE FOR TODAY: But if we walk in the light, as he is in the light, we have fellowship with one another, and the blood of Jesus, his son, purifies us from all sin (1 John 1:7, *New International Version*).

HYMN FOR TODAY: "The Light of the World Is Jesus"

The jailer in Philippi thought he had it all under control. His world was probably all in order, and maybe he was dreaming of a nice promotion as he kept his watch over Paul and Silas in their darkened cell.

Then his world crumbled. That's when he realized that it was he who was in darkness. His secure world was suddenly out of control, and despair set in. No hope! No reason for living! Let's just end it all here and get it over with.

That's when he heard a voice of hope. That voice of hope made him long for light. And as physical lights were brought to him, he was introduced to the One True Light.

"What must I do . . . ?" was answered with, "Believe on the Lord Jesus and you will be saved."

He believed in Jesus as Savior and had his sins washed away. As he and his family experienced the excitement of new birth, a true party began. Their total joy was found purely in the redeeming power of Jesus. Now his life was filled with true happiness.

Have you experienced that same refreshing pure joy? If not, follow the steps of the Philippian jailer and experience newness. Then let the party begin!

PRAYER THOUGHTS: Thank You, Lord Jesus, for freeing us from darkness and sin. We praise You for the joy and light we feel in our souls. May we share Your love with others today. Amen.

HE CAME DOWN TO LIFT US UP

SCRIPTURE: John 1:14-18

VERSE FOR TODAY: The Word became flesh and made his dwelling among us. We have seen his glory, the glory of the One and Only, who came from the Father, full of grace and truth (John 1:14, *New International Version*).

HYMN FOR TODAY: "Joy to the World"

Some people picture God in an ivory palace—doing His own thing—and being totally clueless about what's going on down here on earth.

Then there are others who deny that God even exists. We "just happened," the earth "just happened," and "what will happen will happen."

But the Bible confirms (and nature backs it up) that, yes, there is a God and He is alive and active. And, not only is He alive and active—He stepped down inside His own creation and put on our skin so that He might experience all the pain we go through, and pain even too terrible for us to endure.

It couldn't have been pleasant—zipping up in a suit of humanity with all of its imperfections. A lesser being might have refused, saying, "I don't want to cramp my style." But Jesus gave it all up, prompted by holy love, and focused on the final joy—salvation for His people. The next time you feel that no one understands, remember, Jesus knows. He's been there, too. God paved the way through Jesus. He came down to us so that we might be lifted up to Him.

Joy to the world. The Lord is come!

PRAYER THOUGHTS: Heavenly Father, You came down to our world to save us. What amazing grace! May we accept Your gift with love and humility and praise. We pray in Jesus' holy name, amen.

CHOSEN BY GOD

SCRIPTURE: Ephesians 1:3-14

VERSE FOR TODAY: For he chose us in him before the creation of the world to be holy and blameless in his sight. In love he predestined us to be adopted as his sons through Jesus Christ, in accordance with his pleasure and his will—(Ephesians 1:4, 5, *New International Version*).

HYMN FOR TODAY: "I Was In His Mind"

Dear (insert your name here),

Did you know that you were in the mind of God even before the creation of the world? Did you know that He knew that you would be born on (put your birthday here), and that you would desperately need a Savior?

Take a moment to think that God put on flesh and came to your world—not just for a mass of humanity—but especially for you, personally.

Through Jesus' death on the cross, He can be your loving Father, and call you His own. Allow Him to give you His blessings, to teach you, and share with you His wisdom. Through submission, experience His power through His Holy Spirit. Ask Him to use you so that you can know the fellowship of brothers and sisters in Him.

He's preparing for you a very special place where you can fully enjoy life as it is meant to be, and you will be able to see Him face to face!

May His joy be yours. May His hope be yours. With His wisdom and love flowing through you, put your hand in your Father's hand to enjoy a life beyond compare!

PRAYER THOUGHTS: Lord God, nothing can compare to Your holiness and power. And yet, You have chosen us! May our lives be an eternal song of gratitude and praise to You. Amen.

WHO AM I?

SCRIPTURE: John 1:19-23

VERSE FOR TODAY: John replied in the words of Isaiah the prophet, "I am the voice of one calling in the desert, 'Make straight the way for the Lord'" (John 1:23, *New International Version*).

HYMN FOR TODAY: "Take My Life and Let It Be Consecrated"

A recent television series told the story of a man whose identity had been electronically erased by his enemies. He spent the entire show trying to reestablish who he was, with very little success.

John the Baptist's identity was questioned critically by many who heard him preach and saw the influence he had over others. However, John was not intimidated by the questions or the questioners. He had a clear sense of who he was and who he was not. Most importantly, he knew the purpose for which he had been placed on earth: proclaiming the message of repentance in preparation for Christ. Nothing could pull him away from that purpose.

As Christians, we also may face times when people question us about who we are and what right we have to speak on certain issues. In those times, we also need to draw on our sense of who we are and what God has called us to do. We have His authority to speak His Word and make His will and His love known in this world. Otherwise, we have no identity in Him.

Who are you?

PRAYER THOUGHTS: Dear God, thank You for giving us identity in You. Help us not to be pulled away from the purpose You have given us by any criticism or opposition we might face. Amen.

March 8-14. **Paul Friskney**, his wife, Ann, and their children, Hannah and Ben, live in Cincinnati, Ohio, where he teaches English and Communications at Cincinnati Bible College.

COMPARED TO WHAT?

SCRIPTURE: John 1:24-28

VERSE FOR TODAY: He is the one who comes after me, the thongs of whose sandals I am not worthy to untie (John 1:27, *New International Version*).

HYMN FOR TODAY: "His Name Is Wonderful"

As a teacher, I find it interesting to see how different students react to the same grade. For some, a "C" is a valued treasure while for others it is a slap in the face. The difference comes down to what is used as a standard of comparison. For most, it's their past performance, whether good or bad. Others look to the overall performance of those around them. But the best students consider their performance in light of the highest possible achievement marks and are discouraged when they fall short of that.

Those who came to John the Baptist felt that he was claiming too much authority, but John made it clear that he knew exactly how much authority he had because he compared it to the true standard: the authority of Christ. His self-esteem was based not on what he was doing, but on the One who was far greater than he.

If we base our view of ourselves on what we can accomplish, we will have varying rates of success, but ultimately, we will all fail. Only One has perfect power and authority. He deserves all of our worship, and everything we do ought to point others to Him.

PRAYER THOUGHTS: Dear Lord, help us always to be willing to recognize You for who You are and to point others to You through every aspect of our lives. We pray this prayer in the name of Jesus, the perfect one. Amen.

THE POWER OF A TESTIMONY

SCRIPTURE: John 1:29-34

VERSE FOR TODAY: Live such good lives among the pagans that, though they accuse you of doing wrong, they may see your good deeds and glorify God on the day he visits us (1 Peter 2:12 *New International Version*).

HYMN FOR TODAY: "Living for Jesus"

Why was it powerful when John pointed out Jesus as the Messiah, the One to follow? Why did other people believe him and accept the power of his testimony? The reasons can be found in John's life and testimony.

First, every aspect of John's life showed his commitment to his message. What he ate, what he wore, where he lived, how he spoke—all these things identified him as completely surrendered to seeing God's will fulfilled on this earth.

Second, John's message focused on God and not on his own interests, well being, or advancement. He offered hope to his listeners through two images that represented God's mercy and forgiveness: the lamb and the dove.

The challenge to us is direct and immediate. We need to look at our own testimonies for Christ and how they are received by others. First, are our lives completely committed to God? Second, is our conversation focused on God? Or do we reflect the self-focus that characterizes our society? What needs to change for our testimonies to make an impact on the lives of others?

PRAYER THOUGHTS: Dear God, many times we wish that we could make a stronger impact for You on those around us. Help us to be willing to alter how we live and what we say to make that happen. Amen.

March 11

POINTING THE WAY

SCRIPTURE: John 1:35-42

VERSE FOR TODAY: I myself am convinced, my brothers, that you yourselves are full of goodness, complete in knowledge and competent to instruct one another (Romans 15:14, *New International Version*).

HYMN FOR TODAY: "Freely, Freely"

Today is my mother's birthday, and this passage of Scripture is appropriate for a celebration of her life. My mother instilled in me the desire to follow Christ. She did it through many means (and with much help from my father and others), but most significantly she did it through her complete conviction in the truth of who He is.

John the Baptist pointed Andrew to Christ. Andrew brought Peter to Him. Peter preached to thousands on the day of Pentecost. And the message continues to travel along chains begun there. But what happens if any link in the chain doesn't hook up to another? The chain ends.

As receivers of the message of Christ and as ones who share relationship with Him, we must let others know about the One who provides hope, healing, and salvation. If we keep quiet, we will not be fulfilling our duty, and some will miss out on the chance of eternity with God. You have been given a unique situation in which to spread the message of Christ whether it is more like John preaching to crowds or more like Andrew talking to his brother. God expects you to use that situation to point others to Him. Who do you need to be pointing to Christ today?

PRAYER THOUGHTS: Dear God, we don't have to look far to see others around us who need to be brought to You. Help us to communicate our love for them by telling them of Your love. Thank You for our salvation in Christ Jesus. In His name, we pray. Amen.

GO, TELL WHAT YOU SEE AND HEAR

SCRIPTURE: Luke 7:18-28

VERSE FOR TODAY: Blessed is the man who does not fall away on account of me (Luke 7:23, *New International Version*).

HYMN FOR TODAY: "O for a Thousand Tongues"

In graduate school, I met a woman who struggled with many doubts because of vastly different influences in her life, beginning in a fundamentalist Christian home and ending in ultra-feminist organizations in college. She also had a lot of bitterness toward the church because of the criticism she had received for her doubt.

I pointed out to her that Jesus dealt with doubt very differently from the way our defensiveness leads us to respond. Jesus simply pointed the doubter to evidence to believe. He did it for Thomas by showing the marks in His hands and His sides. And He helped John in his time of doubt by pointing him to the miracles that served as evidence of who Jesus was. The evidence was enough to erase John's doubt and to keep him faithful to God's plan of salvation even to the point of giving up his own life.

To help us in our times of doubt, Jesus Christ offers us the evidence of His Word, His life, His death, His resurrection, and His continuing love for us. The question is not whether we doubt but whether we allow ourselves to be controlled by our doubts or to be freed by His evidence to live the lives He intends for us.

PRAYER THOUGHTS: Dear God, help us to look to Your evidence when we experience doubt and to respond as You would to others who are facing doubt. Help us to focus our vision on who You are and what You do in our world. In the name of Jesus, we pray. Amen.

A FUNDAMENTAL DIFFERENCE

SCRIPTURE: John 3:22-36

VERSE FOR TODAY: The one who comes from above is above all; the one who is from the earth belongs to the earth, and speaks as one from the earth. The one who comes from heaven is above all (John 3:31, *New International Version*).

HYMN FOR TODAY: "Majesty"

My geometry teacher taught me fundamental truths and often reminded me that I could never find the correct answers without them. I remember thinking that his words were truer than he realized. There are certain truths that we must not forget if we are going to find answers.

One of those truths relates to the appropriate distinction between who Christ Jesus is and who we are. Christ is the Son of God, chosen from before the foundation of the world to bring salvation. He is the hope of all mankind and the all powerful King. We are not.

While most of us freely admit that truth, we don't always live by it. We feel responsible for solving the world's problems. We see others as hopeless because of their situations or their characters. We consider sins of others to be directed against us rather than against Christ.

John understood who he was and who he wasn't. He knew where to look for true authority, and he was pleased, not angered, when others turned away from him to the Greater Power. How can we follow his example and let go of our lives or others' lives so Christ can be the only King?

PRAYER THOUGHTS: Dear Father, when we start to feel as if it all depends on us or we feel slighted because we haven't gotten the recognition we think we deserve, focus our eyes on Your glory and Your power. In the name of our Savior, Jesus Christ, we pray. Amen.

FAITHFUL BEYOND DEATH

SCRIPTURE: Mark 6:14-29

VERSE FOR TODAY: Be faithful, even to the point of death, and I will give you the crown of life (Revelation 2:10, *New International Version*).

HYMN FOR TODAY: "I'll Live for Him"

When I was in church camp, one of the favorites for Bible drama night was the story of the beheading of John the Baptist. I'm not quite sure why. It might have been the commitment the story demonstrates, but more likely, it was the opportunity to do a story with a gruesome ending.

John's life did have a gruesome, sad ending. After years of faithfulness and righteousness, acknowledged even by his murderer, John was beheaded at the whim of a child based on the urging of an evil mother—a woman who wanted to keep John from bothering Heriod and thought that she had silenced him forever. But it didn't work. Yes, Herodias was able to have John killed, but Herod obviously still heard his voice. When Herod learned of the teaching of Jesus, the Messiah, his first thought was of John.

John's message and presence are still felt long after his death. When we commit ourselves to the work of Christ in whatever form He chooses, we do not know for certain where it will lead us. However, we can be certain that the thing we are working for and the message we are carrying will outlive us. Christ's work is for eternity. Are earthly, temporary concerns keeping us from being completely committed to the work that will live on long after we are gone?

PRAYER THOUGHTS: Dear God, thank You for the examples of men and women whose commitment to You continued beyond death to make an impact for eternity. Help us to be that same kind of example for those who follow us. Amen.

AN INTERESTING VISIT

SCRIPTURE: John 3:1-10

VERSE FOR TODAY: Therefore, if anyone is in Christ, he is a new creation; the old has gone, the new has come! (2 Corinthians 5:17, *New International Version*).

HYMN FOR TODAY: "Whiter than Snow"

Today's text relates an interesting visit because of when it happened, the persons involved, and the teaching that was given. Nicodemus went to Jesus at night. This was not a cowardly act. Rather, it was a very wise choice. It should be observed that Nicodemus was a Pharisee and a member of the Sanhedrin. Coming at night, he would not jeopardize Jesus or himself with the people or with the Jewish Council.

Nicodemus was a Jewish ruler and a person of high position who had the respect of the people. He regarded Jesus Christ as a teacher par excellence, who was sent by God the Father. He said to Jesus, "Rabbi, we know you are a teacher who has come from God. For no one can perform the miraculous signs you are doing if God were not with him" (John 3:2, *New International Version*). Nicodemus came to Jesus wanting information about the kingdom of God.

Jesus told Nicodemus that he must be born of water and spirit to become a new creation. This is accomplished by the converting, transforming power of the Holy Spirit.

What an interesting visit!

PRAYER THOUGHTS: Father, help us to be people of courage and commitment. May we be grateful for Your saving and transforming power. In Jesus' name. Amen.

March 15-21. **Merle Melton** is a retired Christian minister. He and his wife, Martha, make their home in Iowa City, Iowa, where they continue in service to Christ and His church.

GOD'S LOVE IS FOR ALL

SCRIPTURE: John 3:11-21

VERSE FOR TODAY: This is love: not that we loved God, but that he loved us and sent his Son as an atoning sacrifice for our sins (1 John 4:10, *New International Version*).

HYMN FOR TODAY: "I Stand Amazed in the Presence"

Think of today's topic in a new and imaginative way. God's love embraces all who will receive it. We are to be examples and messengers to a world of needy people.

"World" denotes the cosmos of unrighteousness. This embraces all classes of people and every social level. It includes the entire range of professional people, those in skilled and unskilled trades, and those who work at menial tasks. Also included are people of varying degrees of educational attainment and every level of financial standing. "World" includes the morally approved and the socially rejected. God loves this world, and this is the world that we are to love.

Let's follow Jesus' example as He came not to judge or condemn the world but that through Him the world would be saved. He worked with the morally approved and the morally rejected. Likewise, in the apostolic church there were people of every conceivable background. Please read the following Scriptures from this point of view: 1 Corinthians 6:9-11 and Ephesians 4:17–5:21.

As God's messengers of love, let's be understanding, compassionate, non-judgmental and non-condemnatory. Let's share His love with all people.

PRAYER THOUGHTS: Father, make us keenly aware that it is Your desire that all people come to repentance and live. May we realize that we need Your help and pardon. In Jesus' name. Amen.

NICODEMUS RAISES A LEGAL QUESTION

SCRIPTURE: John 7:45-52

VERSE FOR TODAY: Be strong and courageous. Do not be afraid or terrified because of them, for the Lord your God goes with you, he will never leave you nor forsake you (Deuteronomy 31:6, *New International Version*).

HYMN FOR TODAY: "All for Jesus"

The Sanhedrin is determined to arrest Jesus and have Him killed. They see no other way to eradicate the influence of His teachings. Many are asking if He may not be the Christ. "When the Christ comes, will he do more miraculous signs than this man?" (John 7:31, *New International Version*). The Jewish Council did not want His teachings to continue. To accomplish their goal, the temple guards were sent to arrest Jesus. But when the guards returned they did not bring Jesus with them. The message of Jesus had disarmed them. The guards received the stern reproofs of the Council for their failed attempt.

At this point, Nicodemus raises a legal question, "Does our law condemn anyone without first hearing him . . . ?" (John 7:51, *New International Version*). We have to admire Nicodemus. His integrity would not let him keep quiet. The question asked was wisely worded. He made no commitment regarding the identity of Jesus. He simply questioned the legality of this procedure. To issue this kind of challenge under these circumstances took great courage. May we, like Nicodemus, be courageous witnesses.

PRAYER THOUGHTS: Father, may we be courageous followers of Christ Jesus. Help us not to be timid or to draw back when facing difficult situations. May we act wisely and prudently when we are in adverse circumstances. In Jesus' name. Amen.

REAL COURAGE!

SCRIPTURE: John 19:38-42

VERSE FOR TODAY: Wait on the LORD: be of good courage, and he shall strengthen thine heart: wait, I say, on the LORD (Psalm 27:14).

HYMN FOR TODAY: "Ivory Palaces"

Earlier in their relationship with Jesus Christ, Joseph and Nicodemus did not openly admit that they were His followers. Joseph was a secret disciple and Nicodemus, at an earlier time, had gone to Jesus at night. Let's not misinterpret their actions. They were both prominent Jewish men who were members of the Sanhedrin. To openly admit that they were followers of Jesus would have placed them in very dangerous positions.

In our Scripture, Jesus Christ has just died. These men now act very courageously. Joseph, accompanied by Nicodemus, went to Pilate and asked for the body of Jesus. The request was granted, and Joseph took away His body.

Because the Sabbath would soon begin, they had to act quickly to prepare the body of Jesus for burial. Joseph bought the linen cloth (the linen strips used for burial), and Nicodemus provided seventy-five pounds of myrrh and aloes. Joseph furnished a new tomb that was in a garden near Golgotha. Jesus received a kingly burial.

The death of Jesus transformed these men. They were no longer afraid or fearful. They acted boldly and courageously. May the transforming death, burial, and resurrection of Jesus empower us to demonstrate real courage.

PRAYER THOUGHTS: Heavenly Father, help us to have a deep commitment to the Lord Jesus Christ. May we have a deep love for Him. Grant to us insights that we may know how to handle the hard issues in life and make the right choices in difficult situations. We ask for real courage! In Jesus' name. Amen.

NOTHING BETWEEN

SCRIPTURE: Matthew 19:16-22

VERSE FOR TODAY: What good will it be for a man if he gains the whole world, yet forfeits his soul? Or what can a man give in exchange for his soul? (Matthew 16:26, *New International Version*).

HYMN FOR TODAY: "Lord, I Care Not for Riches"

The rich young man desired the greatest gift, eternal life, and he went to the right person to learn what he needed to do to have this gift. When Jesus told him to sell all that he had and give to the poor, he considered the demand to be too great. "He went away sad, because he had great wealth." His love of possessions came between him and eternal life.

The rich young man shared many of the moral and spiritual traits possessed by Joseph and Nicodemus. All were moral, upright, spiritual people. They had positions of prominence and were respected by the people. Each had wealth.

In the crucial decisions of life, these men took divergent paths. Joseph and Nicodemus, after Jesus' death, acted boldly and sacrificially. They removed the body of Jesus from the cross. They used their wealth to give Jesus a kingly burial. Nothing stood between them and Him. The young man let his wealth come between him and doing the will of Jesus. He was mastered by his wealth. Greed held him in its clutches. He went away sorrowful.

In our lives, let's permit nothing to come between us and Jesus. Let's implicitly follow Him.

PRAYER THOUGHTS: Heavenly Father, we have many decisions to make in life. Help us to make wise decisions. May we make hard choices when these are necessary. May nothing be permitted to come between us and You. May it be our supreme desire to please You. In Jesus' name. Amen.

WHEN IT IS CONVENIENT

SCRIPTURE: Acts 24:22-27

VERSE FOR TODAY: For he is our God and we are the people of his pasture, the flock under his care. Today, if you hear his voice, do not harden your hearts as you did at Meribah, as you did that day at Massah in the desert, (Psalm 95:7, 8, *New International Version*).

HYMN FOR TODAY: "Have You Any Room for Jesus?"

Felix, the governor, and his wife, Drusilla, had a marvelous opportunity to become followers of the Lord Jesus Christ. The apostle Paul, who was a prisoner at this time, was very qualified to instruct them in the Christian faith. Although the lives of Felix and Drusilla were very flawed, he was "well acquainted with the Way," (Acts 24:22, *New International Version*), and she had the advantage of being a Jewess. The time came when they permitted Paul to speak to them about faith in Christ Jesus.

In Paul's presentation of the gospel, he chose the themes that would address their particular backgrounds. He spoke of righteousness, self-control, and the judgment to come. He presented the ethical features of the gospel that require moral changes in daily living. These were changes they were unwilling to make. Felix said, "You may leave. When I find it convenient, I will send for you." Even though they talked frequently, Paul was never again permitted to present the gospel of Jesus Christ to Felix and Drusilla. By their unwillingness to let go of the sins in their lives, they chose to reject the gospel. There was never a convenient time.

PRAYER THOUGHTS: Heavenly Father, make us keenly aware of the dangers of waiting for a more convenient time to do Your will. May we, as Christians, realize that this applies to us the same as it applies to non-Christians. Help us to act decisively in obeying Your will at the present time. In Jesus' name. Amen.

GOD IS OUR REFUGE

SCRIPTURE: Psalm 91:1-16

VERSE FOR TODAY: The eternal God is your refuge, and underneath are the everlasting arms (Deuteronomy 33:27, *New International Version*).

HYMN FOR TODAY: "Under His Wings"

This psalm has been a source of comfort and strength for believers under both Testaments. God's concern for His children and the protective care that He gives to them are presented under a wide range of figures of speech. His protection is against all the perils that we may face in life. He makes it possible for us to dwell safely and securely in Him. We may say of the Almighty, "The Lord is my refuge and fortress" (Psalm 91:2, *New International Version*).

This psalm clearly delineates the type of person who has the promise of God's protective care. The picture is that of a person who has an active faith and trust in God. This person "dwells in the shelter of the Most High" (Psalm 91:1, *New International Version*). He lives in daily communion with God and chooses to obey His will. The believer enjoys God's fellowship. This person lives a life of trust in God. The Christian's whole life is centered in Him. Other characteristics are: the believer acknowledges God's name, he calls upon God's holy name, and he expresses his love for Him. What a beautiful description of a believer!

The believer has the assurance of God's faithfulness. Our love for God is rewarded with His protection in danger. The faithful of both Testaments have dwelt securely in Him.

PRAYER THOUGHTS: Heavenly Father, thank You for Your faithfulness to us. May Your faithfulness challenge us to a greater faithfulness to You. May we place our complete trust in You. Thank You for being our refuge. In Jesus' name. Amen.

RESISTING CULTURAL BIAS

SCRIPTURE: John 4:1-6

VERSE FOR TODAY: So he came to a town in Samaria called Sychar, near the plot of ground Jacob had given to his son Joseph (John 4:5, *New International Version*).

HYMN FOR TODAY: "More Like the Master"

The setting of this Scripture is the town of Sychar in the province of Samaria. In Jesus' day the country of Palestine was divided into three provinces—Judea to the south, Galilee to the north and Samaria in between. Jesus and His disciples had left Judea and were traveling to Galilee through Samaria.

Even though it doubled their traveling time, most Jews by-passed this province when traveling between Judea and Galilee because of an intense hatred for the Samaritan people. The inception of this animosity occurred 700 years earlier when Assyria captured the Northern Kingdom. They deported most of the Jews and settled foreigners in Samaria. Those Jews remaining in Samaria intermarried with the foreigners and produced the mixed race of people known as Samaritans. To the "pure" Jew this was unforgivable. Jesus was not bound by these cultural restrictions. Not only did He travel through Samaria, He stopped to rest at the well of His ancestor, Jacob.

Today's Scripture provides the backdrop for a thought pro-voking question. Are we bound by the cultural restrictions of our society, or do we, like Jesus, cast aside restrictions that promote animosity rather than love?

PRAYER THOUGHTS: Thank You, Father, for the example set by Jesus. May we look to Him and have the courage to walk through the Samarias of our world. In Jesus' name. Amen.

March 22-28. **Martha Melton** is a Language Arts Consultant for the Iowa City Community School District, Iowa City, Iowa, where she makes her home with her husband, Merle.

THE WOMAN AT THE WELL

SCRIPTURE: John 4:7-15

VERSE FOR TODAY: The woman said to him, "Sir, give me this water so that I won't get thirsty and have to keep coming here to draw water" (John 4:15, *New International Version*).

HYMN FOR TODAY: "Fill My Cup, Lord"

The Samaritan woman was astonished when Jesus asked her for a drink of water. Not only was there hatred between the Jews and Samaritans, but it was forbidden for a Jewish Rabbi to speak to any woman in public, and she was a woman surrounded by scandal! Despite these barriers, Jesus offered this woman living water.

Though the woman interpreted Jesus' conversation literally, He was speaking of satisfying that basic longing in the heart of every man and woman which produces a thirst that only He can quench. We may try to satisfy that longing with pleasure, material things, and even by doing charitable acts. Through these we experience some happiness, spurts of joy, and a certain sense of satisfaction, but the longing always returns. It is much like C. S. Lewis' description of his pursuit of joy prior to becoming a Christian. Joy seemed an "esthetic experience" which was always transitory. He concludes by saying, "To tell you the truth, the subject has lost nearly all interest for me since I became a Christian" (*The Joyful Christian*, 1977).

That is precisely what happens when we drink of the living water. The longing is satisfied, and our pursuit is over because we are one with the source of the living water.

PRAYER THOUGHTS: Father, thank You for providing the source of the living water. Fill our cups to overflowing with Your love and compassion. Then help us, Father, to share this love and compassion with others. In Jesus' name. Amen.

ONE WHO LOVES US

SCRIPTURE: John 4:16-26

VERSE FOR TODAY: Then Jesus declared, "I who speak to you am he" (John 4:26, *New International Version*).

HYMN FOR TODAY: "I Surrender All"

A truly great blessing in this life is to find a mate or friend with whom you have intimate rapport. One whom you can trust completely. One who knows your faults and loves you anyway. One who supports you and encourages you to reach the potential others do not see.

When Jesus began to converse with the Samaritan woman, there was immediate rapport. Then suddenly she was jolted by the realization that this man knew her lurid past. As we do so often in disconcerting circumstances, the woman changed the subject. Jesus used the new conversation as an opportunity for making the startling announcement, "I am the Messiah!" As the Messiah, Jesus not only loved this sinful woman, but where her neighbors saw an outcast, He saw a woman who would evangelize her community.

Earthly friends and companions are precious to us, but none can compare with the Messiah. He is the one who knows all of our sins and loves us just as He did the Samaritan woman. He knows what we can become if we surrender ourselves to Him. But we must say, as did the Samaritan woman, "Give me this water that I may not thirst."

PRAYER THOUGHTS: Thank You, Lord, for loving us in spite of all of the sins and transgressions we have committed. Thank You for looking past our earthly weaknesses and seeing within each of us the potential for a higher calling. May we strive to be worthy of Your love. In Jesus' name, we pray. Amen.

RESISTING SOCIAL PRESSURE

SCRIPTURE: John 4:27-42

VERSE FOR TODAY: Just then his disciples returned and were surprised to find him talking with a woman. But no one asked, "What do you want?" or "Why are you talking with her?" (John 4:27, *New International Version*).

HYMN FOR TODAY: "They'll Know We Are Christians by Our Love"

The disciples were astonished when they returned to find Jesus talking to the Samaritan woman, but they asked no questions. They were learning that Jesus did not succumb to social pressure. They offered Him food, but He was already refreshed by the spiritual food of doing His Father's work.

It takes courage to resist social pressure, but when we do not, the results can be disastrous. In the children's book, *Terrible Things, An Allegory of the Holocaust* by Eve Bunting, the animals were content in the forest. Then the "terrible things" began taking away one species of animals at a time. When Little Rabbit asked why, his fellow animals silenced him, saying, "We don't want them to get mad at us." Finally, all of the animals were gone except Little Rabbit who hid among the rocks. At last, he realized his responsibility and how things might have been different if the animals had stood up for what was right.

Do we have the courage to reject social pressure when it is opposed to God's will? Jesus' desire for His disciples is that we seek the same spiritual food that refreshed Him.

PRAYER THOUGHTS: Father, may we seek spiritual food today. May we resist social pressures and love all of those whom You created. Forgive us if we have lacked compassion or have failed to stand for what is right. In Jesus' name. Amen.

DEEDS OF KINDNESS

SCRIPTURE: Matthew 10:37-42

VERSE FOR TODAY: And if anyone gives even a cup of cold water to one of these little ones because he is my disciple, I tell you the truth, he will certainly not lose his reward (Matthew 10:42, *New International Version*).

HYMN FOR TODAY: "A Beautiful Life"

Mosaics, made by interlaying small pieces of varied colored material into designs, are among our most beautiful artwork. The individual pieces may be simple, but together they are lovely. Our lives are like mosaics. Many of the tiles forming the overall design represent the cups of cold water, or good deeds, done or received in the name of Christ. We do the deeds. God gives the reward.

Many years ago, a teenager was facing legal charges. My husband helped him with his problem, and later performed his marriage ceremony. To my husband, this was giving a cup of cold water in the name of Christ. To the couple, it was a life-changing event.

A dear friend of mine frequently gave me a cup of cold water. Often when I was feeling discouraged, a phone call or prayer-gram would come from him. I asked him once how he knew to send those messages, and he replied, "I send them when I want you to know I am praying for you."

I thank God for the tiles in the mosaic of my life. May many of these tiles represent my kindness to others.

PRAYER THOUGHTS: Father, only You can know the fruits that may come as a result of a kindness done. May we accept our responsibility for being kind and serving others, realizing that it is through us, Your children, that Your work is done on earth. Thank You for the opportunity of service. In Jesus' name. Amen.

THE FREE GIFT OF THE WATER OF LIFE

SCRIPTURE: Revelation 22:16-21

VERSE FOR TODAY: The Spirit and the bride say, "Come!" And let him who hears say, "Come!" Whoever is thirsty, let him come; and whoever wishes, let him take the free gift of the water of life (Revelation 22:17, *New International Version*).

HYMN FOR TODAY: "Whosoever Will"

Thirst is a more intense drive than hunger. Water accounts for approximately three-fourths of our body weight, and our bodies must have water to survive. The pangs of thirst produce within us a fervent desire for water. Often the Scriptures use the analogy of water when referring to salvation.

Isaiah says, "Come, all you who are thirsty, come to the waters;" (Isaiah 55:1, *New International Version*). Jesus said, "He who believes in me will never be thirsty" (John 6:35, *New International Version*) and "Blessed are those who hunger and thirst for righteousness, for they will be filled" (Matthew 5:6, *New International Version*). To the Samaritan woman, he offered living water.

Today's Scripture offers the great and final invitation of the Revelation using this same analogy. "Whoever is thirsty, let him come;" (Revelation 22:17, *New International Version*). Whoever has a sincere desire for salvation is assured acceptance—young or old, rich or poor, educated or uneducated, any nationality, the invitation is open to all. What a closing to the greatest book on earth!

PRAYER THOUGHTS: Our Father, it is not possible to express the deep gratitude we feel for Your goodness and mercy. Thank You for the water of life. Thank You for the universal invitation of the gospel. May we share it with others. In Jesus' name. Amen.

THE TRIUMPHAL ENTRY

SCRIPTURE: Mark 11:1-11

VERSE FOR TODAY: Those who went ahead and those who followed shouted, "Hosanna!" "Blessed is he who comes in the name of the Lord!" (Mark 11:9, *New International Version*).

HYMN FOR TODAY: "Jesus Paid It All"

The Triumphal Entry marks the beginning of the end of Christ's earthly ministry. Jesus came into Jerusalem as a king. As He rode into the city, the crowd threw their cloaks upon the road and strewed palm branches in His path. These were common people who could not afford to line the road with the customary flowers, wave expensive banners, and greet the Lord with fanfare. Rather, they used their cloaks and palm branches cut from the fields to line His path, and their fanfare was their voices crying out, "Hosanna!"

This was a wondrous occasion for the Lord, but it was marred by one shadow. These people were praising Him and proclaiming Him the Messiah because they expected Him to deliver the Jewish nation from Roman rule and establish a new kingdom. He alone knew that by the end of the week, their loyalty would be gone, and He would be crucified.

After the celebration, Jesus went out to the peace of Bethany to be with His disciples and gain strength for the week ahead. After three years of giving living water to so many, He must now prepare to pay the price so that we, too, may be partakers of that water.

PRAYER THOUGHTS: Holy Father, may we always be cognizant of the monumental price paid for our salvation. Remind us not only of the crucifixion, but the loneliness, humiliation, betrayal, and abandonment heaped upon Christ during His final days. Thank You for caring so much for each of us. In Jesus' name. Amen.

WHOM DO YOU SEEK?

SCRIPTURE: John 18:1-14

VERSE FOR TODAY: Then Jesus, knowing all that was to befall him, came forward and said to them, "Whom do you seek?" (John 18:4, *Revised Standard Version*).

HYMN FOR TODAY: "'Are Ye Able,' Said the Master"

It was a sad day indeed when Judas Iscariot betrayed Christ Jesus. Jesus had entered into the Garden of Gethsemane, a little garden on the slopes of the Mount of Olives. He was there with His disciples. They went there often for peace and quiet. It was here in the midst of this peaceful garden that Judas the betrayer had plotted the arrest of the Lord. He brought with him a larger than necessary army of Jewish and Roman soldiers. The number of soldiers may have been as few as two hundred or as many as one thousand, far more than needed to arrest one man. But Judas was a coward and desired to insure that his betrayal would not have personal consequences.

Jesus on the other hand was the model of courage. He knew all that was going to happen. Still He went up to Judas and the soldiers in the garden asking, "Whom do you seek?" He was not afraid. Again He asked them, "Whom do you seek?" Then as a further example of His courage, He said, "If you seek me, let these men go."

Every day holds opportunities for faithfulness or betrayal on our part. Whom do you seek?

PRAYER THOUGHTS: Heavenly Father, we grieve for those times that we have betrayed you. Please forgive us. Give us the courage this day to live for You. Amen.

March 29-31. **Dan Lawson** is director of Development at Emmanuel School of Religion in Johnson City, Tennessee. He and his wife, Linda, have two children.

ARE YOU A FOLLOWER OF CHRIST?

SCRIPTURE: John 18:15-27

VERSE FOR TODAY: The maid who kept the door said to Peter, "Are not you also one of this man's disciples?" He said, "I am not" (John 18:17, *Revised Standard Version*).

HYMN FOR TODAY: "Stand Up, Stand Up for Jesus"

When Jesus was arrested in the Garden of Gethsemane after being betrayed by Judas, Peter took a sword in hand to defend the Lord. In fact, he cut off the ear of the high priest's slave, but Jesus forbade him from violence, commanding him to put his sword away. The soldiers took Jesus away, but Peter and another disciple followed. It was obviously Peter's intention to come to the defense of Christ Jesus, but the actions that followed were just the opposite. When questioned about his relationship to Jesus, Peter denied that he was a follower.

Peter's loyalty to Christ was mixed with contradictions. After the arrest of Jesus, the other disciples fled. Only Peter and one other disciple dared to follow Him as the soldiers led Jesus away. Now that is loyalty! But then Peter was guilty of disloyalty when he rejected Christ by saying "No" to the question, "Are not you also one of this man's disciples?"

Our loyalty to Christ is realized when we admit in the privacy of our own heart that every good and perfect gift comes from above. But more importantly, when those around us remain silent and aloof, our loyalty to Christ Jesus is a very public expression when we say, "Yes, I am a follower of Christ!"

PRAYER THOUGHTS: Father, forgive us when we have denied You before others in word or in deed. We know that it is not enough for us to call you "Lord" in the privacy of our own heart and mind. May we stand up for You this day. In Jesus' name. Amen.

THE RESPONSIBILITY OF A CHOICE

SCRIPTURE: John 18:28-40

VERSE FOR TODAY: And if you be unwilling to serve the LORD, choose this day whom you will serve, . . . but as for me and my house, we will serve the LORD (Joshua 24:15, *Revised Standard Version*).

HYMN FOR TODAY: "I Have Decided to Follow Jesus"

Jesus was brought before Pilate to be judged, but Pilate could find no guilt. He questioned Christ; he interrogated Him. He endeavored to push the judgment onto the Jewish mobs. He tried to get personal with Christ through conversation, hoping for some clear answers. After all was said and done, Pilate found Jesus blameless. He was not guilty. He was not a criminal. But Pilate, fearing a riot of the people, decided to give them a choice. Would they have him release Jesus or the robber Barabbas? That was the choice that Pilate gave to the people. It was now their responsibility to make the decision.

Life brings us a choice, a decision to make about Christ Jesus. That choice is our responsibility. We choose to make Jesus our Lord when we become a Christian. But in addition, we make choices daily as we live our lives for Christ. Jesus said, "If you love me, keep my commandments." Each day brings challenges to the Lordship of Jesus over us. Yes, Joshua's words hold true for us as we choose whom we will serve. Will we serve mammon, material possessions, or will we serve the Lord? Our task is to follow Jesus. May His will be our will to obey.

PRAYER THOUGHTS: O Holy Father, guide us to a greater understanding of Your will. Help us to know how we might serve You not only in the motives of our lives, but also in each deed. We long to be Yours and to have Your Holy Spirit dwell within us. In Jesus' name. Amen.

DEVOTIONS™

April

photo by Ward Patterson

VERDICT BY MOB

SCRIPTURE: John 19:1-16

VERSE FOR TODAY: He who finds his life will lose it, and he who loses his life for my sake will find it (Matthew 10:39, *Revised Standard Version*).

HYMN FOR TODAY: "I'll Live for Him"

It is justice to condemn a criminal or a wrong-doer. It is injustice to find guilty one who has done nothing wrong. Americans come from a society that has high regard for a system of justice where one is presumed innocent until proven guilty. In the western world, there are courts, judges, juries, lawyers, and verdicts. All of these are part of the judicial order through which guilt or innocence is determined.

Pilate said to the mob, "I find in him no fault at all" (John 18:38). You would have reason to conclude that a judge had made a judgment, and the case was thus closed. Not so. The mob apparently ruled the day. Pilate, the judge, became more afraid. Try as hard as he could to release Jesus, the mob condemned an innocent man. Even today, mob violence can be irrational and justice will find no friend.

Faith is a positive judgment based on evidence. The Christian is one who makes a positive judgment that Jesus is the Christ, the Son of the living God. On the basis of positive judgment, the believer makes Jesus the Lord and Ruler of his life. It is not a decision to condemn Him, but rather it is a decision to live for Him.

PRAYER THOUGHTS: Father in Heaven, we love You and seek to live for You. May we be found faithful. Use us this day to lead others to Christ Jesus, in whose name we pray. Amen.

April 1-4. **Dan Lawson** is the Director of Development for the Emmanuel School of Religion in Johnson City, Tennessee. He and his wife, Linda, have two children.

IT IS FINISHED

SCRIPTURE: John 19:17-30

VERSE FOR TODAY: When Jesus had received the vinegar, he said, "It is finished"; and he bowed his head and gave up his spirit (John 19:30, *Revised Standard Version*).

HYMN FOR TODAY: "Were You There?"

In the city of Jerusalem today there are two probable sites for the burial of Christ Jesus. To some, the favorite is the garden tomb site near what is called Gordon's Calvary. At one end of this beautiful garden is a carved-out cave in which it is believed that our Lord was buried in the borrowed tomb of Joseph of Arimathea. But at the other end of the garden is a jagged hillside that looks very much like Golgotha. Rock impressions in the side of the hillside cause the rock to look much like a skull.

As you visit this site, you are awestruck because you are reminded that our Lord and Savior Jesus the Christ died His sacrificial death on our behalf. He did not die because He did something wrong, as a common criminal has. He did not die because He deserved to die. He died for a purpose—to pay the price for our sinfulness.

There is something sad about reading the words of Christ when He said, "It is finished." He could have meant that His life was done. He may have meant that His life's work was accomplished. He came to earth for a purpose, and that purpose was now accomplished. He came that those who believe in Him should not perish but have life that lasts forever. Victory is His! Victory is ours!

PRAYER THOUGHTS: "Thank You, Lord, for saving my soul, Thank You, Lord for making me whole; Thank You, Lord, for giving to me Thy great salvation so rich and free." (from the chorus, "Thank You, Lord")

THROUGH DAYS OF PREPARATION

SCRIPTURE: John 19:31-42

VERSE FOR TODAY: But one of the soldiers pierced his side with a spear, and at once there came out blood and water (John 19:34, *Revised Standard Version*).

HYMN FOR TODAY: "Rock of Ages, Cleft for Me"

It was the day of preparation for the Sabbath. According to the Jewish law, it was illegal for bodies to remain on the cross. The soldiers hurried death and broke the legs of the criminals on either side of the Lord. When the soldiers came to Jesus, they saw that He was already dead. A soldier pierced His side, and blood and water came out of the side of Christ.

Here we have the two symbols of the two great sacraments of the Church. The sacrament of baptism is based on water. The old life, where sin is put to death, is buried in order that the new life, where Christ is Lord, may be resurrected. A new life is born, a life committed to the likeness of Christ Jesus.

The sacrament of the Lord's Supper is based on the blood. The cup of wine, yes, the cup of blessing, is our participation in the blood that Christ shed upon the cross. When the Christian shares in that Supper, he does so out of an effort to remember the sacrifice that was made by Christ on the cross.

The Christian needs to participate in a time of preparation. Baptism prepares us not as the washing of the body, but as the appeal before God of a clear conscience. The Lord's Supper prepares the Christian by reminding him of God's grace. When we remember Christ's sacrifice, we cannot help but confess our sins and seek His forgiveness.

PRAYER THOUGHTS: Heavenly Father, thank You for an abundant life now and an eternal life to come. In the name of the Savior, amen.

MINE EYES HAVE SEEN THE GLORY

SCRIPTURE: John 20:1-18

VERSE FOR TODAY: Mary Magdalene went and said to the disciples, "I have seen the Lord"; and she told them that he had said these things to her (John 20:18, *Revised Standard Version*).

HYMN FOR TODAY: "Battle Hymn of the Republic"

Christ died and was buried; an apparent passing like any other mortal man. His life appeared to come to an end in defeat. But then something happened that proved that Jesus was indeed the Son of God. He conquered death. He was God over life and God over death. The cross could not still Him. The grave could not keep Him. He rose from the dead. Mary Magdalene and the disciples saw Him dead in the tomb, and then saw Him alive.

It was Mary who first discovered the tomb empty. She stood outside the tomb weeping when she was approached by Jesus. Assuming Him to be the gardener, she asked where the Lord's body had been taken. Once she found out that He was the Lord, she went to the disciples and declared, "I have seen the Lord!" (John 20:18, *Revised Standard Version*).

Mary and the disciples have had the opportunity to see the Lord with their own eyes. It is the testimony of those who have seen Him that draws us to the Savior even today.

After appearing to Mary, Jesus appeared to Thomas, the disciple, and said, "Because thou hast seen me, thou hast believed: blessed are they that have not seen, and yet have believed" (John 20:29). The Lord was speaking of us.

PRAYER THOUGHTS: Heavenly Father, we thank You for the hope that is ours. We know that because You arose from the dead, we, too, will someday arise from the grave, victorious on our way to Your Heaven. We look forward to Heaven where we will live in Your holy presence. Amen.

April 5

PARALYZED BY FEAR

SCRIPTURE: John 20:19-23

VERSE FOR TODAY: On the evening of that first day of the week, when the disciples were together, with the doors locked for fear of the Jews, Jesus came and stood among them and said, "Peace be with you!" (John 20:19, *New International Version*).

HYMN FOR TODAY: "Stand Up, Stand Up for Jesus"

My friend and I were hunting on an African mountain. Above us on a rocky ledge, a troop of baboons nervously paced and howled as they stared into the bush near us. Suddenly, my curiosity about their behavior gave way to fear when a leopard growled, warning us that we were getting too near. We, the bold hunters, were almost paralyzed by fear. Our only movement was our eyes searching the bush for a glimpse of the predator. The hunters had become the hunted.

John wrote, " . . . with the doors locked for fear of the Jews." Ten strong men, chosen by Jesus to change a hostile world, were prisoners of fear. Their sanctuary had become their prison. Go out and save the world had become stay in and save your skin.

Is fear a barrier in your life? Does it keep you from joy? Does it multiply guilt? Does it paralyze or retard your effective service? Hear the voice of Jesus, "Peace be with you! As the Father has sent me, I am sending you." Christians are not the prey, they are the hunters, sent to seek and to save the lost. "Peace be with you!"

PRAYER THOUGHTS: Father, give us the courage to enjoy the peace offered by Jesus. Let us learn to stand up, stand up in Him. Amen.

April 5-11. **Dr. David Grubbs** is the president of the Cincinnati Bible College and Seminary in Ohio. For many years, he and his wife, Eva, served the church as medical missionaries to Zimbabwe.

BELIEVING IS SEEING

SCRIPTURE: John 20:24-29

VERSE FOR TODAY: Then he said to Thomas, "Put your finger here; see my hands. Reach out your hand and put it into my side. Stop doubting and believe" (John 20:27, *New International Version*).

HYMN FOR TODAY: "Only Trust Him"

Are you a show-me person? Thomas was. A show-me person says, "If I can't see it, or smell it, touch it or taste it, hear it or conclude it, then it doesn't exist." Mr. Show-me reserves the right to be the standard for truth.

I had a strange experience. I was quite young and was sitting under the backyard shade tree on a hot summer day. It was so quiet that "not a creature was stirring, not even a mouse." In my isolation, it occurred to me that I was the only living creature on earth. I wondered, "Do other things really live and move, or do they do that only in my presence?" That attitude is called egocentrism (self-centered existence) and while normal during a brief period in childhood, it is an illness in an adult. It is the show-me attitude.

Some people see with their eyes, others with their finger tips. Some trust intellect, while others live life in a world of complex emotions. Jesus instructs us to live by faith. He said, "For judgment I have come into this world, so that the blind will see and those who see will become blind" (John 9:39, *New International Version*). Faith has 20/20 vision. Believing is seeing. Do you believe? If you do, seeing the truth of His Word will be easy.

PRAYER THOUGHTS: Dear Father, we cry out to you today as people of old did to Jesus, "I believe, please help my unbelief." Forgive us for our failure to live by faith for Jesus. Amen.

THE LAST TO KNOW

SCRIPTURE: Luke 24:13-27

VERSE FOR TODAY: One of them, named Cleopas, asked him, "Are you only a visitor to Jerusalem and do not know the things that have happened there in these days?" (Luke 24:18, *New International Version*).

HYMN FOR TODAY: "Open My Eyes, That I May See"

Mark Twain, on being told that it was rumored that he had died, replied, "Reports about my death have been greatly exaggerated." Many of us are not happy to be the last to know about something that it important to us.

Have you played the little game called *Whisper*? In it a story is whispered from ear to ear during common conversation in a crowded room. At the end of the party, the person who began the story and the last person to hear the story each relate their accounts to the crowd. The difference is often not only humorous, but frightening in the amount of distortion that takes place. The constant occurrence is the failure of the last person to hear truth.

The news of Jesus' death was so urgently important that Cleopas wondered if Jesus was the last to hear. The tragedy was that Cleopas failed to believe a greater news—that Jesus had conquered death. Although Cleopas knew the details, he lacked a confident faith.

If you were to meet the last person on earth, and he had not heard the good news of Jesus, would he end this day in confident faith?

PRAYER THOUGHTS: Dear Father, make us conduits for the greatest news ever told. Open our eyes to those who have never heard, and fill us with confidence. For Jesus' sake. Amen.

IT IS TRUE!

SCRIPTURE: Luke 24:28-35

VERSE FOR TODAY: Then the two told what had happened on the way, and how Jesus was recognized by them when he broke the bread (Luke 24:35, *New International Version***).**

HYMN FOR TODAY: "There's a Quiet Understanding"

A volunteer missionary was returning from Africa to her home in Ohio. Her brother was doing a mission internship in Austria, but time and money did not permit her to arrange to visit him. However, she and her traveling companion had some free time to visit the historic city of Venice. While standing beside the canals, she was suddenly interrupted when a young man called her name. It was her brother who had heard her laugh and said to himself, "That is my sister's laugh." He accurately identified her presence when he heard her voice.

He came to them in the breaking of the bread. Was it the prayer or the gentle generosity of offering bread to them? Was it a stirring memory of another meal at another time? Did the Holy Spirit open their eyes to Him? Whatever it was, truth came in the person of Jesus. Their hearts "burned" when He opened the Scripture, and truth was confirmed in His person.

The end of the struggle for truth is the person of Jesus. He rarely comes like the earthquake, like a violent wind in a storm, or as fire from heaven. He gently and persistently breaks bread with us, and it is in the breaking of the bread that we see Him.

PRAYER THOUGHT: Holy Father, may the blessed Lord Jesus come to us in the activities of the day. Stir our memories and let our hearts burn within at the warning of His presence. We need Him. Amen.

PEACE BE WITH YOU

SCRIPTURE: Luke 24:36-43

VERSE FOR TODAY: While they were still talking about this, Jesus himself stood among them and said to them, "Peace be with you" (Luke 24:36, *New International Version*).

HYMN FOR TODAY: "The Savior Is Waiting"

Shalom! The common greeting in the Near East is "Shalom" (Peace). "Peace be with you." How strange that in a land divided by religious wars and ethnic hatred, the shared greeting is a prayer for peace. The word is always spoken but often empty, meaningless.

The purpose of a greeting is to show one's purpose or intention. When people meet, there is often the unspoken question, "Does this person mean to bring me harm?" The universal custom is to show submission by bowing or nodding the head and extending one or both hands, open to show that no weapons are being held. The gestures and the words say, "I am a person of peace and I mean no harm to you."

Like those early disciples, we live in a world of locked doors with chain bolts and security peep-holes. Our neighborhoods band together hiring private police to patrol the streets. We are searched in airports, and our children pass through metal detectors at their schools. Politicians promise peace, but peace is elusive and the search for it is expensive.

But while we are "still talking about this," Jesus silently comes into our lives through our closed doors saying, "Peace be with you"—bringing eternal peace.

PRAYER THOUGHTS: Lord of Peace, we know that peace will never come until the Prince of Peace rules in our lives and in our world. Help us to proclaim Him! In His wonderfully satisfying name, amen.

FORGOTTEN PEOPLE

SCRIPTURE: Luke 24:44-52

VERSE FOR TODAY: Repentance and forgiveness of sins will be preached in his name to all nations, beginning at Jerusalem (Luke 24:47, *New International Version*).

HYMN FOR TODAY: "We've a Story to Tell to the Nations"

It was a two-hour flight across dense jungle from the mission station to the narrow airfield in the forest. It took another thirty minutes to walk from the field to the leper village. About one hundred people met us when we arrived. Most of them were Christians. Some had fingers, toes, or portions of their nose and ears missing. All of them suffered from leprosy.

Exiled from their people because of their disease, and neglected by their government, they were a pocket of forgotten people. It had been over ten years since a doctor had visited their village. At intervals, a nurse or another medical worker would come and leave medicines. Forgotten and neglected by men, they were constantly in the mind of Christ.

Most people have sufficient problems and stresses of their own. There is little motivation to take on the concerns of others. Like the priest on the Jericho Road, we find it more comfortable to pass by on the other side, and to forget. Our world is full of forgotten people. Their cry is distant and indistinct, but our heavenly Father remembers even a sparrow that falls. The invitation to share Heaven with Him will be preached to all nations.

PRAYER THOUGHTS: Dear Father, open our eyes and minds today to people who are often invisible and easily forgotten. Open our hearts and our mouths that they may hear Jesus' offer of forgiveness. In Him, amen.

COME AND HAVE BREAKFAST

SCRIPTURE: John 21:1-14

VERSE FOR TODAY: Jesus said to them, "Come and have breakfast." None of the disciples dared ask him, "Who are you?" They knew it was the Lord (John 21:12, *New International Version*).

HYMN FOR TODAY: "I Will Serve Thee"

It was a coincidence, or was it? We were stranded in a small town in Africa. We had no vehicle, no friends, and there was "no room in the inn." Repeated visits during the day to the hotel clerk had the same result. "The hotel is fully booked and there is no way we can give you a place to sleep." Our prospects of spending the entire night sitting in the middle of a border town in Africa caused us to cry to the Lord for help.

And then it happened. We happened to meet a friend we had not seen for a long time, who happened to have an extra hotel room because the people he had reserved it for happened not to be able to use it. So much happened in such a short time, or had it been happening for longer than we knew? It has been said that many of earth's coincidences are God's providence.

Jesus anticipates our need. He is always prepared. With fish and bread on the fire he says, "Come and have breakfast." After a long night of empty nets and empty hearts, of tired bodies and numbed emotions, we smell the fresh aroma of baking bread and broiled fish. Leap into the water and wade ashore. Breakfast is ready.

"None of the disciples dared ask Him, 'Who are you?' They knew it was the Lord."

PRAYER THOUGHTS: Heavenly Father, You know what the day holds for us. You know what we will need and are already making provision for those needs. Help us to see Your hand at work. Thank You! In Jesus' name. Amen.

VERY TRICKY!

SCRIPTURE: John 6:1-15

VERSE FOR TODAY: We live by faith, not by sight (2 Corinthians 5:7, *New International Version*).

HYMN FOR TODAY: "Open My Eyes, That I May See"

"Where shall we buy bread for these people?" With this question, Jesus tested Philip. Consider this question which implies that provisions must be purchased. By formulating it as He did, Jesus focused Philip's attention on the improbability of finding a source of food for so many people. Mark makes it clear that Jesus' comments had the desired effect, for Mark reports that the disciples responded with incredulity, asking Jesus whether He really intended for them to spend a large sum of money on food for the huge crowd.

If Jesus had simply asked, "What shall we do to provide for these people?" the disciples might have considered whether the solution to the riddle lay in Jesus' miraculous powers. He didn't, however, and they didn't.

Isn't this also how God tests us? He allows situations to arise—situations that lead us to focus on them rather than Him. God does not speak to remind us that He can provide a solution. Instead, He waits and watches to see whether we will remember that He is with us, to see whether we will trust Him to resolve the situation according to His will.

PRAYER THOUGHTS: How often, O God, have we looked at situations from a purely human point of view. We have failed to remember Your divine presence. Open our eyes and our ears and our hearts, that we may live and walk with You. In Jesus' name, amen.

April 12-18. **Robin Smith** is an attorney who lives in Baltimore, Maryland, with his wife, Lois, and their twin daughters, Kathryn and Kelsey.

ROW, ROW, ROW YOUR BOAT

SCRIPTURE: John 6:16-24

VERSE FOR TODAY: We are hard pressed on every side, but not crushed; perplexed, but not in despair; persecuted, but not abandoned; struck down, but not destroyed (2 Corinthians 4:8, 9, *New International Version*).

HYMN FOR TODAY: "We Have an Anchor"

Within Michigan's upper peninsula lies Brevort Lake, where my family vacationed when I was a child. One memorable day we launched a rowboat to picnic on the opposite side of the lake. As we were finishing our meal, we noticed dark clouds beginning to build, so we hastened to make our return. A stiff wind sprang up against us, and a chill rain began to fall while we were still far from shore. Anxiously Mom, Sister, and I watched Dad battle the wind and the waves to bring his family to the warmth and safety of our cottage.

As Christians we find that the rowing is often surprisingly hard. We expect that with God on our side, the wind will always be at our backs. We are surprised that it is not, as we had expected our experience to be like that of Jesus' disciples. They rowed for miles across the storm-tossed sea but only until Jesus entered the boat. Once He was aboard, the boat immediately reached the shore. More apt for us, however, is the experience of the apostle Paul, who was shipwrecked not once but three times. God saved him, but only after he abandoned his sinking ship and swam to shore.

PRAYER THOUGHTS: Dear God and Father, You are the God who keeps His promises. Therefore we will keep pulling at the oars when the storm builds and the winds blow. We trust in You to bring us safely to shore, in Your own time and way. In Jesus' name, amen.

HEIGH-HO, HEIGH-HO!

SCRIPTURE: John 6:25-40

VERSE FOR TODAY: Who is it that overcomes the world? Only he who believes that Jesus is the Son of God (1 John 5:5, *New International Version*).

HYMN FOR TODAY: "Faith Is the Victory"

My three-year-old daughter Katie asks me, "Are you going to work today, Daddy?" Depending on the circumstances, I tell her either, "Yes, I have to go to work today" or "No, I'm staying home with you today." I would rather stay home with her every day, but often I "have to go" to work in order to provide food, shelter, and clothing for Katie, her sister, and her mother. Work is foremost in my life. But I am not speaking of the work that takes me away from my family.

I am speaking of the work of believing in Jesus, which pervades my life at home and away. Jesus called it work, and rightly so, for it is often difficult to maintain faith in Him. When my marriage is on the rocks, when my job is in jeopardy, when my loved ones are living in sin, when a dear friend is wracked by injury or disease, it is not easy to keep trusting Jesus. Like the crowd by the lake, I feel as if I need a miracle if I am going to keep on putting my hope and trust in Jesus. Yet somehow, even without that miracle, I keep at the work of believing. Though buffeted by the vicissitudes of this world, I still believe that the rewards of trusting in Jesus will eventually surpass my temporal troubles.

PRAYER THOUGHTS: O Lord God, You are the source of our strength. We put our hope in You. You have never failed those who love and trust You, and we know that You will not fail us. Strengthen our hands and our feet for the work we have to do. You are our help in times of trouble. Great is Thy faithfulness! Amen and amen.

EAT, AND LIVE FOREVER

SCRIPTURE: John 6:41-51

VERSE FOR TODAY: "I am the living bread that came down from heaven. If anyone eats of this bread, he will live forever. This bread is my flesh, which I will give for the life of the world" (John 6:51, *New International Version*).

HYMN FOR TODAY: "Break Thou the Bread of Life"

Nothing is more satisfying than good bread. Sweets are alluring, meats filling, and vegetables appealing, but nothing beats bread for long-lasting satisfaction. *Good* bread that is. There are bagels, and there are *bagels*. There are biscuits and there are *biscuits*. Don't try to ply me with some fancy store-bought shortbread; only my Scottish grandmother's home-made shortbread will do. No leaden frozen bagels for me; only crusty, fresh-baked bagels will pass these lips!

The Israelites had some good bread while they were on the Sinai peninsula. Provided by God Himself, this bread was referred to as "the bread of angels!" (Psalm 78:25, *New International Version*). It was apparently flavorful, being variously described as tasting like something made with olive oil and like wafers made with honey. But as good as it was, it could not save the Israelites from death in the desert. The bread they ate was of little value to them because they did not combine it with faith. And likewise the bread we eat is of little value to us unless we also partake of the divine bread which God has provided for us. Unless we hold firmly till the end our confidence in Christ Jesus, the bread of life, we, like those Israelites, will surely die.

PRAYER THOUGHTS: O Lord God above, thank You for the spiritual food You have provided. Strengthen our hearts, to continue trusting in Jesus until that final day. In His name we pray, amen.

TO TELL THE TRUTH

SCRIPTURE: John 6:52-59

VERSE FOR TODAY: Jesus said to them, "I tell you the truth, unless you eat the flesh of the Son of Man and drink his blood, you have no life in you" (John 6:53, *New International Version*).

HYMN FOR TODAY: "Jesus Saves"

"This is a hard teaching. Who can accept it?" (John 6:60, *New International Version*). This comment and question by Jesus' disciples hits the mark, for Jesus' Messianic claim was, and is, hard to accept. The question of that day is the question of the ages: Who can accept that Jesus of Nazareth, the son of Joseph, was God incarnate, the One whom all races, nations, and people of every language will inevitably, inexorably worship? Who can accept that the carpenter's son has received sovereign authority over the billions of people on this planet? Who can accept that Jesus will rule over the Einsteins, Beethovens, Napoleons, Rousseaus, and Hegels who have passed across the stage of human history? Who can accept it?

Finding the answer to this question is one of our principal tasks in life. We dare not assume that those who *have not* accepted Jesus *cannot*. We must periodically broach the "hard teaching" of Jesus' Lordship with our friends and acquaintances. Jesus dared to speak the truth, to say that eternal death awaits all who refuse to take Him into their lives. Is there anyone with whom I can discuss eternal matters today? A life hangs in the balance.

PRAYER THOUGHTS: Dear God, give us courage and love to confront those we love with the truth about eternity. Thank You for shining the light of Christ into our hearts and allowing us to receive Him as our Lord and Savior. Open our eyes to opportunities to spread the message of salvation to those we meet today. Through Jesus we pray, amen.

TODAY IS THE DAY

SCRIPTURE: Nehemiah 9:6-15

VERSE FOR TODAY: Therefore God again set a certain day, calling it Today, when a long time later he spoke through David, as was said before: "Today, if you hear his voice, do not harden your hearts" (Hebrews 4:7, *New International Version*).

HYMN FOR TODAY: "Count Your Blessings"

Today I will review my prayer diary. Compiling a list of answered prayers will remind me of God's mighty works on my behalf. As He did for Israel, God has provided what I have needed when I have needed it. He has graciously provided not what I deserve but what I need, and even more.

Through His acts, God has made a name for Himself which remains to this day: Immanuel! The name symbolizes God's willingness and ability to rescue, to deliver, to save those in need. God was with Israel and delivered her from enslavement in Egypt. The people who witnessed that mighty deliverance did not take possession of the promised land, however. They rebelled against God and died in the desert.

Immanuel has performed mighty works in my life. Through Jesus Christ, I have experienced a mighty deliverance. But I have not yet reached the promised land. Only by eating the bread that came down from Heaven, drinking the living water, and holding firmly till the end my confidence in Jesus' atoning work, will I finally reach that rest which God has prepared for those who put their hope in Him.

PRAYER THOUGHTS: Thank You, Father, for the promise of a Sabbath rest. Thank You for the heavenly home You have prepared for Your children. Thank You for the opportunity to fall on our knees in gratitude and worship. Your gift of Your Son has made it possible for us to have life with You now and in eternity. Hosanna! Amen.

HOW SOON WE FORGET

SCRIPTURE: Psalm 78:17-29

VERSE FOR TODAY: Again and again they put God to the test; they vexed the Holy One of Israel. They did not remember his power—the day he redeemed them from the oppressor (Psalm 78:41, 42, *New International Version*).

HYMN FOR TODAY: "Lead Me to Calvary"

God parted the sea, and the Israelites went through on dry ground. After this display of divine power, the people trusted God. Their trust evaporated during a three-day desert march, however, and when with parched lips they arrived at an oasis, they grumbled against God because the water was unpalatable. God sweetened the water at Marah, but then the Israelites began to grumble about a lack of food. Quail and manna miraculously appeared, but then the people grumbled when water again became scarce. Again God responded, enabling a rock to provide water to quench the people's thirst and, albeit temporarily, their complaints.

The psalmist succinctly summarizes the Israelites' sorry bent to disbelief in the questions that they posed during their journey: "Can God spread a table in the desert? When he struck the rock, water gushed out, and streams flowed abundantly. But can he also give us food? Can he supply meat for his people?" (Psalm 78:19, 20, *New International Version*). When stated so starkly, we see how foolish it was to doubt God. And when I remember the day God redeemed me from the Oppressor and consider God's providential provision for me since that day, I realize how silly is my wondering whether he will be able to rescue me again.

PRAYER THOUGHTS: You, O Lord, are the God who can feed us the spiritual food we need to eat and live. We will glorify Your name. Amen.

JESUS SHOWS THE WAY

SCRIPTURE: John 8:12-20

VERSE FOR TODAY: I am the light of the world: he that followeth me shall not walk in darkness, but shall have the light of life (John 8:12).

HYMN FOR TODAY: "The Light of the World Is Jesus"

We were driving at night on unfamiliar roads in the hill country when a fog settled in. If there had been a place to stop overnight, we would have taken advantage of it immediately, but there was none. So we crept along, with every nerve tense and eyes straining to see through the reflection of our own headlights in the mist. After some time the yellow fog lights on a truck appeared in our rear view mirror and we welcomed the first opportunity to let the trucker go by. His rig was well lighted, front and rear, and he was traveling at a reasonable pace, so we settled gratefully at a comfortable distance behind and followed through the foggy miles. What a relief to find a leader who had been there and obviously knew where he was going!

So it is with Jesus as our light and leader on the way of life. He knows the way and He shows the way, not only with His directing Word, but especially with His bright example providing guidance thorough what is otherwise an impenetrable fog. He is the light of life, relieving us of the strain of trying to make it alone.

PRAYER THOUGHTS: Thank God fervently for Jesus, the way, the truth, and the life, who makes possible for us a saving relationship with God. Pray for steadfastness to follow Him faithfully and to help others find in Him the light of life.

April 19-25. **Edwin V. Hayden** is a Christian minister and retired editor of the *Christian Standard*®. He continues to write and edit from his home in Cincinnati, Ohio.

CONVINCING DEMONSTRATION

SCRIPTURE: John 8:21-30

VERSE FOR TODAY: Jesus said, . . . "The Father . . . has not left me alone, for I always do what pleases him." Even as he spoke, many put their faith in him (John 8:28-30, *New International Version***).**

HYMN FOR TODAY: "Fairest Lord Jesus"

Boy Scouts work with cords and ropes, learning to tie knots. These are described and pictured in the *Scout Handbook*, but there is a better way to learn knot tying. It is by demonstration, as when a leader puts a cord in the boy's hands and then guides those hands through the movements of tying the desired knot. The resulting skill can be useful for a lifetime.

Jesus was the best of all teachers at showing what He wanted His followers to learn. When He was asked where He was lodging, He said, "Come and see" (John 1:39). They caught on. When Nathanael asked if any good could come from Nazareth, Philip answered, "Come and see" (John 1:46). Nathanael met Jesus and was convinced. Samaritans at Sychar became convinced that Jesus was the Messiah, not because their neighbor told them, but when they saw Him for themselves (John 4:41, 42). Jesus wanted His disciples to became useful servants rather than proud bosses, so He reminded them that He had come not to do His own will and be served, but to do God's will and to serve Him (John 6:38; Mark 10:45). Jesus demonstrated that service by washing the disciples' feet (John 13:2-17). It was a convincing demonstration.

PRAYER THOUGHTS: Thank and praise God for the love that sent His one and only Son into the world as a perfect demonstration of the Father's will and way. Pray for eyes to see, and a heart to understand, and the will to follow in the way He has shown.

HOW TO BE FREE

SCRIPTURE: John 8:31-38

VERSE FOR TODAY: Jesus said, "If you hold to my teaching, you are really my disciples. Then you will know the truth, and the truth will set you free" (John 8:31, 32, *New International Version*).

HYMN FOR TODAY: "Joy in Serving Jesus"

She was thirteen years old and her father had said she was to eat her vegetables because they were good for her. But at age thirteen she found that she had a mind and personality of her own that must be respected, first by herself and then by other people, including her parents. She had no great dislike for vegetables, but she felt that she was neither a child nor a slave, to take orders from anyone. The confrontation that ensued was to be repeated many times before she discovered that the way to be really free was to love God as she found Him in Jesus, and to love and respect her parents and others in authority so much that she really wanted to please them. She was that much like the younger son in Jesus' story found in Luke 15:11-31. He was not really free until his greatest desire was to be with his father.

Jesus is the way, the truth, and the life (John 14:6). Eternal freedom is to be found only in the grateful love that chooses Him, His way, and His company above all else. In rejecting Him, a person is enslaved to self, to sin, and the destruction that awaits the world and its followers.

PRAYER THOUGHTS: Mention to God some things that Jesus did and said for which you are most thankful. Praise God for the truths that Jesus taught and exemplified. Thank God for the joy you have found in following Him, and for the increasing joy that is still available as you approach His presence in Heaven.

LIKE FATHER, LIKE SON?

SCRIPTURE: John 8:39-47

VERSE FOR TODAY: "If you were Abraham's children," said Jesus, "then you would do the things Abraham did" (John 8:39, *New International Version*).

HYMN FOR TODAY: "A Child of the King"

My grandfather liked to tell of the day in 1874 when General (later President) Garfield walked up behind him on a college campus and asked, "Young man, which Hayden sired you?" Garfields and Haydens had been neighbors in a community nearby, and the General knew Haydens well enough to recognize one by the way he walked.

Family traits may show in other ways—bodily structure, speech, face, general behavior, or abilities. You may stay close to your family heritage in some ways, but not in others. Among the later kings of Judah, for example, there were wicked sons of godly fathers and godly sons of wicked kings.

Godly faith and moral character are always more important than physical characteristics, and Jesus expected the descendants of "Father Abraham" to reflect their ancestor as the "father of the faithful!" Otherwise those descendants had rejected their inheritance. While Abraham rejoiced to see in Jesus the fulfillment of God's promises (John 8:56), some of Abraham's descendants sought to destroy Jesus. More happily, even those who have no fleshly connection with Abraham may still be his heirs in godly faith.

PRAYER THOUGHTS: Give thanks for the faith of "Father Abraham" and for our opportunity to be his heirs in faith. Praise God for the fulfillment of His promises to Abraham through the Lord Jesus. Pray for steadfastness as a child of God and spiritual heir of Abraham and for faithfulness to live up to that family tradition.

THE WAY OF LIFE

SCRIPTURE: John 8:48-59

VERSE FOR TODAY: Jesus said to her, "I am the resurrection and the life. He who believes in me will live, even though he dies; and whoever lives and believes in me will never die" (John 11:25, 26, *New International Version*).

HYMN FOR TODAY: "Because He Lives"

"Don't give us that junk! When yer dead, yer dead, and that's all there is to it!"

Not many folk in the big city had found their way into his small chapel, so the preacher had taken his message of Christ and the resurrection to the street. A few curious ones had paused to observe. One loud youngster put into words what many others seemed to think, but were reluctant to say. "That junk" is hard for a lot of worldly wise folk to swallow. When you're dead, you're dead. Period. So they think.

Jesus faced the same kind of disbelief, especially when He presented himself as the eternal Son of God and the way to everlasting life. Even the leaders of the religious community accused Him of being crazy—demon possessed—and promoting himself in a way that dishonored God. But God was the very one who proved Jesus' claims to be true. God spoke His approval at Jesus' baptism. He worked miracles at Jesus' word and touch. He revealed himself in Jesus' teaching and demonstration of unchanging truth. And He was to raise Jesus from the dead. That is the resurrection and life Jesus desires to share with believers in Him.

PRAYER THOUGHTS: Praise God for showing us things too marvelous for us to understand, like the wisdom and power of Jesus and the nature of life eternal. Pray for faith to believe what we can't see, because of what we have already seen in Christ our Lord.

SEEING AND FOLLOWING GOD'S WAY

SCRIPTURE: Ephesians 5:1-14

VERSE FOR TODAY: "Put your trust in the light while you have it, so that you may become sons of light" (John 12:36, *New International Version*).

HYMN FOR TODAY: "Stepping in the Light"

A cat can't see in total darkness any better than you can. It doesn't require much light, though, for the cat to see plainly. Its eyes are adaptable to admit all the light there is. Similarly, a young person's eyes admit more light than those of an older person, so the young person can see to read or drive an automobile in light that leaves the older person virtually helpless.

Wicked people depend on darkness to hide all kinds of misbehavior (John 3:19-21). They think no one will see and know; but God sees perfectly, even in total darkness (Psalm 139:11, 12). Good lighting can reduce crime and make a roadway safer, but it will make no difference in divine judgment.

Spiritually, though, it is a different matter. God has provided the bright light of His Word and His Son to show the way of life. We have no excuse for stumbling and making wrong turns. It is foolish to try to hide. We can adjust our spiritual eyesight by fixing our attention on what Christ reveals, and by opening our minds wide to admit the light of His teaching. Old age can improve our spiritual vision by making us more attentive to it.

PRAYER THOUGHTS: Glory in the grace of God that He has given His Son to become the light of our lives. Ask for wisdom to fix mind and attention on what He reveals. Pledge faithfulness in following the path in which He leads. Pray to reflect His light and example to others.

THIS IS THE WAY; WALK IN IT

SCRIPTURE: Psalm 43:1-5

VERSE FOR TODAY: Whether you turn to the right or to the left, your ears will hear a voice behind you, saying, "This is the way; walk in it" (Isaiah 30:21, *New International Version*).

HYMN FOR TODAY: "Lead, Kindly Light"

We asked for careful directions before we started toward the camp ground in the hills. "It's very simple," we were told. "Just go out from town on the Hardy Hill Road and follow the double yellow line till you get there. You'll find crossroads and other ways, but no other road will have the double line in the middle. That will give you the direction, and it should also keep you in your own lane! Good going!" So for twenty miles of hills, curves, and choices of direction we followed the double line to our destination.

The psalmist writer of our text prayed for direction on life's way and for protection from dangers and discouragements created by the enemies of his soul. The direction, keeping him on the right side of the right road, had to come from the light and the truth of God's Word. By following that, he would come into God's presence, safely and rejoicing.

As Christians we have more certain guidance from Jesus and the available power of His Spirit and His Word. In following Him, we are freed also from the fear and uncertainty that plague the uninstructed traveler. Our direction and destination is Jesus.

PRAYER THOUGHTS: Give glory to God, who has not left us without direction in the way of life. Thank Him again for His Son, whom we may follow with complete confidence to His very presence. Ask God for a Christlike spirit that will seek and draw others into the glad way of life eternal.

KNOWING AND UNDERSTANDING

SCRIPTURE: John 12:20-26

VERSE FOR TODAY: He who loves his life loses it, and he who hates his life in this world will keep it for eternal life (John 12:25, *Revised Standard Version*).

HYMN FOR TODAY: "Where He Leads Me"

This portion of Scripture reveals two things. First, the chain of events that brought the Greeks under the influence of Christ and His teachings. They had heard about Christ and they wanted to know more; then they turned to Philip, whom they apparently knew was close to Christ. In turn, Philip appealed to Andrew who took the request to Christ. So it is today—we may simply be a channel whereby someone is directed to a person who can lead them to Christ.

This desire to know and understand Christ continues to be the greatest need of the world today. The power that is revealed by the God of the universe through His Son, Jesus Christ, is available and ready to change the world today. Our goal, as Christians, is to become Christ-like, not in theory, but in actuality, as we share the pain and humility of His suffering.

Second, this incident reveals the opening of a door through which the whole world would see and know the God of the universe, who was revealed in Christ. That door is still open today and waiting for us to show others the way through.

PRAYER THOUGHTS: Open our eyes, Father, and help us to see Jesus in His love and humility, as well as His redemptive glory and then to share it with others. Place a burden on our hearts for lost souls. Amen.

April 26-30. **Garnet Dixon** is a retired school teacher who enjoys her volunteer work as a recorder for the blind and at Kosair Children's Hospital in Louisville, Kentucky, where she makes her home. She has continued her life-long study of the Word of God by taking a trip to the Holy Lands.

THE PURPOSE OF CHRIST'S COMING

SCRIPTURE: John 12:27-36

VERSE FOR TODAY: "But I, when I am lifted up from the earth, will draw all men to myself" (John 12:32, *New International Version*).

HYMN FOR TODAY: "Lift High the Cross"

Christ describes himself as the Son of Man, and we see His humanity revealed in these verses. As He looks back on His short ministry, He praises God, but the shadow of the cross falls across His path. We see here the questioning and uncertainty in Christ's mind as He faces the cross. We also see clearly that He knows with certainty His purpose in coming into the world and He accepts what lies ahead calmly and serenely. We must slip, slide, and sometimes fall before we can achieve our goal, yet, just like Christ, our faith will carry us through to ultimate victory.

As we struggle through our trials, striving to bring honor and glory to Him, we have the assurance that He has been there, too, and for our sakes. We die in order to live; we lose our life in order to find it more glorious.

Often we take God for granted. We sin and then turn to Him for forgiveness. His heart must be saddened by our callousness. In the Scripture text for today, Christ emphasizes the power of the cross and promises that men will be drawn to it if it is lifted up. Are we holding it high so others can see it and be drawn to it?

PRAYER THOUGHTS: Heavenly Father, we turn our eyes upward, remembering Your promise that You will love us and forgive us if we keep focused on You. Help us to live so others may see You in us. Help us to keep shining in a dark and sinful world. In the name of our Savior, Jesus Christ, we pray. Amen.

BELIEF IS NECESSARY

SCRIPTURE: John 12:37-43

VERSE FOR TODAY: For they loved praise from men more than praise from God (John 12:43, *New International Version*).

HYMN FOR TODAY: "Almost Persuaded"

We live in a society that finds it more and more difficult to believe in the word of other people. Not many years ago a promise and a handshake were a bond that the promise would be fulfilled. Men often bought and sold great plots of land with simply their word and a handshake.

Today we are bombarded with promises in the news media that we find hard to believe. This is in contrast to what we know of the Word of God. It is the same yesterday, today, and forever. The Word of God can be depended on and we know that nothing changes it. We are assured that the promise of salvation and an eternity with God is awaiting all those who accept and obey the Word of God.

As we look at the transient gods of the material world we sometimes worship, we wonder how we can be so blind. Let's ask ourselves these questions, "Do I have idols today? Have I put my belief and trust in something other than the true and living God?" It is comforting to know that our God is an "awesome God" and He will be the same today and forever.

PRAYER THOUGHTS: We praise You, our Father, for the knowledge that You are the one and only true God of the universe and that we can build our lives upon that belief. We are overwhelmed by the love You have shown to us, making life today wonderful and the hope of eternity something to desire. Help us to live our lives in truth that comes only from You. In the name of Your Son, and our Savior, Jesus Christ. Amen.

THE RESULT OF BELIEF

SCRIPTURE: John 12:44-50

VERSE FOR TODAY: I have come as light into the world, that whoever believes in me may not remain in darkness (John 12:46, *Revised Standard Version*).

HYMN FOR TODAY: "The Light of the World Is Jesus"

Jesus Christ came into a dark and depressed world to bring light and encouragement. Many heard His message, believed, and accepted the promise it offered. Others heard, wanted to believe, but were too afraid of their religious leaders to speak openly of their belief. There were also those who heard the good news but openly rejected it.

Today, we see the same situation. There are those who are sure that Jesus is the Christ and have made Him their personal Savior. There are those who mentally accept the belief in Christ but are afraid that someone will discover their belief and reject them. There are those who hear the Gospel and reject it without giving it much thought.

Sometimes it is hard to believe in something we cannot see, yet the book of Hebrews gives ample proof of such believers in both the Old and New Testaments. When we, like them, stand firm in our belief, God will bless us and lift us up. We need to examine ourselves, pray for guidance as we study, and assurance will be given to us that we belong to the vast host of those who believe. This will fill us with "joy unspeakable."

PRAYER THOUGHTS: Dear heavenly Father, we thank You for the promises You have made to those who believe in You. We know we join a select company when we become a part of that great body of believers who have gone before us and we are humbled. We pray this prayer in the name of our Savior, Jesus Christ. Amen.

SEEKING THE MIND OF CHRIST

SCRIPTURE: Philippians 2:1-11

VERSE FOR TODAY: Let this mind be in you, which was also in Christ Jesus: (Philippians 2:5).

HYMN FOR TODAY: "May the Mind of Christ, My Savior"

Does your mind reflect the mind of Christ? Does my life reflect the mind of Christ? Has He entered your life and changed you into a different person? Has he entered my life? Can you see a difference in me because I have the mind of Christ? Paul emphasizes to the Philippians the good things that resulted when they became Christians. He points out the danger they are in because of the intervention of worldly disagreements in their midst. He paints a picture of the relationship between God and Christ.

When we accept Jesus as our personal Savior, we put on the mind of Christ. And in so doing, we do away with selfish ambition and vain conceit.

Let us show our faith by our actions. It is good to see those around us who have the mind of Christ and find ways to carry out His work here on earth. Let us find a way today to help the poor, to give care to the homeless, to show compassion to those who hurt, both physically and spiritually, and to feed the hungry.

This expression of love to others will bring joy and fulfillment ot life.

PRAYER THOUGHTS: Almighty God, our heavenly Father, help us to see the needs of those around us and to show our love for Christ by forgetting ourselves and helping others. Help us to show tenderness and compassion to our fellowmen. Make us a blessing to someone today and every day. Help us, dear Father, to have the same attitude as that of Christ Jesus, our Lord. Amen.

My Prayer Notes

_____

_____

_____

_____

_____

_____

_____

_____

_____

_____

_____

_____

_____

_____

_____

_____

_____

_____

_____

_____

_____

_____

DEVOTIONS™

May

photo by Dr. Ward Patterson

SEEING THE INVISIBLE GOD

SCRIPTURE: Colossians 1:9-20

VERSE FOR TODAY: He is the image of the invisible God, the firstborn over all creation (Colossians l:15, *New International Version*).

HYMN FOR TODAY: "Immortal, Invisible"

We often see ourselves revealed in our children and grand-children. My grandson, a kindergartener, was coming home each day with much of his lunch uneaten. When questioned about this, his reply was that he talked to his friends and didn't have time for lunch. Neither his mother nor I were surprised to hear this for we, too, do our share of talking.

This portion of Scripture emphasizes that God revealed Himself to us through His Son, Jesus. Our conception of the world and its meaning is found in terms of the spiritual ends which are confirmed in Christ. The created universe with all its spiritual and physical aspects is an unfolding of the mind of God in Christ. In a lesser fashion, we see this revealed in our physical universe in the beauty of spring and fall.

We know God fully when we know and believe in Christ, the animating Spirit who brings His church to life. The peace that Christ brings through His blood reconciles men to God but also brings them into harmony with each other. The kind of lives we live as Christians should reveal the invisible God as well as Jesus Christ to those whose lives we touch.

PRAYER THOUGHTS: Dear Lord, help us to open our hearts to Thy Word. May Christ show us the way to better see and understand You so that You will be visible to others. Amen.

May 1, 2. **Garnet Dixon** is a retired school teacher who enjoys her volunteer work as a recorder for the blind and at Kosair Children's Hospital in Louisville, Kentucky, where she makes her home. She has continued her life-long study of the Word of God by taking a trip to the Holy Lands.

GOD REVEALED THROUGH CHRIST

SCRIPTURE: Colossians 2:1-15

VERSE FOR TODAY: And you have come to fulness of life in him, who is the head of all rule and authority (Colossians 2:10, *Revised Standard Version*).

HYMN FOR TODAY: "I Know Whom I Have Believed"

Through Christ, God was revealed to the world, and His love shines forth in Christ's earthly ministry and was culminated in His death on the cross. Yet this was not the end, for His resurrection brought hope that man had never had before—the hope of an eternity to be spent with God, the Father, and Christ, the Son. As Paul has written, we now see through a glass, darkly, but in Heaven the mystery will be solved and we will see clearly (1 Corinthians 13:12). The faith and dependence we have had in our earthly parents—and continue to have in our husbands, wives, children, and grandchildren —help us to understand this better—but how much greater is our faith and trust in Christ.

As Christians we form the body of Christ and, if that body is to be strong, every part must be strong and carry out its purpose. Spiritual maturity comes by growth and growth comes by sharing in the loving relationships of a believing and serving Christian community. Just as a child's physical and mental growth approaches maturity through instruction at home and in school, so we Christians need the spiritual nurture that comes from prayer, Bible study, and meeting with other Christians.

PRAYER THOUGHTS: Dear Lord, we thank You for the fellowship that we enjoy with others who know and love You. There is much we don't know and understand, but we are sure that You love us and sent Christ to die for us and are here to lead us through Your Spirit. Amen.

THE ORDER OF THE TOWEL AND BASIN

SCRIPTURE: John 13:1-11

VERSE FOR TODAY: Having loved his own who were in the world, he now showed them the full extent of his love (John 13:1, *New International Version*).

HYMN FOR TODAY: "Make Me a Servant"

Jesus' service did not proceed from a sense of worthlessness or powerlessness. Jesus was secure in His origin, destiny, and identity. Out of that assurance, He could pick up the towel and the basin. Too often we want to be served rather than to serve. When we do serve, we often do so because of a sense of unworthiness. We could learn well from Jesus that true service is a sign of strength. It could even be argued that service that is not voluntary is not true service at all. Jesus was clearly superior to the disciples in every way. He was superior in holiness, power, and intellect. Yet it did not bother Him to do the menial tasks usually relegated to the least of the servants.

The one who should have received the bowed knee of worship displayed the bowed knee of service. The one who should have worn the royal robe wore a towel. The one who should have carried a scepter carried a basin.

That day, Jesus gave His disciples a picture they would never forget. Jesus spoke of love often, but on this occasion He displayed love through His actions. He showed them the full extent of His love. They never could get that picture out of their minds and neither should we.

PRAYER THOUGHTS: O God, help us to sense the sweetness of serving. Help us to be more like our Lord who came not to be served but to serve. Help us to not only speak of love, but also show it. Amen.

May 3-9. **J. Michael Shannon** is senior minister at First Christian Church of Johnson City, Tennessee.

FOLLOW THE LEADER

SCRIPTURE: John 13:12-20

VERSE FOR TODAY: I have set you an example that you should do as I have done for you (John 13:15, *New International Version*).

HYMN FOR TODAY: "Follow On"

When you were a child, did you ever play "Follow the Leader?" It's a simple game and rarely lasts long. One person is designated the leader and the rest of the group has to follow. The game goes well enough until the leader makes the actions so hard, or the road so difficult, that the followers drop out.

The disciples wanted to follow Jesus. They had said as much several times. Some even vowed to follow Jesus to the death. Nevertheless, they found one action very difficult. Jesus had taught them to serve. This they did not want to do. What's the use of being a leader if you can't have a lot of people serving you? Was this not the sign of prestige?

Jesus was showing them a different way. He was leading them to value service. Why is service so valuable? First, it is a check on our arrogance and pride. It is difficult to look down on a person when you are lifting them up.

Second, there are real people with real needs out there. Someone needs to care for them. Someone needs to put aside pride and convenience to notice them, approach them, and meet their needs in Jesus' name. It's not easy, but we must do it if we want to play "Follow the Leader" with Jesus.

PRAYER THOUGHTS: Dear Father, we submit to Your leadership. We commit to following You even if that commitment takes us places we would rather not go. Help us to see people not as nuisances, but as opportunities to show forth Your love. We do not claim to be better than Your Son, so let us see that we are never too important to serve. Through Christ. Amen.

WHEN FRIENDSHIP FAILS

SCRIPTURE: John 13:21-30

VERSE FOR TODAY: As soon as Judas took the bread, Satan entered into him (John 13:27, *New International Version*).

HYMN FOR TODAY: "'Are Ye Able,' Said the Master"

How do you feel about betrayal? If you don't know, just think of names like Benedict Arnold, Brutus, Quisling, and Judas. Even the word *betrayal* leaves a stain in our minds. Betraying a friend is one of the worst acts we can imagine. If you have ever felt the sting of betrayal, then you know how painful and long lasting it can be. Ask yourself this question: Would you invite a betrayer to dinner? Jesus did. Would you be kind and courteous to your betrayer? Jesus was.

Isn't it striking that Judas enjoyed the blessings of the Last Supper along with the rest of the disciples?

He too experienced the washing of his feet by the Lord. He too heard the teachings. He too experienced the fellowship meal. Just how he could experience that and still turn Jesus in is one of the great mysteries of the Scriptures. The fact that we are told is an unfortunate testament of the depths of depravity to which a human can descend. Even greater, however, is the picture it gives us of the heights of holiness. More striking than the offense of Judas is the kind, understanding heart of Jesus. We are only left to wonder that if Judas had understood this great truth how his story might not have ended at the potter's field, but in the upper room.

Forgiveness could have been his, if he had thought to ask.

PRAYER THOUGHTS: We are reminded each Lord's day, dear God, how wonderful is Christ's love. Each Lord's day, He invites us to His table, unworthy as we are. Help us to be as forgiving to others as our Savior is to us. In the name of our merciful Lord. Amen.

SOMETHING OLD, SOMETHING NEW

SCRIPTURE: John 13:31-35

VERSE FOR TODAY: "A new command I give you: Love one another. As I have loved you, so you must love one another" (John 13:34, *New International Version*).

HYMN FOR TODAY: "They'll Know We Are Christians by Our Love"

Jesus describes His command to love one another as a new command. How can this be? The old law reminds us to love God with all our heart, mind, and strength and to love our neighbor as ourselves. This was not a new command, but an old one. Yet there is something new about it. First, this love is now a greater priority.

While love has always been a quality of God, it is given front page treatment in the ministry of Jesus. It is also new in the sense that we have a greater example of that love. No one taught it or exemplified it like Jesus. It is also new in the sense that it has a greater purpose. Jesus chose love as the one quality that should be present and evident in the Christian life. So much so, it would be the identifying factor in the Christian life. If love is of such great importance, how are we doing? Do people see the love in us they ought to see? If not, why not? We might choose to put a Christian bumper sticker on our car or to wear Christian jewelry or listen to Christian music. But the mark of the Christian, according to Jesus, is the measure of our love.

PRAYER THOUGHTS: Dear God, we pray that You teach us to love. We need it so much, but show it so little. Our capability to love is so impaired we ask You to enlarge our hearts that we may reach out in love to others. Give us the kind of love the Lord Jesus had that people may know that we know Him. Through our loving Lord. Amen.

NOW THAT'S A SERVANT

SCRIPTURE: Isaiah 42:1-9

VERSE FOR TODAY: A bruised reed he will not break, and a smoldering wick he will not snuff out (Isaiah 42:3, *New International Version*).

HYMN FOR TODAY: "More Like the Master"

It's not as if they weren't warned. Most people in the ancient Jewish world were looking for a militant Messiah. We can understand their desire. They were a vulnerable and often mistreated people. When Jesus came, He did not fit into their pre-conceived molds of what a Messiah should be like. Jesus came as a gentle Messiah. He was, as Isaiah predicted, a suffering servant. The problem was that people interpreted this as weakness. They were wrong. There is nothing stronger than the strength of a gentle hand. Isaiah was able to see that even with these compassionate qualities, the Messiah could bring justice to the earth. Only a Messiah of this type could bring about the desired results. Strength without compassion often leads to oppression. The gentleness of the Messiah is made all the more striking by the fact that He has the power to overcome any foe. The hand that would not break the bruised reed nor snuff the smoldering wick could have been raised to the heavens to summon twelve legions of angels. He didn't raise His hand because He came not to be our kind of Messiah, but the Father's kind.

PRAYER THOUGHTS: Dear Lord, help us to see Jesus. We want to see Him as He really is, not as we have constructed Him in our own minds. Thank You for Your Word, which provides the portrait. Having seen Him, help us to be like Him. Allow us to wed, as he did, strength and gentleness. Amen.

THE MARKS OF TRUE GREATNESS

SCRIPTURE: Matthew 23:1-11

VERSE FOR TODAY: The greatest among you will be your servant (Matthew 23:11, *New International Version*).

HYMN FOR TODAY: "Humble Thyself in the Sight of the Lord"

How does this world measure greatness? If we were giving a greatness test, what qualities would we try to quantify? The shallow may measure it according to a person's financial statement or the important people he knows. The slightly more sensitive might measure it by talent or accomplishments. Very few, even the wisest among us, would measure a person by how he serves.

Yet the one whose judgment is most important does measure it that way. Jesus talked about how the teachers and the Pharisees loved to order other people around and be seen as a leader of men. They loved to be seen doing "good" deeds and to be praised for them. They loved to be called by exalted titles. Jesus then warns us not to be like them. These things do not reveal a person's true greatness; sensitivity to the hurts and needs of others does. Arrogance and pride take no special virtue; humility and love demand the best from us. That is why service is the measure of true greatness.

So if you want to be great, don't look for a trophy, look for a cross. That is where you will find the true heroes.

PRAYER THOUGHTS: Father, You are great and greatly to be praised. Great also is Your Son. Truly believing in Your greatness, we ask to be made great as well. We want to have servant hearts. We pray that when You apply Your yardstick to our lives, we will measure up. Amen.

IN HIS STEPS

SCRIPTURE: 1 Peter 2:18-25

VERSE FOR TODAY: For it is commendable if a man bears up under the pain of unjust suffering because he is conscious of God (1 Peter 2:19, *New International Version*).

HYMN FOR TODAY: "How Firm a Foundation"

Have you ever seen a child try on his father's shoes and walk around the room? He thinks he looks grown up and sophisticated, but he looks quite comical.

It must look something like that sometimes when we try to imitate Jesus. When we try to be like him, we don't realize all it involves. It involves, among other things, a rather strange attitude toward suffering.

Most people accept suffering with either resignation or resentment. Peter tells us we were called to a life of suffering for the cause of Christ and that it is commendable. The way some people talk, you would think that the Bible promised us we would never have to suffer. Not only does the Bible never make that promise, it explicitly warns us that we will suffer.

Yet our suffering is redemptive, because in it we continue the legacy of Jesus and in some mysterious way make a personal connection with Him. If Jesus, the only perfect person ever to walk this earth, suffered, why should we think we will be immune? Isn't it amazing how often Jesus turned His own suffering into something good and beneficial for mankind? We can do that, too. We have His promise on it.

PRAYER THOUGHTS: Dear Father, we do not ask to be spared all suffering, for we know it is our common lot. We pray that we may glorify You as we face trials of various kinds. We know through the sufferings of our Lord that redemption was wrought, so we pray this prayer through Him who bore scars for us. Amen.

THE PRUNED VINE

SCRIPTURE: John 15:1-11

VERSE FOR TODAY: "He cuts off every branch in me that bears no fruit, while every branch that does bear fruit he prunes so that it will be even more fruitful" (John 15:2, *New International Version*).

HYMN FOR TODAY: "I Have Decided to Follow Jesus"

The firm decision to follow Jesus in this life is not one to make flippantly, without due consideration of the cost. It may cost earth's bounties; it may cost a life, friends, business—whatever unduly restricts a committed service in His kingdom. It will certainly call for pruning away all things which might prevent doing whatever the Lord's work requires.

Every profitable vineyard demands that the vines be pruned each autumn. When you look upon such a pruned vineyard, the impression is that the vintner has certainly overdone his work—the remaining trunks look decimated; and they are, temporarily. His wisdom is not evident until the refreshed vine sends forth several shoots, which bear an abundance of clusters. If the nutrients taken in had been shared with the old vine, as well as bringing about the new growth, the harvest would have been minimized.

By worldly standards, self-pruning for the Lord's service may seem to be foolish—even wasteful. But only the totally committed Christian—pruned of all self-will, all taint of sin—yields full and fruitful service to our Lord Jesus Christ.

PRAYER THOUGHTS: Father, prune us! Cut from our heart all taint of sin, and bring forth fruitful growth through the strength of the Holy Spirit; and all to Your greatest glory in Jesus Christ! Amen.

May 10-16. **Brant Lee Doty** was Professor Emeritus at Great Lakes Christian College in Lansing, Michigan, until his death on January 23, 1998.

THERE IS NO GREATER LOVE

SCRIPTURE: John 15:12-17

VERSE FOR TODAY: Greater love has no one than this, that he lay down his life for his friends (John 15:13, *New International Version*).

HYMN FOR TODAY: "O Love That Wilt Not Let Me Go"

Americans often make a travesty in the use of the word "love," robbing it of its unique expression of supreme affection and inextinguishable fidelity. Do you really *love* that new car? or the neighbor's artistically landscaped lawn? or chocolate ice cream sundaes? Perhaps we have forgotten that clear distinction between those things we may only *like* and those we may truly *love*.

There should never be any real doubt or confusion: in its purest sense, we can truly *love* only that which is human or divine, for love is the supreme emotion of the human breast. It is shared carefully with those who may properly receive and return that love in kind and degree.

It is of the greatest significance that love may be shared; indeed, it must be shared if it is to endure and increase. That young lad who sets his affections on a pretty young lady, only to find his attentions totally ignored or rebuffed, must turn elsewhere for lasting happiness. Does it not follow then, that those who do not respond to the earnest love of Jesus Christ will find themselves ultimately outside of His circle? Can you honestly and sincerely say, "I love Jesus Christ"?

PRAYER THOUGHTS: O God, how clearly we have seen Your power and righteousness in the love and life of our Lord Jesus Christ. May we never permit our love and service for Him to grow cold, and may we be channels through which His love reaches all mankind. Amen.

TREASURED WORDS

SCRIPTURE: Job 23:1-12

VERSE FOR TODAY: I have treasured the words of his mouth more than my daily bread (Job 23:12, *New International Version*).

HYMN FOR TODAY: "Wonderful Words of Life"

There she lay—tiny, silver-haired and prim, all four feet eleven inches of her—drawing each breath with difficulty and her voice barely audible: "Lee, be a good boy!" Those were the last words I heard from the lips of "Nanaw" (Grandmother) MacRoberts, my mother's mother. They were spoken to me when I was an ash-blond six-year-old who knelt by her bedside, tears brimming my eyes as I watched life slowly ebb from the elderly, little, white-haired lady I loved.

"Nanaw" had been a real pal to me—I never forgot my first shopping trip downtown! Hand in hand, I and my stately companion marched to the five-and-ten cent store. "Here's a dime," she said. "Buy whatever you want!" That was like "sic 'em" to a dog! Around and around I walked, slowly evaluating the potential purchases. I finally settled for a metal camel bank.

"Nanaw," widow of a banker, thoroughly approved of the choice, and, appropriately, gave me a nickel (quite a sum of money then) for my first deposit!

"Be a good boy?" Who could possibly fail to give it his best shot after that! The very memory still brings a challenge to my heart and tears to my eyes. I wish everybody had a grandmother like my grandmother!

PRAYER THOUGHTS: O Father, we never know how deeply our lives may affect the lives of others, or where our influence ends. May we always live in such a manner that others are edified and challenged to love You dearly and serve You well. Amen.

ABOUT FACE!

SCRIPTURE: Acts 9:10-19

VERSE FOR TODAY: Christ Jesus came into the world to save sinners—of whom I am the worst (1 Timothy 1:15, *New International Version*).

HYMN FOR TODAY: "There Is a Fountain"

Saul was a devout Jew. As such, he considered Christians to be nothing more than pagans, attributing divine status to their Jesus. He translated his convictions into murderous actions, slaughtering whomever he might until, by direct, divine confrontation, he was suddenly turned "about face" on the road to Damascus. From that day, he never ceased to proclaim this same Jesus "both Lord and Christ!"

His "about face" could hardly have been more complete, or more effectual.

Following Jesus in our day demands nothing less than a genuine commitment to Him—often a complete turn-about in our own lives. In the words of the chorus, *Things Are Different Now*,—"Things I loved before have passed away; things I love far more have come to stay!" We call this indispensable step in our conversion "repentance." The promise we claim is gloriously inspiring: attesting to our faith, and turning resolutely from past sins, we permit our body to be washed—literally and symbolically—in baptism, rising to walk in a new life!

As Saul/Paul devoted his life to winning souls to Christ among all peoples, so should we; and we may have no farther to go than around the block or to another part of town!

PRAYER THOUGHTS: Dear Father, when You see us marching to the beat of the wrong drummer, *turn us around!* Satan is wily and strong; but You are much wiser, much stronger, and we must put ourselves totally under Your command. Guide us in the footsteps of Jesus. Amen.

ON DIVINE DISCIPLINE

SCRIPTURE: Romans 11:13-24

VERSE FOR TODAY: Consider therefore the kindness and sternness of God: sternness to those who fell, but kindness to you, provided that you continue in his kindness. Otherwise, you also will be cut off (Romans 11:22, *New International Version*).

HYMN FOR TODAY: "Footprints of Jesus"

When the term "discipline" is used, some people have an erroneous concept of the implication of the word. They think of corporal punishment. The original thought of the Greek word is a matter of instruction: taught, and not necessarily punishment. Ideally, of course, any punishment for wrongdoing should have this concept as the significant lesson to be learned —a "please don't do it again . . . or else!" type of thing.

I know of a little fellow who thought he had his third grade teacher precisely where he wanted her. She was a member of the church where his Dad preached, and that gave him a superior and exempt status, his nine-year-old mind reasoned.

While her back was turned, he poked the little girl in front of him, and she gave a subdued yelp—subdued, but loud enough to be heard. The teacher whirled about, instantly analyzing the situation, and sent him to stand in the time-out area for what, to him, seemed an eternity.

That was true discipline: the teacher *never* was disturbed by the little imp (me) again! He learned respect for the teacher and the little girl he had tormented, and that his claim to exemption from discipline was groundless.

No wrongdoer is exempt from discipline.

PRAYER THOUGHTS: Dear Father, lead us to live so that others may see in us the very love and goodness of our Lord Jesus Christ. In Jesus' name. Amen.

THE QUALITY OF MERCY

SCRIPTURE: Romans 11:25-36

VERSE FOR TODAY: Judgment without mercy will be shown to anyone who has not been merciful. Mercy triumphs over judgment! (James 2:13, *New International Version*).

HYMN FOR TODAY: "At Calvary"

One of the famous quotations from Shakespeare's plays is the so-called "Mercy Speech" of Portia in *The Merchant of Venice*. Young Antonio has fallen into the clutches of the shrewd moneylender, Shylock, and cannot repay an honest debt. He pleads for mercy; Shylock is not at all inclined to listen. Portia, disguised as a lawyer, pleads in Antonio's behalf: "The quality of mercy is not strain'd, It droppeth as the gentle rain from heaven Upon the place beneath: it is twice blest; It blesseth him that gives and him that takes: . . . "

Perhaps we have thought of mercy only from one perspective—that of the person who receives. Is it possible that God, too, is blessed in extending His mercy to the penitent sinner? It would certainly be reasonable, establishing once for all that divine characteristic which should be inherent in us all.

Why is it often difficult to forgive one who has offended us? If any of us had never been offended, this might be beyond understanding; but which of us has never been guilty of offending another? Which one can "hurl the first stone," boasting innocence everywhere, at all times, toward all people?

Even so, without exception we must all plead for the mercy of God, available through our Lord Jesus Christ.

PRAYER THOUGHTS: How marvelous is Your mercy toward us all, O Father! We abjectly bow, confessing that we have sinned often against You. And we plead for pardon, knowing that You have made it available to the penitent one through our Lord Jesus Christ. Amen.

THE ULTIMATE GIFT

SCRIPTURE: Mark 12:1-12

VERSE FOR TODAY: This is love: not that we loved God, but that he loved us and sent his Son as an atoning sacrifice for our sins (1 John 4:10, *New International Version*).

HYMN FOR TODAY: "Give of Your Best to the Master"

Jesus made it abundantly clear that following Him faithfully may well demand, of some, the supreme sacrifice—death itself.

Historically, this is true. The pages of church history run red with the blood of countless devout Christians who have been called upon to renounce their faith or be slaughtered; and they have chosen the latter. Polycarp, the second-century "venerable bishop of Smyrna," was taken by Roman guards to be put to death. He invited them to share a feast before completing their mission. After they had eaten he asked for an hour of prayer, which being overheard, brought his guards to repent; they refused to carry out the orders.

Others, however, seized him, and he was condemned by the proconsul, then burned at the stake. Just prior to this he said, when asked to deny the Christ, "Eighty and six years have I served him, and he never once wronged me; how then shall I blaspheme my King Who has saved me?"

If God wills, we of this generation may never be confronted with such a circumstance. Should it ever come to pass, may we have both the devotion and the courage to face death willingly rather than repudiate our Lord, Jesus Christ.

"Only one life; 'twill soon be past. Only what's done for Christ will last." Amen, and praise the Lord!

PRAYER THOUGHTS: O Father, may our lips never be silent, under any condition, if silence means a denial of that faith in Christ. Amen.

THE REASON FOR OBEDIENCE

SCRIPTURE: 1 John 14:15-24

VERSE FOR TODAY: We love him, because he first loved us (1 John 4:19).

HYMN FOR TODAY: "My Jesus, I Love Thee"

There are many reasons why people obey orders. The soldier obeys because he understands the importance of military discipline. The worker obeys because of self-interest. If he does not do what his employer tells him, he will be fired. The student obeys the teacher because he knows that if he does not complete the assignment he will receive a failing grade. The weakling obeys the bully out of fear. The threat of violence can be a strong motivation.

The strongest motive of all is love. We want to do our best to please someone we love. The little child wants to please the parent. The lover wants to please his beloved. Jesus gives us the very best reason for obeying Him. It is not simply respect for who He is, although we know that He is the Son of God. It is not just fear of His judgment, although we know that He will judge. We are obedient to Him because we know that "God commendeth his love toward us, in that, while we were yet sinners, Christ died for us" (Romans 5:8).

The apostle Paul also tells us, "The love of Christ constraineth us" (2 Corinthians 5:14).

PRAYER THOUGHTS: Father, we love You and know that You love us. You have given us everything we have, and most of all, You have given us salvation. We pray that we may be faithful and obedient in response to Your love. In the name of Him who loved us and died for us. Amen.

May 17-23. **Ross Dampier** is a frequent writer of DEVOTIONS. He is Minister Emeritus of the Central Christian Church in Bristol, Tennessee.

BE FILLED WITH THE SPIRIT

SCRIPTURE: John 14:25-31

VERSE FOR TODAY: If we live in the Spirit, let us also walk in the Spirit (Galatians 5:25).

HYMN FOR TODAY: "Spirit of God, Descend upon My Heart"

I heard once of an ol' farmer who had a friend who was going to Texas. They got together for a parting drink of moonshine. The man was very discouraged. "I have a brother in Texas," he said. "Tell him that the crops have failed, my hogs have died, and I don't know if I'll get through the winter." After a few drinks, he had forgotten his troubles and was feeling much better. "I have a brother in Texas," he said. "Tell him we are doing fine and if he needs anything to let me know and I'll be glad to get it for him."

The euphoria produced by a few drinks is well known. Well known, too, is the hangover which is the inevitable result of a few drinks too many. One of the problems of being filled with wine is that the effect is temporary. "And be not drunk with wine, wherein is excess; but be filled with the Spirit" (Ephesians 5:18)

The beauty of being filled with the Spirit is that the results which are produced are not temporary. The love and joy and peace which are the fruit of the Spirit are not fleeting, but when we are faithful they become a permanent part of our Christian experience. When we have this fruit in our lives, we can really make ourselves available to help others in the name of Christ.

PRAYER THOUGHTS: Lord God, we thank You that Your Holy Spirit is in our lives every day. We thank You that through Your Word, He reveals to us a better way of solving our problems. Thank You, Lord, for His direction and His comfort. Amen.

FINDING A SENSE OF DIRECTION

SCRIPTURE: John 16:4-15

VERSE FOR TODAY: Now if any man have not the Spirit of Christ, he is none of his (Romans 8:9).

HYMN FOR TODAY: "Greater Is He That Is in Me"

People experienced in Arctic exploration tell us that snow, ice, and cold are not the greatest hazards of Arctic travel. The most serious problem is what is known as "white-out." It is produced by haze which blots out everything. You lose your sense of direction. Worse than that, you get disoriented. You can even lose your sense of balance. Since there is no horizon and you cannot see the ground, you become confused as to up, down, and sideways.

Jesus promised to give us the Holy Spirit. Trying to live without Him in a wicked world can be as confusing as trying to navigate in a white-out. Without the Word of God, we are left without a sense of direction because there is no horizon and no pole star of absolute values. It is easy to become confused about right and wrong. The failure to use the Scripture as a guidepost has resulted in an ethical crisis in our world which affects every aspect of our lives.

When Jesus talked about the Spirit taking things from Christ and making them known to us, He was referring to the guidelines and words of encouragement which we have today in the Bible. As God's Word, it enables us to keep a sense of direction and balance in a topsy-turvy world.

PRAYER THOUGHTS: Father, guide us in all the decisions we have to make today. May we take no action which does not meet the prayer test of Your approval. In a world of situation ethics, keep our lives on course by showing us the direction of Your Word. In Jesus' name. Amen.

THE PROMISE OF FREEDOM

SCRIPTURE: 2 Corinthians 3:12-18

VERSE FOR TODAY: Ye shall know the truth, and the truth shall make you free (John 8:32).

HYMN FOR TODAY: "Breathe on Me, Breath of God"

As Christian and Hopeful made their way in *Pilgrim's Progress*, they came to Doubting Castle where they were captured by Giant Despair. He put them in a dungeon and tortured them cruelly. He even encouraged them to commit suicide, and poor Christian cried, "I know not whether it is better to live thus or to die." Hopeful, on the other hand, encouraged his friend to patience. On Saturday night about midnight they began to sing hymns and to pray, and they continued singing and praying until the break of the Lord's Day. Then Christian cried, "What a fool I have been to lie thus in this dungeon when I could walk at liberty! I have a key in my bosom called Promise, and it will open any lock." Then he tried the key and the door of Doubting Castle flew open and they were free.

In our Scripture for today we are told that the Holy Spirit produces freedom. Each one of us carries in our heart the secret of overcoming doubt and discouragement. The promise of Christ to be with us through the Holy Spirit will deliver us not only from depression but it will also free us from ignorance and from sin. We are to demonstrate in the way that we live the liberating power of the Lord Jesus Christ.

PRAYER THOUGHTS: Keep us from discouragement, O God. Fill our lives with a divine optimism which comes from putting our trust in Your promises. Let us know that even when the outlook is discouraging, the uplook is always good. In Jesus' name. Amen.

A CHILD OF THE KING

SCRIPTURE: Galatians 4:1-7

VERSE FOR TODAY: For as many as are led by the Spirit of God, they are the sons of God (Romans 8:14).

HYMN FOR TODAY: "A Child of the King"

An African chief was invited to appear at the court of Queen Victoria. As a young man, he had been captured and sold by Arab slave traders, but he escaped and returned to his people and became their chief. Because of his support of British rule in Africa, he was invited by Queen Victoria to come to England to appear at court. When asked what impressed him most he said, "I cannot describe the splendor of it. Many things impressed me, but the greatest surprise of all was that I, who was once a slave, should find myself welcomed as the child of the great white mother."

As self-confident Americans, we may find it difficult to understand that the surprise of the chief was genuine. We must not overlook the fact that although we were the slaves of sin, God loved us enough to send His Son to die for us. And He has made us His children by the new birth, and has prepared a place for us in Heaven which is more beautiful that anything we can imagine.

This sense of relationship with our heavenly Father should not be a source of pride but the basis of a deep humility. Our relationship is not a result of our own efforts but as a result of His love and mercy and grace.

PRAYER THOUGHTS: Father, help us to cherish the relationship which we have as a part of Your family. We call You Father because, through Jesus Christ, we have become a part of Your family. May we live lives worthy of the sacred name by which we are called, even the name of Jesus Christ. Amen.

THE SOURCE OF POWER

SCRIPTURE: Ephesians 3:14-19

VERSE FOR TODAY: For God hath not given us the spirit of fear; but of power, and of love, and of a sound mind (2 Timothy 1:7).

HYMN FOR TODAY: "Where the Spirit of the Lord Is"

The setting of the movie *Star Wars* was situated in a far away galaxy. Evil men were trying to destroy the Galactic Empire. Only a few Jedi-Knight pilots stood against them. Among the pilots were young Luke Skywalker and his mentor, Obi Wan Kenobi. Kenobi had magical abilities and knew of the secret powers of The Force.

This force was a system of beliefs meant to give powers to the defenders of the Empire in time of danger. Their watch word was, "May the Force go with you." Luke Skywalker does not understand the Force and Kenobi tells him, "You will know when the Force is with you, for you will receive power."

As Christians, we must be aware that we have a power given to us by Christ. It is the power for which Paul prays (Ephesians 3:16). It is the power which unites us with all the saints (Ephesians 3:18). It is the power which works in us (Ephesians 3:20).

Like Luke Skywalker, we may not always understand, but we seek to learn from God's Word all we can about the Spirit of God which dwells in us. It is this Spirit which sustains us in all the difficult times of life; it is absolutely essential that this Christ-given power be with us. "Now if any man have not the Spirit of Christ he is none of his" (Romans 8:9).

PRAYER THOUGHTS: Father, we know that the world tempts us with many kinds of power. Deliver us from the temptation to depend upon worldly influence. May the power in our lives be the power of Jesus Christ shown through His Spirit. In Jesus' name. Amen.

GOD'S ADOPTION

SCRIPTURE: Romans 8:12-17

VERSE FOR TODAY: Ye are all the children of God by faith in Christ Jesus (Galatians 3:26).

HYMN FOR TODAY: "The Family of God"

Jesus taught us that we become children of God by being born again. Paul used a different illustration to demonstrate to us the same point. He tells us that we are the children of God by adoption.

Adoption was familiar to the people in Paul's day. Roman citizenship was a valuable asset. Sometimes it was purchased for a great deal of money. If a man had a slave that he wanted to reward, he could adopt him.

When the requirements for adoption were met, a number of things happened. The slave became a free man. He was made a Roman citizen. He took the family name. He became an heir or a joint heir with other members of the family.

Paul implies all these things when he tells us that through the Holy Spirit we are called to be children of God. He implies that this is a blessing which can be received by anyone. There has been a lot of discussion about what is meant by, "and by this we cry, Abba, Father." The word *Abba* is an Aramaic word which is not translated. It is an informal word for *father*, like Daddy. The word translated *father* from the Greek is more formal. I believe that Paul was saying that however we speak to God, in whatever language, that God accepts us and makes us His children.

PRAYER THOUGHTS: We pray to You, Father, for those who are our brothers and sisters in the family of God. May we help bear the burdens of those who are in need. May we depend upon one another, and upon You, in time of need. In Jesus' name. Amen.

PRAISE HIM!

SCRIPTURE: John 17:1-5

VERSE FOR TODAY: These words spake Jesus, and lifted up his eyes to heaven, and said, Father, the hour is come; glorify thy Son, that thy Son also may glorify thee: (John 17:1).

HYMN FOR TODAY: "Praise Him! Praise Him!"

Jesus' prayer that God would glorify Him occurred near the end of His ministry. Ironically, the glorification He prayed for came through His death on the cross. We have great difficulty understanding how such a brutal death could bring Him glory. Yet, many times in the past, martyrs who have died for a great cause have, in their death, done more for that cause than in the activities of their life.

Jesus was glorified through His death because it signaled the completion of His mission on earth. Christ left His heavenly throne for the very purpose of dying on the cross.

Jesus was further glorified through the cross because His acceptance of such a cruel death was a act of obedience to His heavenly Father. His whole life and ministry were dedicated to doing the will of the Father, even to the acceptance of death.

Jesus' death on the cross also glorified Him because it purchased our salvation. We may not understand all of the theology involved in His death on the cross, but one thing we know for certain—He died for us. Hallelujah!

PRAYER THOUGHTS: Dear God, we thank You that You answered Jesus' prayer that He be glorified. Even though we cannot be glorified in the same way as our Lord, we can learn obedience to Your will in such a way that it will bring glory to Your name. Amen.

May 24-30. **John Wade** is a professor, author, minister, and former editor for Standard Publishing Company. He and his wife live in Fayetteville, Georgia.

THEY HAVE KEPT THY WORD

SCRIPTURE: John 17:6-10

VERSE FOR TODAY: I have manifested thy name unto the men which thou gavest me out of the world: thine they were, and thou gavest them me; and they have kept thy word (John 17:6).

HYMN FOR TODAY: "I'll Go Where You Want Me to Go"

Today's Scripture continues Jesus' prayer to the Father. In these verses He prayed specifically for the twelve whom He had called to be His close companions during His ministry. They came to be known as apostles. These men, who came from various backgrounds, were quite ordinary individuals by most human standards.

For three years they had followed Jesus, leaving behind their businesses, their homes, their friends, and their families. The three years spent learning at the feet of the Master Teacher had left their mark upon them, and they were changed men. They had come to believe that God had sent Jesus into the world on a special mission. That knowledge gave them a changed view of the world. Others had heard Jesus preach and teach, but many who heard did not—indeed, would not—believe Jesus. The apostles were different because in Jesus words, "they have kept thy word" (John 17:6).

Yet ironically, all of the apostles did not prove faithful. Even as Jesus was praying this prayer, Judas was carrying out his scheme to betray his Master. His traitorous actions came because he had not kept the word. We must give care to keep the word lest we fall into the same temptation.

PRAYER THOUGHTS: O God, we give You thanks that men and women down through the centuries have kept the faith. Give us the spiritual strength to hold firm to our faith in You and Your Son that we might give faithful service to You. Amen.

SENT INTO THE WORLD

SCRIPTURE: John 17:11-19

VERSE FOR TODAY: As thou hast sent me into the world, even so have I also sent them into the world (John 17:18).

HYMN FOR TODAY: "So Send I You"

In the portion of Jesus' prayer used in today's devotion, He turns His attention to the disciples. Jesus first points out that while He will soon be leaving the world, the disciples must remain in the world. He gives them a warning that they will be hated by the world, even as He had been hated by the world. But they need not fear the threats of the world. While He was with them, He had protected them. Now that He is leaving them, He assures them that God will watch over them so long as they carry out His mission.

Even after nearly two thousand years, Jesus' words have meaning for us. We have a commandment to carry the gospel to the uttermost parts of the world. Jesus' warning that those who serve Him will be hated by the world is just as meaningful for us today as it was in the first century when He first spoke them. Yet we also have His assurance that God will watch over us if we are faithful to Him.

While few of us will face physical threats or dangers because we serve King Jesus, we will be the targets of sneers and verbal abuse. Further, we will face subtle temptations to compromise our convictions. But when those temptations come, remember, God and Christ are with us.

PRAYER THOUGHTS: We rejoice, dear Father, that we have been called to serve You. As we work and serve, let us never forget that we are always under Your protective watch care. May that give us strength for the task before us. In Jesus' name. Amen.

UNITED WE STAND

SCRIPTURE: John 17:20-26

VERSE FOR TODAY: Neither pray I for these alone, but for them also which shall believe on me through their word; that they all may be one; as thou, Father art in me, and I in thee, (John 17:20, 21).

HYMN FOR TODAY: "They'll Know We Are Christians by Our Love"

A Peanuts cartoon strip opened with Linus quietly watching television. Then Lucy walked in and demanded that he change the channel to the program that she wanted to watch.

"What right do you have to come in here and make me change to your program?" asked Linus.

"See these five fingers," responded Lucy. "When I close them like this, they make a fist. Now do you understand?"

"What program was it you want to watch? I'll turn to it immediately," replied Linus timidly.

The closing panel showed Linus holding up his hand and looking at his five fingers. "Why can't you guys ever get together like that?" was his comment.

We may smile at this cartoon strip as just a childish episode. But it conveys a pointed truth to us. Jesus prayed that His immediate disciples be one, but His prayer also extend to all of His followers in the generations to come. As we look about us, we see His followers often divided and even fighting one another. As a result, our efforts against the forces of evil often fall short. Do you suppose Jesus ever looks upon this scene and asks, "Why can't you guys ever get together?"

PRAYER THOUGHTS: Our Father, we repeat the prayer of our Lord that all of His followers may be one. At the same time we must pray for forgiveness for the divisions we may have caused within Your holy church. Amen.

I AM THIRD

SCRIPTURE: Luke 22:24-32

VERSE FOR TODAY: But ye shall not be so: but he that is greatest among you, let him be as the younger; and he that is chief, as he that doth serve (Luke 22:26).

HYMN FOR TODAY: "Make Me a Blessing"

A student at the college where I teach served his summer internship at a youth camp. At the end of the summer when he turned in a report on his activities, he brought me a placard which had written on it these words: "I Am Third." Then he told me its meaning.

The camp receives a great deal of its financial support from a generous Christian gentleman who owns a large and very successful fast food chain. Every two weeks when a new group of campers arrived for their session, he spoke to them about his Christian faith. He encouraged them to put Christ first, others second, and themselves third, and as a reminder he gave each a placard reading, "I Am Third."

This man was born into an impoverished home and spent his early years in a public housing project. Eventually he was able to work his way out of that situation and start a restaurant. In his business he applied the same principles that he spoke about to the campers: Christ first, others second, and oneself third. There is no doubt that much of the success of his business has come from his commitment to serve God and others before he served himself.

Let's apply this lesson today.

PRAYER THOUGHTS: Gracious God, forgive us our selfish ways. May we look to Jesus, Your divine Son, as one who was willing to become a lowly servant for our sakes. Give us the grace to say, "I am third," as we reach out to serve God and others. In Jesus' name. Amen.

WATCH AND PRAY

SCRIPTURE: Matthew 26:36-46

VERSE FOR TODAY: Watch and pray, so that you will not fall into temptation. The spirit indeed is willing, but the body is weak (Matthew 26:41, *New International Version*).

HYMN FOR TODAY: "Rise Up, O Men of God"

A minister friend told of an occasion when he was preaching—a man in the audience fell soundly asleep and began to snore. He snored so loudly that soon he could be heard all over the sanctuary, and the audience broke out in laughter that woke up the sleeper. My friend quickly responded: "That's the trouble with the church today. Half of the Christians are asleep, and the other half think it's funny."

When Jesus returned from His prayer vigil, He didn't laugh at the three disciples whom He found asleep. Instead, He realized that the hectic pace of the preceding hours had left them exhausted. But their sleepiness at one of the most critical moments in Jesus' ministry serves as a sobering lesson for all of us. Physical sleepiness is not the most serious problem we experience in the church (although in the hectic, sleep-deprived pace we sometimes set, it can be a very serious problem). The real problem is spiritual drowsiness. We become so absorbed in our jobs, our school, our recreation, and our responsibilities, that we fall asleep spiritually to the vital issues that we face. My preacher friend had a point—half the church members are fast asleep and the other half think it's funny.

PRAYER THOUGHTS: Gracious God, forgive us when we have grown weary or bored in Your service. Help us to be always alert and watchful that we may protect ourselves from the wiles of the Devil even as we labor in Your vineyard. Give us strength to follow You. In the name of Jesus Christ, our Lord, we pray. Amen.

GOD ALWAYS LOVES US

SCRIPTURE: Romans 8:31-39

VERSE FOR TODAY: Nor height, nor depth, nor any other creature, shall be able to separate us from the love of God, (Romans 8:39).

HYMN FOR TODAY: "Because I Have Been Given Much"

A farmer once had a weather vane on the top of his barn. On it were the words, "God Loves Us." One day his minister happened to be visiting him and noticed the weather vane and commented, "Are you suggesting that God's love varies with the wind? That every time the wind changes directions, God's love changes?"

"Oh, no," responded the farmer. "I mean that regardless of which direction the wind is blowing, God always loves us!"

In an age in which it seems that everything is changing and it seems that we cannot depend for very long on any one or any thing, we need to be assured that God always loves us. Once we come to believe, really believe, that God loves us, we will find ways to cope with the threats and disappointments that all of us must face in this life.

While nothing can really separate us from the love of God, because we have freedom of choice, we can turn away from Him and reject His love. As long as we continue to rebel against Him, we forfeit many of the blessings of His love. Only as we accept His love can we know and enjoy the richness of its fruits.

PRAYER THOUGHTS: O Father, open our eyes to Your love that surrounds us on every side. Forgive us when we have ignored that love. May we acknowledge that love and commit ourselves to serving You and our fellowmen. Let our lives express Your love. In Jesus' name. Amen.

THE LIGHT OF THE WORLD IS JESUS

SCRIPTURE: Genesis 1:1-5

VERSE FOR TODAY: When Jesus spoke again to the people, he said, "I am the light of the world. Whoever follows me will never walk in darkness, but will have the light of life" (John 8:12, *New International Version*).

HYMN FOR TODAY: "The Light of the World Is Jesus"

Light is indispensable. Not only do we need light to be able to see, but light is the great sustainer of life. Plants use light energy through photosynthesis to convert carbon dioxide in the air into the food they need to live and grow. Various animals in turn eat the plants, turning them into the food energy that they need. When still other animals eat the plant-eating animals, they too are nourished by the light energy used in the first place by the plants.

In view of this, it is not surprising that one of the first things God created—even before the formless and empty earth was molded and filled—was light.

The first verses of the Gospel of John are parallel in many ways to the opening verses of Genesis. Both begin with the words, "In the beginning. . . . " Both mention light. But in John, the light has a name. Jesus is both light and life.

In the physical world, the light of the sun sustains life. In the spiritual realm, Jesus Christ gives us life, and sustains it through the light of His presence.

PRAYER THOUGHTS: God, our heavenly Father, and Jesus, Light of Life, we praise You as the source of both physical and spiritual life. Help us to see clearly by Your light. Amen.

May 31. **Benjamin Rees** and his wife, Karen, serve in cross-cultural ministry to Chinese and Filipinos in Hong Kong. Their two children, Matthew and Megan, were both born in Hong Kong.

DEVOTIONS™

June

photo by Dr. Ward Patterson

NOT MYTH BUT MIRACLE

SCRIPTURE: Genesis 1:6-13

VERSE FOR TODAY: By the word of the LORD were the heavens made, their starry host by the breath of his mouth (Psalm 33:6, *New International Version*).

HYMN FOR TODAY: "How Great Thou Art!"

Most ancient cultures have some kind of "creation myth," describing how the world and mankind were made. Some use this fact to argue that the biblical account is no more than another such myth, telling how ancient people with no knowledge of modern science tried to explain their origins.

When we compare the biblical account with such myths, however, we immediately notice an immense difference. The Chinese story of P'an Ku (or Pan Gu) is typical. The universe is said to have been formed from the body of the first man, P'an Ku. When he died, his eyes became the sun and moon, his blood and his sweat formed rivers, his body became soil, and his hair grew into trees and plants.

In contrast, the biblical record has a simplicity and dignity that myths lack. It is true that the Bible does not give us all the scientific details of how certain events took place. Few, if any of us would understand these if it did. But it tells us the essentials without the elaboration of ancient myths. "God said . . . " and everything happened as God commanded.

PRAYER THOUGHTS: God of creation, we thank You for the world You made. We thank You for the Bible, which gives us a reliable record of Your work. Help us not to be misled by myths, no matter whether ancient or modern, but always to trust in You and Your Word. Amen.

June 1-6. **Benjamin Rees** and his wife, Karen, serve in cross-cultural ministry to Chinese and Filipinos in Hong Kong. Their two children, Matthew and Megan, were both born in Hong Kong.

REFLECTING HIS LIGHT

SCRIPTURE: Genesis 1:14-19

VERSE FOR TODAY: "You are the light of the world. . . . let your light shine before men, that they may see your good deeds and praise your Father in heaven" (Matthew 5:14, 16, *New International Version*).

HYMN FOR TODAY: "Let the Lower Lights Be Burning"

On the first day of creation, God brought light into the universe. But this light seems initially to have lacked a specific source apart from God himself. On the fourth day, two specific sources of light were created (or perhaps made visible to the earth). These specific sources of light were the "great light" of the sun by day, and the "lesser light" of the moon at night.

Some people argue that the moon is not really a "light," since it does not produce light itself. But the moon does illuminate the earth with light it reflects from the sun.

In a similar fashion, as Jesus is "the light of the world" (John 8:12), so Christians also are called "the light of the world" (Matthew 5:14).

Just as the moon has no light of its own, but provides light that it reflects from the sun, so we have no spiritual light of our own to give the world, but we become lights to the world as we reflect the light of Jesus to them through our words and especially through our deeds.

Let us aim always to be good reflectors of Christ's light in this world so that people can give glory, not to us, but to Him whose light we reflect.

PRAYER THOUGHTS: Our Father in Heaven, we thank You for sending Jesus to be our spiritual light. We thank You also for the privilege of representing Him as lesser lights in this world. Help us to be well-polished reflectors that will truly show His light to those who see us. Amen.

GOD SAW THAT IT WAS GOOD

SCRIPTURE: Genesis 1:20-23

VERSE FOR TODAY: How many are your works, O LORD! In wisdom you made them all; the earth is full of your creatures (Psalm 104:24, *New International Version*).

HYMN FOR TODAY: "For the Beauty of the Earth"

Despite the fact that Hong Kong, where I have lived for more than 25 years, is one of the most densely populated territories in the world, it is also home to an amazing variety of wildlife. Birds are especially prolific.

Sparrows frequently forage in the window boxes that adorn our high rise apartment block. A more exotic window box visitor is the crested bulbul. Unlike many cities, there are not many pigeons, but we often see spotted doves. Kites and other large birds of prey wheel overhead, occasionally dipping down to the level of our windows on the fifth floor. One sign that winter is here—since it never gets very cold—is the noisy crowd of migratory gulls over the harbor. In Hong Kong's country parks and few remaining rural areas, we often see egrets and herons.

If the variety of birds in the wild were not enough, Hong Kong also has several aviaries where we can see peafowl, flamingos, and many varieties of parrots.

The immense variety of birds, with their many colors and great assortment of different habits, is testimony to the truth of God's own comment on His creation, "that it was good" (Genesis 1:21, *New International Version*). Let us remember to give Him thanks for that.

PRAYER THOUGHTS: Thank You, Father, for the goodness of life and the beauty around us. Help us to enjoy it afresh and praise You for it anew each day. Amen.

CHRISTIANS, STEWARDS OF THE ENVIRONMENT

SCRIPTURE: Genesis 1:24-31

VERSE FOR TODAY: "The land must not be sold permanently, because the land is mine and you are but aliens and my tenants" (Leviticus 25:23, *New International Version*).

HYMN FOR TODAY: "This Is My Father's World"

Are Christians to blame for the world-wide environmental crisis? Some people say so, and they point to today's Scripture passage as the cause.

The reasoning of these people goes like this: "The current crisis has been caused by careless over-exploitation of natural resources. The Bible's teaching that God told mankind to subdue and rule over the earth gives Christians a license to exploit the earth's resources at will. This has led to Christians pillaging and plundering the earth with no thought of the consequences to the ecology."

This view overlooks two important points. First, it is not only Christians who have carelessly exploited the earth. Some of the most serious examples of environmental destruction today are in so-called "developing" countries, with largely non-Christian populations, where the desire for economic progress supersedes all other considerations.

Second, God's people are called to be stewards of all that God gives us, including our earthly environment. Let's treat it as the home God has given us, and take care of it.

PRAYER THOUGHTS: Creator of Heaven and earth, we humbly ask Your forgiveness if we have plundered or "trashed" this world You have given to us. Help us learn to be wise stewards who will use whatever You give us for Your glory. Amen.

MANKIND NEEDS A SABBATH

SCRIPTURE: Genesis 2:1-4

VERSE FOR TODAY: Six days you shall labor, but on the seventh day you shall rest; even during the plowing season and harvest you must rest (Exodus 34:21, *New International Version*).

HYMN FOR TODAY: "Take Time to Be Holy"

A friend who visits Hong Kong occasionally on business once told us that he enjoys being in Hong Kong for the first two or three days. After that he feels a need to get away and slow down. It is a very busy place. It is also very stressful. Some people who have lived in both Hong Kong and New York City say that they find New York restful by comparison.

Most people in Hong Kong work long hours, and in the hours when they are not working at their first job, many take second jobs or enroll in night classes to improve their chances for a better job.

Unfortunately, it is not only Hong Kong where the pace of life makes it difficult to slow down, relax, and rest. On recent trips to the United States I have found more and more Americans living this kind of life.

The Sabbath law of the Old Testament ensured that God's chosen people took time for two things: time to acknowledge God and worship Him, and time for needed relaxation and rest. Even though we are no longer strictly required to keep this law, we do still have these needs and must make sure that we take time to satisfy them.

PRAYER THOUGHTS: Holy Father, in this busy world there are so many demands on our time. It is hard to find time for all we want to do or feel we should do. We are encouraged to know that even You found time to rest. Help us to take time for worship and time to rest. Amen.

WITHOUT EXCUSE

SCRIPTURE: Psalm 104:24-35

VERSE FOR TODAY: For since the creation of the world God's invisible qualities—his eternal power and divine nature—have been clearly seen, being understood from what has been made, so that men are without excuse (Romans 1:20, *New International Version*).

HYMN FOR TODAY: "Joyful, Joyful, We Adore Thee"

Psalm 104 speaks of the greatness of God as shown in the things He has made.

In his letter to the Romans, Paul uses the things God has made to demonstrate mankind's accountability before God. A lack of familiarity with God's written law is no excuse, he argues, because the most essential qualities of God are clearly demonstrated in the universe He created.

What can we know about God and His divine nature from His creation? Psalm 104 shows us a few things.

Verse one begins by praising God's greatness, and much of what follows is a demonstration of how great and powerful God is. Who can gaze at the stars on a clear night, or peer into the depths of the Grand Canyon, or watch the tons of water thundering over Niagara Falls, without being impressed by the greatness and power of God?

Verse 24 stresses God's wisdom. Scientists are still laboring to unlock the secrets of the universe. God knew these from the beginning, and put everything together to make this amazingly complex world we live in.

God's power, wisdom, and other divine qualities are indeed clearly visible in His creation. Therefore we are, as Paul says, "without excuse" if we do not honor Him as God.

PRAYER THOUGHTS: O God, we praise Your power and wisdom. Help us always to give You the honor that is due You. Amen.

INGRATITUDE

SCRIPTURE: Genesis 2:4-14

VERSE FOR TODAY: O give thanks unto the Lord; for he is good (Psalm 136:1).

HYMN FOR TODAY: "If I Have Wounded Any Soul"

In a small Georgia town a young couple was walking home from their work in the cotton mill. Their friendly foreman walked with them till they came to his home. In the front yard was a small tree with three huge peaches.

"What beautiful peaches!" the young wife exclaimed.

"Wait a minute," the foreman said. Generously he picked two of the peaches and gave them to the couple." Enjoy," he said.

Do you know what? The two sneaked back when no one was looking and stole the one remaining peach.

In the Garden of Eden, God gave Adam not only a peach, but "every tree that is pleasant to the sight, and good for food." There was only one tree in the whole garden that God reserved for himself. You know the rest of the story. Adam and his wife sneaked in and stole fruit from the one tree that was forbidden.

Shame on them! But think a minute. After all the good things God has given you to enjoy, is there some forbidden thing Satan has convinced you that you must have?

PRAYER THOUGHTS: Though Eden is far behind us, our Father, You have surrounded us with comforts that Adam never knew. Besides, You have given us the promise of everlasting life. In return we promise to obey You. Help us to keep our promise, we pray in Jesus' name. Amen.

June 7, 8. **Orrin Root** of Cincinnati, Ohio, is a retired editor of Standard Publishing. He continues to write for a variety of Christian publications.

WHEN TWO ARE ONE

SCRIPTURE: Genesis 2:15-25

VERSE FOR TODAY: They shall be one flesh (Genesis 2:24).

HYMN FOR TODAY: "Blest Be the Tie"

A young couple on the verge of divorce went to their minister for counseling. He gave each one a pencil and paper, saying, "Make a list of things you want more than you want happiness and peace with your mate."

They both frowned at the paper for a while and decided there was nothing like that to list.

The minister asked, "Why did you quarrel yesterday?"

"I want a dishwasher."

"I want some money in the bank for emergencies."

"OK," the minister said cheerfully. "You both know something you want more than peace and happiness. Write it down on the paper."

"We'll get a dishwasher," he conceded.

"No," she answered, "I'd rather have money in the bank."

When two become one, sometimes the question seems to be, "Which one?" Each may want to change the other. The answer, of course, is, "Neither one." Each one gives up some things he or she likes so both can enjoy what both of them like. When top priority is given to harmony, a lot of selfish personal wishes can be postponed or forgotten.

PRAYER THOUGHTS: Though You began the human family with only two people, our Father, in their story is a message for all of us. May we think less of ourselves, more of one another, and most of all of You. In Jesus' name we pray, amen.

ONE PLUS ONE EQUALS ONE

SCRIPTURE: Ephesians 5:18-33

VERSE FOR TODAY: "For this reason a man will leave his Father and mother and be united to his wife, and the two will become one flesh" (Ephesians 5:31, *New International Version*).

HYMN FOR TODAY: "Savior, Like a Shepherd Lead Us"

In God's arithmetic, one plus one equals one. This does not mean that a person loses his or her identity, but the two become "one in name, one in aim, and one in a holy destiny." It is often said that a couple begins to look alike after years of marriage. One congregation held a contest to see if there could be any truth to this. It was agreed that some couples did look alike. Probably it was because they had adopted the same mannerisms and facial expressions.

It is in a larger sense that the Bible speaks of two becoming one. It means that the couple is not competing with one another nor fighting against one another. It means that they are working together for common goals in a cooperative spirit. Newspapers recently carried the story of a couple in the Soviet Union who were married for 100 years. He was 119 years old and she was 115. We wonder what advice they could give us! But it would be no more helpful than the advice Paul gives in this passage. When a wife respects her husband and a husband cherishes his wife, marriage is a little bit of Heaven on earth.

PRAYER THOUGHTS: Dear Father, when You created us, You created marriage. Help us to develop qualities that will lead us toward Your ideal for our lives. Through Christ our Lord, amen.

June 9. **Robert Shannon** has enjoyed a varied career as minister, missionary, and college professor. He is now enjoying retirement in Valle Crucis, North Carolina.

CHRIST OUR FOUNDATION

SCRIPTURE: Matthew 15:1-9

VERSE FOR TODAY: See to it that no one takes you captive through hollow and deceptive philosophy, which depends on human tradition and the basic principles of this world rather than on Christ (Colossians 2:8, *New International Version*).

HYMN FOR TODAY: "The Church's One Foundation"

What are your family traditions? Often someone in the family assumes the duty of keeping traditions, memories, and reunions intact. Sociologists call these people, "Kinkeepers." I value my family kinkeeper and the extraordinary effort she puts into maintaining the family heritage.

In Jesus' time the religious traditions were often too hampering. God had a plan for the Jewish nation and eventually the whole world, but the people allowed the traditions of the elders to replace the law of the Lord.

A United Press release in a midwestern city told of a hospital where officials discovered that the fire fighting equipment had never been connected. For 35 years it had been relied upon for safety in case of emergency, but it had never been attached to the city's water main. The pipe that led from the building extended four feet underground and there it stopped. The medical staff and the patients had felt complete confidence in the system. Theirs was a false security. Although the costly equipment was adequate for the building, it lacked the most important thing—water!

It is the Word of God that links us to the Heavenly Father.

PRAYER THOUGHTS: Father, forgive our shortsightedness when we rely on things of this world to guide us. In the name of Jesus, amen.

June 10. **Dr. Willard Walls** and his wife, Ruth, minister in the United Kingdom.

June 11

THE SURRENDER THAT ENDS IN VICTORY

SCRIPTURE: Matthew 19:16-22

VERSE FOR TODAY: With man this is impossible, but with God all things are possible (Matthew 19:26, *New International Version*).

HYMN FOR TODAY: "Be Thou My Vision"

With our lives surrendered to God, we can face every moment. Our material possessions and achievements are inadequate to meet life. But our Lord is always sufficient.

Everyone fails. The atheist Edwin A. Robinson knew that. His poem, "Richard Cory," is of the young man whom everyone admired. He appeared to have life together. But one day Richard Cory went home and put a bullet through his head. "All have sinned and fall short of the glory of God" (Romans 3:23, *New International Version*).

The life surrendered to God means a life that can face the day. Material goods will never impress enough nor fulfill enough to bring contentment. The English author Samuel Johnson summarized the conflict in our minds after he visited a beautiful castle: "These are things which make it difficult to die." But such "things" will not see us through life. Earthly problems take heavenly solutions.

We can rely on God to meet the day's tasks. The crucial issue is surrendering it all to Him. When we make that surrender we find victory and we can face the day.

PRAYER THOUGHTS: Almighty and loving heavenly Father, I would surrender those parts of my life that are not yet wholly Yours. I cannot know contentment with material goods and achievements. You alone are sufficient to meet the tests and trials of this day. I would live the victorious life in Thee. Through Jesus Christ, my Lord, I pray. Amen.

June 11. **John Wakefield** is a hospital chaplain in Cincinnati, Ohio.

THE SACREDNESS OF MARRIAGE

SCRIPTURE: Mark 10:1-9

VERSE FOR TODAY: Therefore what God has joined together, let man not separate (Mark 10:9, *New International Version*).

HYMN FOR TODAY: "O Perfect Love"

One day when his regular secretary was absent, a young businessman had another girl work for him. She brought some papers for his signature, and as she leaned over the desk, she let her hair trail across his face. He fought his feelings, but by the end of the day, he touched her, and she responded with a kiss. Even as he kissed her, he visualized his wife and children waiting for him at the door. He hated what he was doing, but he kept on. This was just the beginning of a struggle between lust and love that went on for weeks. Finally, he sought the help of a Christian counselor.

With the husband's consent, the counselor told the wife the whole story. Although fearful, she and the counselor went to her husband's office. He was expecting them, and as the couple embraced, she said, "I know. I love you. Everything will be all right."

Then the secretary was called in. The counselor told her of the couple's love for each other and then began to witness to her of Christ.

PRAYER THOUGHTS: Lord, help us never to forget the sacredness of marriage. Help us to love each other with the love that is possible only through knowing You. In Jesus' name, amen.

June 12. **Mary Kay Mosby** is a Christian writer who lives in Alton, Illinois.

THE RESURRECTION BODY

SCRIPTURE: 1 Corinthians 15:42-49

VERSE FOR TODAY: When the perishable has been clothed with the imperishable, and the mortal with immortality, then the saying that is written will come true: "Death has been swallowed up in victory." "Where, O death, is your victory? Where, O death, is your sting" (1 Corinthians 15:53, 54, *New International Version*).

HYMN FOR TODAY: "Beyond the Sunset"

When the apostle Paul preached in the Areopagus in Athens, some of those who heard mocked him for speaking about the resurrection of the dead. It was not the idea of life after death that they found strange. What they found hard to swallow was the idea of a bodily resurrection.

Most religions teach some kind of life after death, but the Bible is almost alone in teaching a bodily resurrection.

The doctrine of a bodily resurrection does raise certain questions. My mother is now in her 80s, and is suffering considerable back pain as a result of osteoporosis. My brother lost a leg in an accident a few years ago. For them to be reunited with the bodies they now have would hardly be a blessing. They look forward to a new body in Christ Jesus.

In today's Scripture passage, Paul calls the speculation of a bodily resurrection foolish. The body we will receive at the resurrection is as different from what we now have as the tree is from the seed or the sun is from the moon.

PRAYER THOUGHTS: We praise and thank You, Father, that we have the promise of a new body that is spiritual, immortal, imperishable, full of glory, and free from the weaknesses and infirmities of our present existence. In the name of Him who made it possible, amen.

June 13. **Benjamin Rees** and his wife, Karen, live in Hong Kong. They have two children.

SIN LURKS WHERE WORSHIP FADES

SCRIPTURE: Genesis 4:1-7

VERSE FOR TODAY: "If you do what is right, will you not be accepted? But if you do not do what is right, sin is crouching at your door; it desires to have you, but you must master it" (Genesis 4:7, *New International Version*).

HYMN FOR TODAY: "Come, Thou Fount"

In Autumn 1978, I rented an old gambling hall in which to hold Bible classes. The hall was in the center of Lung-ku-taan, a small Hakka village on the South China coast.

Like Cain before them, the residents of Lung-ku-taan had let healthy adoration of God decline. As we spruced up the old hall, several residents derided Jesus and teased me in front of others with words like, "Look, a foreign devil that talks Jesus." "Jesus stinks!" "He's dead, so what's the fuss?" "Only barbarians like you would believe in Jesus." "Give the kiddies cakes and candy instead of Jesus."

That attitude took its toll on their lives. They were notorious sea-pirates, hijackers, bank robbers, blackmailers, and murderers. A dozen or so of the able-bodied men spent most of their time drinking and gambling.

One day, a two-year-old boy was harmed while his father sat drinking and gambling only two hundred yards away. When the father reached the toddler, he himself cried like a baby, but no one comforted him. In fact, what comfort is there apart from giving Jesus His place of adoration in their lives?

PRAYER THOUGHTS: Heavenly Father, we pray Jesus Christ may again have first place as Lord in the hearts of Your people. Amen.

June 14-16, 18-20. **Gary Anderson** ministers in Emmett, Idaho. For many years he served among the Chinese people in Hong Kong. He and his wife, Joyce, have three children, Sandra, Steven, and David.

YOU DIDN'T SEE THAT

SCRIPTURE: Genesis 4:8-16

VERSE FOR TODAY: This is the verdict: Light has come into the world, but men loved darkness instead of light because their deeds were evil (John 3:19, *New International Version*).

HYMN FOR TODAY: "Stepping in the Light"

Oh, how tempting it can be to imagine, like Cain, that no one knows what harm we do.

Last Sunday I determined to eat lighter at the adult Bible class social, but someone brought homemade vanilla ice cream. I savored it and contemplated having more. I saw that everyone was busy visiting, so I reasoned that they wouldn't notice if I had more. But as I ladled some into my bowl, I noticed a face trying to catch my eye. When I looked, a young man smiled and said, "Ahem, that's your third bowl."

Some time ago a dear church lady had personalized her car license plate to be a Bible text. However, she was so troubled that her aggressive driving might bring dishonor to Jesus' name that she had the car horn disconnected.

How much kinder we would be, how much less we would shove and push and scowl and cut someone off for a parking spot and speak harshly on the phone if we were each identified with tags that said, "Hello, I'm so-and-so and I'm a Christian. How am I doing? Please notify my heavenly Father." Indeed, nothing we do is ever really unseen.

PRAYER THOUGHTS: O God in Heaven, nothing is hidden from You. Purify us and remind us often, we pray, to keep relying on You so that we can live so purely that others will be drawn to You because we were willing to be transparent. In the name of Jesus, the Savior of the world, we pray. Amen.

FRESH STARTS HAPPEN

SCRIPTURE: Genesis 4:17-26

VERSE FOR TODAY: At that time men began to call on the name of the LORD **(Genesis 4:26,** *New International Version***).**

HYMN FOR TODAY: "Morning Has Broken"

My high school years had some real minuses. Among the school's four thousand students, I knew of only a few Christians. Many actions among the student body leaders were depressing. Much of the student body and some of the teachers showed ungodly behavior.

It seems that during the decade of the sixties, many found a way of life without Christ. Remembering the evils that happened around me in my youth, in my school, my community, and evils reported in the media, I felt that there were few Christians in the world. Like Eve after the loss of Abel, I found the future bleak.

Then last Sunday evening, I felt like middle-aged Eve at Seth's birth. Joyful tears flowed as I watched a national video documenting the serious commitment to Christ by millions of high schoolers—dedicating themselves for Him and gathering at their school flag poles to pray for their nation, their schools, their teachers, and their fellow students.

Today I have the feeling of a new beginning. Men are once again turning to God. Once again men see the need for living godly lives. Praise God!

PRAYER THOUGHTS: O thank You, heavenly Father, for a new generation determined in Your strength to take on the evil of the world. Guide them. Empower them. Protect them from the sins that to easily beset us and from the destructive onslaught of the evil one. We know that prayer can awaken us to a new beginning. Our prayer today is in the name of our Savior and Lord, Jesus Christ. Amen.

SEPARATED FROM GOD

SCRIPTURE: Isaiah 59:1-15

VERSE FOR TODAY: It is your iniquities that raise a barrier between you and your God, because of your sins he has hidden his face so that he does not hear you (Isaiah 59:2, *The New English Bible*).

HYMN FOR TODAY: "Nothing Between"

A couple was riding along a highway. The wife, sitting close to the door, looked over at her husband who was driving and complained, "We don't sit as close to each other as we once did."

Glancing over at her, he replied, "I haven't moved."

If there is a barrier between you and God, it is a barrier you have erected, not God. He cannot stand sin. When Christ took upon himself the sins of the world at Calvary, God turned His face from Him.

Sometimes the barrier is only temporary. One morning everything was going wrong for me. I had a writing assignment to finish, and my typewriter suddenly broke. In the background a television announcer kept repeating, "We have temporarily lost the video portion of our program, but we will continue with the audio portion. Please stand by." And I thought, *Sometimes when we cannot see God, we can still hear Him.* We must "stand by" in faith, so that the separation between ourselves and God will not become permanent.

PRAYER THOUGHTS: O Lord, it seems a long time since I have heard Your voice. Other voices, louder and noisier, have been making themselves heard. Let me tune in so that I may hear Your quiet voice leading and guiding me in the paths in which I should walk. Amen.

June 17. **Gordon Chilvers**. ©1978, *DEVOTION*™, Standard Publishing Company, Cincinnati, Ohio. Reprinted by permission.

DISCLOSING HEALS

SCRIPTURE: Proverbs 28:9-14

VERSE FOR TODAY: He who conceals his sins does not prosper, but whoever confesses and renounces them finds mercy (Proverbs 28:13, *New International Version*).

HYMN FOR TODAY: "Cleanse Me"

Who hasn't wanted to run and hide when we did something embarrassing? But such a plan is both weak and dangerous. That very desire warns us that we may have done wrong.

Excuses, time, blaming others, blaming circumstances, calling sins nice names, and busying ourselves at good works, won't conceal sins from the Lord, but only conceal His prosperous blessings from us. Our hearts start hardening.

In an episode of the TV series, *Touched by an Angel*, the main character was a prominent news anchor-woman. While she was hurriedly driving her car and became distracted, she accidentally hit and critically injured a star athlete. In deep embarrassment that such a prominent person as herself would hit someone, she hopped in her car and fled from the scene before medical help arrived.

Later, she made a full confession, but she still lost her privilege to drive for a long while, and her career was seriously endangered. Yet, if she had just stayed with the injured man and not tried to conceal her mistake, she probably wouldn't have been charged with any serious crime, and public sympathy would have gone out to her. How much more the Lord's abundant mercies?

PRAYER THOUGHTS: Lord, please forgive us. By sinning, we trifled with Your holiness and authority. By hiding we treated You as if You were too ignorant to know. We alienated ourselves from others and our own hearts. Forgive and heal by Christ's work in us, we pray. Amen.

CHRIST RECONCILES

SCRIPTURE: Matthew 5:21-26

VERSE FOR TODAY: Leave your gift there in front of the altar. First go and be reconciled to your brother; then come and offer your gift (Matthew 5:24, *New International Version*).

HYMN FOR TODAY: "Make Me a Blessing"

Yellowstone National Park lies northeast of our Emmett, Idaho, home, but we travel to Yellowstone by first traveling southeast around the Sawtooth Mountains. Likewise, we cannot always give directly to God. An obligation to a brother or sister may loom up like a great mountain between us and worshipping Him.

Before worship last Sunday, I promised a lady that I would find some Bible lesson for her neighbor children, but by the time church was over I had forgotten. Now I cannot rest until I have the needed lessons in hand to give her. The Lord would not ignore such a promise, so neither can I.

It may be that we have caused someone to be quite upset at us. We owe it to them, and to the Lord, to carefully, honestly, listen to their complaint without attacking them or dwelling on their wrongs. Then let us take responsibility for our part—confess our shortcomings, ask God to help us change obstinate ways, and seek to repair all that is lacking. And we shall find that the other person will be enabled to join us in giving whole-hearted worship and praise to the Lord.

PRAYER THOUGHTS: Eternal Father of both me and him whom I have wronged, forgive me for obstructing his enjoyment of You. Cleanse me until You can use me to right the wrong so that he and I can rejoice in Your name together. Amen.

OH, JOY, FORGIVEN!

SCRIPTURE: Psalm 32:1-11

VERSE FOR TODAY: You are my hiding place; you will protect me from trouble and surround me with songs of deliverance (Psalm 32:7 *New International Version***).**

HYMN FOR TODAY: "You Are My Hiding Place"

Our old church building is so full of nooks and crannies that children and teens in the building for evening socials delight in nothing more than playing a form of hide and seek known as, "Sardines." A boy, for example, squeezes into some hiding place. Each person who finds him joins him in silent anticipation until only one person is left. Together they know the nervous stillness that makes one almost afraid to breathe as they keep hidden.

All the more, people who have lived through the terror of war and search parties of enemies or bandits know the breathless silence of hoping with their whole lives that their hiding places would not be discovered.

To try to hide our sins from God only produces the oppressive sense of His watching. He sees all. But Jesus was exposed on the cross with *no* hiding place, so that we might expose our sins to God. This empowers us to hug the Lord with all the delight of a personal *my* as our hiding place. From then on we are surrounded right and left and covered above and beneath with joyful deliverance songs right in the midst of even very public lives.

PRAYER THOUGHTS: Merciful Father, forgive our hiding. We have hidden our true selves not so much from You as from ourselves. Empower us, we pray, to open up to You so that You might indeed be our true and eternal hiding place. Amen.

TOO FAR GONE

SCRIPTURE: Genesis 6:5-22

VERSE FOR TODAY: Now the earth was corrupt in God's sight and was full of violence (Genesis 6:11, *New International Version*).

HYMN FOR TODAY: "In the Hour of Trial"

Termites are such a pain. They'll eat your house, your furniture, your books, your magazines, and anything else that is made from wood. In Hawaii, as in south Florida, there's nothing to slow them down. We had to replace most of the stage area in our church building because of termite damage, and we've been advised that the parsonage "would fall down if the termites ever quit holding hands." Although we don't usually wear shoes in houses in Hawaii, my wife couldn't wear high heels in the parsonage because the heels might sink down through the termite-eaten floor. We're thankful to have a parsonage to live in, and over the years many repairs have been made on the house, but the church just can't go on trying to fix this one up. So a new one is being planned. Sometimes you just have to tear an older house down and start all over with new materials. You can't save the old one.

That's pretty much what God had to do with the human race. Man was too corrupt. Warnings to repent went ignored. God saved the seed, eight souls in the ark, and then started over. In so doing, He, of course, rescued humanity from total extinction. Like termites, sin destroys.

PRAYER THOUGHTS: Father, thank You that we today don't have to die in our sins. Thank You for cleansing us and saving us from destruction by sending Jesus to save us. In His name, amen.

June 21-27. **Donnie Mings** and his wife, Charlotte, are former missionaries to Japan. They now serve the Hauula Church of Christ, Hauula, Oahu, Hawaii.

GOD FOUND A RIGHTEOUS MAN

SCRIPTURE: Genesis 7:1-16

VERSE FOR TODAY: But Noah found favor in the eyes of the Lord (Genesis 6:8, *New International Version*).

HYMN FOR TODAY: "I Would Be True"

The motto of the State of Hawaii is written both in English and in the Hawaiian language. Although not on the state flag, this motto is prominently included in the great seal of the state, wherever that is displayed. It states: "The Life of the Land is Perpetuated in Righteousness." The authors of that statement correctly noted the connection between righteousness and survival. Evil brings destruction.

Noah was a righteous man. The new human race would start from a position of faithfulness and obedience to God. Humanity would continue, but not in its corruption. The life of the race must be perpetuated in righteousness. Noah's righteousness stood out in contrast to the sin of his contemporary society. His faithfulness to God continued as he obediently built the ark exactly as God had instructed. And although he probably had never seen rain before, he believed God and prepared for it. Noah carefully made provision for, and took into the ark, all those animals as God had asked him to do. And then he and his family obediently entered that big lifeboat, to be divinely carried above and beyond the flood. His righteousness and obedience was rewarded.

PRAYER THOUGHTS: Heavenly Father, thank You for Noah and his righteousness and example of trust. And thank You that in Jesus we can be righteous, too. Strengthen us as we do our best to be faithful and true to You every day. In the name of Jesus, our Lord and Savior, amen.

GOD'S FAITHFULNESS

SCRIPTURE: Genesis 7:17–8:5

VERSE FOR TODAY: Know therefore that the LORD your God is God; he is the faithful God, keeping his covenant of love to a thousand generations of those who love him and keep his commands (Deuteronomy 7:9, *New International Version*).

HYMN FOR TODAY: "O God, Our Help in Ages Past"

Have you ever forgotten to feed a pet? What if it were caged or tied or otherwise restricted and unable to get out and find food and water? What could have happened to the pet that was put in your care? Sometimes people are careless and forget their responsibilities. Thankfully, God is always faithful and does not forget us. He keeps His covenant with us.

The flood waters just kept coming. They rose above the mountains and lifted the ark so that it floated on the surface. All other animals and birds perished, and all mankind died except for those in the ark. And then the rain stopped. The heavens ceased their downpour, and the springs of the deep were stopped. And Noah and his family waited.

God did not forget the precious cargo in the ark. He sent a wind, and the waters started to go down, slowly but surely. He had the situation under control. Not too many days afterward the ark came to rest on Mount Ararat. Just as God took care of the first man and woman in the Garden, so now God was faithfully watching over Noah, his family, and the animals, so that they would live and soon be able to walk out of the ark onto dry ground. God had a schedule, and He was keeping it.

PRAYER THOUGHTS: Dear heavenly Father, we praise You and thank You for Your faithfulness. Just as You watched over Noah, his family, the animals and the birds of the air so long ago, we know You'll watch over us. Thank You for Your everlasting faithfulness. Through Jesus, amen.

WALKING ON DRY LAND AGAIN

SCRIPTURE: Genesis 8:6-22

VERSE FOR TODAY: Then God said to Noah, "Come out of the ark, you and your wife and your sons and their wives" (Genesis 8:15, 16, *New International Version*).

HYMN FOR TODAY: "This Is My Father's World"

The ark was home to Noah and his family for just over a year. That's a long time to be cooped up in a restricted space, but it's what saved their lives.

The flood waters, after continuing to rise until they covered the mountains, reached their highest point, and then the waters started to recede. Gradually over a period of months, the waters dried up until they were eventually all gone. The day finally came when God called to Noah to come out of the ark and to release the animals. How happy they must have been to be able to get out and run around on dry land again! The cleansing of the earth was completed, and it was now ready to be inhabited again.

Most of us are familiar with many forms of cleaning or washing, all the way from brushing our teeth to dry cleaning our clothes and sand blasting the side of a building. Various soaps and chemicals are often used, some with water. God used water to purify the earth morally and spiritually. After cleaning, it had to dry. Noah waited patiently, and finally God called him out. Noah and his family gladly came.

It is wonderful to know that when we wait upon the Lord, He gives to us what is good. We can trust Him.

PRAYER THOUGHTS: Thank You, heavenly Father, for the cleansing You have accomplished in us who have received Jesus. Thank You for washing us in the blood of the Lamb and taking away our sin and guilt. We gladly submit to that cleansing. In Jesus' name, amen.

A NEW BEGINNING

SCRIPTURE: Genesis 9:1-7

VERSE FOR TODAY: Therefore, if anyone is in Christ, he is a new creation; the old has gone, the new has come! (2 Corinthians 5:17, *New International Version*).

HYMN FOR TODAY: "Dear Master in Thy Way"

When a person gives his life to the Lord Jesus, there is a new beginning. The old self is gone, and a new person is born spiritually. The old self and its sinful nature are cleansed away. The stain of sin is removed. A washing or purging takes place, and there is a fresh, clean start. Life is new.

After the flood experience was over, Noah and his family came out of the ark to a new life. We read in today's Scripture that God then blessed Noah and his sons, and gave them some instructions that remind us of God's instructions to Adam and Eve in the beginning. Like Noah, Adam and Eve were blessed by God. Genesis 1:28 tells us that God charged them also to "Be fruitful and increase in number; fill the earth" (*New International Version*). In both cases their food was designated. In both cases, their relationship to the animals was stated and there were warnings about what was forbidden. Just as Adam and Eve started in a clean, new world, now Noah and family were starting life anew in a freshly cleansed world. God alone can accomplish that total purifying work in the earth, and in mankind.

PRAYER THOUGHTS: Thank You heavenly Father, for the new birth and newness of life that You give us when we receive Jesus. Thank You for blessing us and providing for us, as we strive to serve and be faithful to You. In Jesus' name. Amen.

A SIGN IN THE SKY

SCRIPTURE: Genesis 9:8-17

VERSE FOR TODAY: I have set my rainbow in the clouds, and it will be the sign of the covenant between me and the earth (Genesis 9:13, *New International Version*).

HYMN FOR TODAY: "What God Hath Promised"

A rainbow is an awesome thing. Its dazzling beauty reminds some people of colors such as in paintings or in the familiar box of crayons. Others see it as a cheerful sign in the sky that the rain is over. Some folks think of a pot of gold at its end or of a song sung in a famous movie. Science tells us that the rainbow is the result of the refraction of light in the particles of moisture in the air.

But God tells us in today's Scripture that the rainbow is the sign of a covenant, a promise that He made long ago. When we see it in the sky, we are reminded of God's commitment to never again destroy all life with a flood. God makes commitments, too. He made this one not only with Noah and his descendants, but the Scripture says that He also made it with every living creature that was with Noah—the birds and animals as well. We wonder if the animals can possibly be aware of that. But we can be. And God is, too. He says twice in this passage that He also will remember His promise when the rainbow appears in the clouds. And God is faithful. He always keeps His promises.

PRAYER THOUGHTS: Dear heavenly Father, thank You for the rainbow and for Your great promise that You made when You put the first rainbow in the clouds. Thank You for all of Your many promises to us. As Your children, we claim Your promises. Amen.

GOD'S MERCY

SCRIPTURE: Genesis 9:18-28

VERSE FOR TODAY: The LORD is compassionate and gracious, slow to anger, abounding in love (Psalm 103:8, *New International Version*).

HYMN FOR TODAY: "There's a Wideness in God's Mercy"

I recently read about a lady who was arrested and thrown in jail for putting coins in parking meters, helping others avoid parking tickets. She wanted to do someone a favor. However, she was told that remetering was against the local laws. While I may not know all of the circumstances involved in this particular case, this punishment seems too harsh and cold.

We are saddened a bit as we read the last part of the Scripture about Noah. We're disappointed by his drunken stupor and the way in which his youngest son handled his immodest behavior. And we are surprised that Noah would pronounce a curse on one of his own sons. There's a lot that we don't understand about how Ham disgraced his father. Did he make fun of his father or broadcast his father's nakedness? Did Noah overreact in anger when he found out about it? Was what Ham did sufficient reason for this harsh condemnation?

How thankful we are that God is merciful and compassionate, rescuing us from the curse and slavery of sin by sending His Son, Jesus Christ, to die for us on the cross! His willingness to redeem us and show His mercy to us is wonderful!

PRAYER THOUGHTS: Father in Heaven, thank You that You are merciful and compassionate. Thank You that we can experience Your love and forgiveness by becoming Your children. Help us also to be loving and compassionate to others. Help us to show mercy. In Jesus' name, we pray. Amen.

MOVING ON

SCRIPTURE: Genesis 11:27-32

VERSE FOR TODAY: By faith he made his home in the promised land like a stranger in a foreign country; he lived in tents, as did Isaac and Jacob, who were heirs with him of the same promise (Hebrews 11:9, *New International Version*).

HYMN FOR TODAY: "All the Way My Savior Leads Me"

At the end of chapter 11 of Genesis, we find Terah setting out with his family to find another home. He must already have felt the call to go to the promised land, for we are told that even before the call came to Abram, Terah set out to "go to Canaan." Perhaps he was disgusted with the moon worship prevalent in Ur, or perhaps he was looking for a closer relationship with God.

In Acts 7, the perspective is from the standpoint of Abram, while in Genesis it sounds as if Terah is the one who took the initiative in leaving Ur. Whichever it was, the family moved. However, they didn't get very far. They wound up settling in Haran, in northern Mesopotamia. Apparently it was not God's will for Terah to go to Canaan, but rather for his son to fulfill the vision and the call.

God may move us from a certain place. We may never know the full reason. It may lie in something our children will do rather than something we will do. The call may not be supernatural, but it will be real nonetheless, and it will have eternal consequences. When the call comes, we must move.

PRAYER THOUGHTS: Thank You, Father, for the knowledge that You lead us, and that You will take us all the way to that special place which You have for our lives. Help us to trust You. In Jesus' name. Amen.

June 28-30. **Lonnie Mings** lives with his wife, Coral, in Jerusalem, Israel.

THE CALL OF ABRAM

SCRIPTURE: Genesis 12:1-9

VERSE FOR TODAY: By faith Abraham, when called to go to a place he would later receive as his inheritance, obeyed and went, even though he did not know where he was going (Hebrews 11:8, *New International Version*).

HYMN FOR TODAY: "Guide Me, O Thou Great Jehovah"

When God called Abram, he didn't give him a map or show him light at the end of the tunnel. In the Jewish Torah readings, this portion of Scripture is called *Lek lekha*—"Get up and go." Abram, get up and go. *Where, Lord?* "It doesn't matter; I'll show you where you're going as you go along. You don't need to know the details. As far as you're concerned, you're going to play this by ear. But I'll be in control."

God then proceeded to give several amazing promises to Abram including the promise to bless him, to make him into a great nation, and to bless others through him.

Thus encouraged, Abram set out on his journey. At Shechem, the very heart of the rich hill country of Canaan, God appeared to Abram and said, "To your offspring I will give this land" (Genesis 12:7, *New International Version*). A little later Abram moved on toward the Negev. In other words, from north to south he was surveying the land God had promised him and his descendants.

When God calls us, what He has in mind to give us is so much greater than what we may have left behind, that the former pales in comparison.

PRAYER THOUGHTS: Thank You, O God, for the example which we have in Abraham. Thank You also that You love us, as You loved him, and that You are in complete control of our lives. Amen.

THE DEATH OF THE VISION

SCRIPTURE: Acts 7:1-8

VERSE FOR TODAY: He gave him no inheritance here, not even a foot of ground. But God promised him that he and his descendants after him would possess the land, even though at that time Abraham had no child (Acts 7:5, *New International Version*).

HYMN FOR TODAY: "Be Thou My Vision"

Stephen, in his sermon in Acts, says Abraham was given no inheritance in Canaan, not so much as a foot of land; but, rather, God promised that he and his descendants would later possess the land. One of the reasons was that the Amorites' cup of iniquity "was not yet full" (Genesis 15:16).

Something happened at that point which is sometimes referred to as the "death of the vision." First, God gives a vision. In this case, it was the promise of a wonderful, fruitful land, where Abraham and his people could live in peace. But then something happened. Abraham himself lived there until his death, but his grandson had to gather up his large family, leave everything behind, and go to Egypt. That resulted in the death of the vision. In other words, it appeared that God's promise would not be fulfilled. The land would not be theirs.

But no, it was only a temporary setback. God had in mind to give it to them a little later. Often God gives us a vision or a promise. This is followed by some kind of setback in which it appears the promise will not be fulfilled. But it's only a test of faith. God will fulfill it—in His own time and in His own way.

PRAYER THOUGHTS: Father, thank You for the visions which You place in our hearts. Help us to trust You that when You have given us a promise, You will in Your own time bring it to fruition. Amen.

My Prayer Notes

_____

_____

_____

_____

_____

_____

_____

_____

_____

_____

_____

_____

_____

_____

_____

_____

_____

_____

DEVOTIONS™

July

photo by Ward Patterson

ARE YOU LISTENING?

SCRIPTURE: 1 Samuel 3:1-10

VERSE FOR TODAY: The Lord came and stood there, calling as at the other times, "Samuel! Samuel!" Then Samuel said, "Speak, for your servant is listening" (1 Samuel 3:10, *New International Version*).

HYMN FOR TODAY: "I Heard the Voice of Jesus Say"

One night while the boy, Samuel, was serving with Eli in the Tabernacle at Shiloh, God called Samuel's name three times. Each time Samuel thought it was Eli calling. Finally, Eli told Samuel, "Go back and if he calls again, say, 'Speak, Lord, for your servant is listening.'" This Samuel did. God then revealed things to Samuel which were going to happen in the near future. God gave Samuel a miraculous call. A call to be a prophet. A call to anoint—and even rebuke—kings.

But God couldn't reveal anything to Samuel until Samuel said, "Speak, Lord, for your servant is listening." This brings us to the crux of the matter. Does God speak today? Of course He does. How many of us are listening? I'm not talking about an audible message, though I wouldn't rule that out. The voice of God is usually the "still small voice." The point is, He is much more anxious to speak than we are to hear.

Some of us complain: God never speaks to me. Is it that He never speaks, or is it that we're seldom listening? He does want to speak to us, and it would be well worth our time to listen to Him.

PRAYER THOUGHTS: Heavenly Father, it is so hard to hear Your voice over the cacophony of the modern world. Help us to be still and listen, and help us to develop a sensitivity to the still small voice, as You seek to direct our lives. In Jesus' name. Amen.

July 1-4. **Lonnie Mings,** a college professor and missionary, lives with his wife, Coral, in Israel.

GOD ALSO USES FARMERS

SCRIPTURE: Amos 7:10-15

VERSE FOR TODAY: But the LORD took me from tending the flock and said to me, "Go prophesy to my people Israel" (Amos 7:15, *New International Version*).

HYMN FOR TODAY: "Take My Life, and Let It Be Consecrated"

Amos didn't brag about his call. In fact, he only related the story in answer to the false prophet Amaziah who was telling him to get out of Israel and go back to Judah, because he brought an unpleasant message. In response, Amos revealed his credentials. "The Lord . . . said to me, 'Go, prophesy to my people Israel'" (Amos 7:15, *New International Version*).

Amos had originally been a shepherd and one who tended sycamore-fig trees. But God called him from his farming to deliver a message. It was not to the rich and famous, not to those living in palaces and wearing soft garments, that the Spirit of God came. It was to one of the simple shepherds of Tekoa that God gave His message concerning Israel.

God loves to confound the wise by using the simple. He loves to circumvent the rich and visit the poor. He delights to use farmers, shepherds, fishermen, fig-gatherers, and tax collectors. Why is this so? Probably because these people are more likely to be attuned to God's voice. Being "poor in spirit," being empty, they have great capacity to contain the grace and the message that God wants to pour into their hearts.

PRAYER THOUGHTS: Father, we also want to be used. Please place Your message in our hearts, and then send us out to proclaim Your Word to the sin-sick world around us. Give us courage for the rejection which will inevitably come. In Jesus' name. Amen.

FROM PERSECUTOR TO PREACHER

SCRIPTURE: Acts 9:1-9

VERSE FOR TODAY: He fell to the ground and heard a voice say to him, "Saul, Saul, why do you persecute me?" (Acts 9:4, *New International Version*).

HYMN FOR TODAY: "Why Do You Wait?"

Saul of Tarsus, rooted in rabbinic Judaism, did not believe God had become incarnate in Jesus of Nazareth. Deeming the Jesus movement a heresy, he did his best to destroy it. With letters from the authorities, he set out for Damascus for the purpose of extraditing believers and bringing them back to Jerusalem for punishment. On the way, the Lord, who rules over hearts and minds, appeared to him and brought about a change of plans.

Not every call is as sudden and dramatic as Saul's. But it took a lot to turn Saul around. No Christian apologetic could have changed this man. It took a blinding light, a fall to the ground, and a voice from Heaven. Perhaps God's Spirit had been working in his heart with no results. Perhaps, observing the stoning of Stephen, Saul's heart had tried to tell him something which he suppressed. As a result, God saw that He was going to have to knock this man down to get his attention.

When God's call comes to our hearts, for whatever purpose, let us be attentive. For as we know from the story of Saul, He does have other ways to get our attention.

PRAYER THOUGHTS: Lord God, thank You for Your sovereign grace through which You choose your servants. Thank You that You turned Saul around and gave him a heart through which You could speak even to future generations. In Jesus' name. Amen.

JESUS CALLS US

SCRIPTURE: Mark 1:16-20

VERSE FOR TODAY: "Come, follow me," Jesus said, "and I will make you fishers of men" (Mark 1:17, *New International Version*).

HYMN FOR TODAY: "Hark, the Voice of Jesus Calling"

In today's Scripture Jesus calls the twelve for special training in the ministry of saving souls. They were a motley group, these men, and they came from all walks of life. At first they were not sure to what they were being called, and they were not even sure who Jesus was, but eventually, convinced that He was the Messiah, they gave their lives for him.

Whatever it was they were doing, when they heard His voice, they laid down their work and got up and followed. "We have left everything to follow You!" Peter said (Mark 10:28, *New International Version*). Jesus told them that whatever they had left—houses or brothers or sisters or father or mother or children or fields—for His sake, they would receive a hundred times as much, as well as eternal life.

So today He calls us "o'er the tumult" of our frenzied lives. Today, as then, He demands no half-hearted trailing along in His wake, but a decision to walk in step with Him, a total commitment of our lives. He demands, in other words, that we give Him our best. In return, He promises His best. He promises to make us no less than co-heirs with Him of the eternal riches of God the Father.

PRAYER THOUGHTS: Eternal Father, thank You that You have not left us alone but that You have called us to be Yours. Help us to make a decision today that we will be done with compromise and that we will commit our lives solely to You. Through Jesus we pray, amen.

A STAR IS BORN

SCRIPTURE: Genesis 15:1-6

VERSE FOR TODAY: And he brought him forth abroad, and said, Look now toward heaven, and tell the stars, if thou be able to number them: and he said unto him, So shall thy seed be (Genesis 15:5).

HYMN FOR TODAY: "The God of Abraham Praise"

Picture the clarity of a brilliant night sky of Abram's time. No pollution from fossil fuels. No interfering glow from a city's artificial daylight. Abram could **see** stars! Countless stars. And God challenged him to count them. For, God promises, Abram's offspring will be as countless as the stars.

But it all had to begin with the birth of one "star" who will come from Abram's own body, his heir. Though that child would never have a star on his dressing tent, he would be God's star, the first in what would become a spiritual and cosmic sky full. All who become God's children—and Abraham's—are the stars of that sky.

Stars are easily seen on the deep black background of space. God's "stars," His lights, must be as easily seen on the sin-darkened backdrop of life's stage. When the contrast is dimmed by an evil haze, when the light flickers and fades, God's celestial witness wanes.

God might say to His children, "Twinkle, twinkle, little Star, let the world see who (and Whose) you are!"

PRAYER THOUGHTS: Great God of Abraham, thank You for making us Your stars. Forgive us when we fail to give light to a dark world. Give us the strength of a countless sky full of brilliant luminaries. You are light, O God; help us to be like you. Amen.

July 5-11. **Ronald G. Davis** was for twenty-six years a teacher in the Education Department of Cincinnati Bible College and Seminary. His wife, Ruth, works in Christian journalism.

EQUALIZING UNEQUALS

SCRIPTURE: Genesis 15:12-20

VERSE FOR TODAY: In the same day the LORD made a covenant with Abram, saying, Unto thy seed have I given this land (Genesis 15:18).

HYMN FOR TODAY: "Great Is Thy Faithfulness"

From the sparkly luminescence of a star-lit night to the utter blackness of a deep sleep, Abram fell. God's good news had to be interrupted. Abram's offspring, with the blessing of their own land and nation, would not avoid the penalties of sinful living. Slavery was inevitable. Yet not even that interlude of enslavement was any sign of a broken covenant. God's covenant with Abram was to be an eternal one. Faith in God's promises autographs the covenant; a covenant equalizing unequals. Unequal to God in purity, power, and holiness, man still signs the covenant—as if he were God's equal—by God's grace!

The conditions of the covenant are well beyond fair. Eternal principles of fairness are simple: "The wages of sin is death" (Romans 7:23). But God has a gift beyond the punishment: eternal life.

For Abram's family there is a blessing after consequence. And the blessing is as certain as the consequence. Abram's covenant, offered freely by God, has God's seal on it. It is as sure as God Himself.

PRAYER THOUGHTS: God of Covenant, we come to Your table of covenant as unequals. So we must come humbly. Yet You have allowed us to enter boldly into Your presence. Thank You for Your gracious, eternal covenant with all of us children of Abraham. Amen.

GOD'S PROMISES AND MAN'S PLANS

SCRIPTURE: Genesis 16:1-16

VERSE FOR TODAY: And Sarai said unto Abram, Behold now, the Lord hath restrained me from bearing: I pray thee, go in unto my maid; it may be that I may obtain children by her. And Abram hearkened to the voice of Sarai (Genesis 16:2).

HYMN FOR TODAY: "Trust and Obey"

Abram believed God . . . but he "hearkened to the voice of Sarai." How much so like another man who was walking with God when his wife suggested an alternate plan! Both choices had dire consequences. Against Abram and his heirs, Ishmael would raise his hand, from that first generation to this one. Against Adam and his heirs, Satan would raise his hand as they become "easy prey" in every generation.

God keeps His promises. No one need doubt Him. No one need help Him fulfill those promises. Timing is irrelevant. Method is neither here nor there. God will do what He says. God's person has only one task: believe . . . and wait. Sarai obviously gave up on God's promise—at least the waiting part. Perhaps she began to believe she had to help God. Either decision is a foolish one. God needs no help. God will do what He has promised. Abram should have known better, but he let Sarai's disbelief sway his own commitment and patience. The person of God must never let another weaken his resolve of faith.

PRAYER THOUGHTS: Promise-making God, we await the grand fulfillment of Your Word. Forgive our impatience. Strengthen us when our faith wanes in the waiting. We praise Your faithfulness. Amen.

WHAT'S IN A COVENANT NAME?

SCRIPTURE: Genesis 17:1-14

VERSE FOR TODAY: And I will establish my covenant between me and thee and thy seed after thee in their generations, for an everlasting covenant, to be a God unto thee and to thy seed after thee (Genesis 17:7).

HYMN FOR TODAY: "Is My Name Written There"

Family and friends from my childhood still call me "Ronnie," though for years I have called myself "Ron." Such childhood names often stick . . . and sometimes grate lightly! Abraham's childhood family and friends knew him as "Abram." Finally, as Abram completes a century of living, God gives him a new name, a covenant name of new meaning.

At the time of today's conversation with God, Abram was father of a thirteen-year-old son. But God is ready to make him "father of many nations." From his physical lineage, a multitude of Semitic nations will arise. Yet of greater significance, from his spiritual lineage, God will raise up an innumerable host of those God will call "Friends" even as Abraham would be called "The Friend of God."

To the point of this face-to-face meeting with God, Abram had lived his life for himself and his earthly family. Abraham is now being called to live his life for God and His spiritual purpose. Such a confrontation parallels God's face-to-face with every person: live the life of purpose—His purpose. Far better to have a covenant name from God than a name of earthly parents. Far better to have God call you by His name!

PRAYER THOUGHTS: We thank You, God, for letting us know Your many names. We humbly praise You for allowing us to wear Your name and that of Your glorious Son. Forgive us when we besmirch it with our sins. Help us to make You proud to call us "Friends." Amen.

HAPPY EVER PRINCESS

SCRIPTURE: Genesis 17:15-27

VERSE FOR TODAY: Beloved, now are we the sons of God, and it doth not yet appear what we shall be: but we know that, when he shall appear, we shall be like him; for we shall see him as he is (1 John 3:2).

HYMN FOR TODAY: "I Belong to the King"

In one famous fairy tale, the Queen Mother declares the True Princess with the pea-poke test. No matter how many mattresses separate her from the strategically placed pea, the True Princess is sensitive enough to feel it . . . and complain! Sarai did not show quite the same high level of sensitivity, especially spiritually, but God called her "Princess"—Sarah. He knew what she was capable of being.

Sarah probably felt little like a princess. Her prince, Abram, has a rather confined and highly mobile realm. No castle was her home. Only a tent. No gilded throne, her seat. Only a rock or a rolled up rug. Yet God calls her "Princess." She is a princess indeed. For out of her shall come one who will be King of kings. One day, as true for all of God's princes and princesses, Sarah will sit in the throne room with the King. The King will have His court. Hallelujah!

Sarah will have her robes of splendor. She will have a be-jeweled seat of gold. She is Princess. And she shall reign with Christ in a kingdom of majesty and infinity. "Beloved, now are we the children of God" (1 John 3:2). And we shall reign as princesses and princes. Hallelujah!

PRAYER THOUGHTS: King of Heaven and earth, we sometimes feel like paupers and aliens in this kingdom of the earth. Our thanks to You for making us royalty—royal ambassadors for our King. Give us our proper regal bearing as we speak on His behalf. Amen.

LAUGHTER AND THE SOUL

SCRIPTURE: Genesis 18:1-15

VERSE FOR TODAY: Is any thing too hard for the LORD? At the time appointed I will return unto thee, according to the time of life, and Sarah shall have a son (Genesis 18:14).

HYMN FOR TODAY: "Down In My Heart"

Both out of sight and out of hearing, Sarah's laughter was still heard by the Lord. Her "inside" laugh, inside the tent, mattered not to the Living God Who Sees, as Hagar had labeled Him (Genesis 16:13). He both sees and hears. Sarah could not conceal her skepticism from Him.

Joy's laughter enriches the soul. Doubt's laughter denies the soul . . . for it denies God's power to do what He says He will do. Sarah laughed in doubt: "Will I really have a child, now that I am old?" (Genesis 18:13, *New International Version*). She had every reason to laugh in joy for, "Is anything too hard for the LORD?" (Genesis 18:14, *New International Version*). Faith is soul food . . . and brings great joy. Doubt is soul disease . . . and brings great distress. Faith nourishes. Doubt destroys. Sarah's soul lies in precarious peril.

For every believer whose mind raises the doubt game, one question should suffice: "What has God said He will do which He cannot and will not do?" Sarah forgot to ask that all-important question. So God kindly but strongly reminds her and us, "Is there anything too hard for the Lord?" A hardy laugh of joy should be the answer. The believer has every reason to laugh. The doubter has absolutely none.

PRAYER THOUGHTS: God of the Sure Promise, we do believe. Help us when we allow our belief to waver. Give us today the laughter of confidence in Your sure promises. Remind us everyday that there is nothing too hard for You. Amen.

LAUGHING FOR THE RIGHT REASON

SCRIPTURE: Genesis 21:1-7

VERSE FOR TODAY: And Sarah said, God hath made me to laugh, so that all that hear will laugh with me (Genesis 21:6).

HYMN FOR TODAY: "Standing on the Promises"

Did anyone laugh when they saw a pregnant ninety-year-old woman? Such incongruity is at the heart of humor. No doubt some laughed . . . *at* Sarah, shaking their heads at such a "joke." But Sarah herself is now no longer holding back an inside laugh. She now laughs aloud, because, "*God* has made me laugh!" (Genesis 21:6). It is the laughter of delight, the laughter of rejoicing, the laughter of faith fulfilled. Sarah now laughs for all the right reasons.

Sarah predicts that "all that hear will laugh with me" (Genesis 21:6). Have you had a good laugh lately about Sarah's good news for Abraham: "I have borne him a son in his old age?" (Genesis 21:7). God's faithfulness, God's fulfilling of His redemptive plan ought always to bring the exultant jubilation of faith.

Sarah and Abraham had a son of promise. Their faith in God was tangibly confirmed. Likewise, every Christian has the Son of Promise. All the prophets promised Him—though some of God's people tired of waiting; though some pretended. He had earlier come; though some refused to believe His appearing, God finally gave tangible, bodily confirmation to His promise: a Son is born, a Son of Promise. Have a good laugh of redemption today! Laugh with Sarah.

PRAYER THOUGHTS: O Great God of Joy and Laughter, You have given us every reason to rejoice. In a world that brings grief and tears, we thank You that we have the soul-satisfying Son of Promise. Put gladness in our hearts and on our faces, by the presence of Your Spirit. Amen.

GOD TESTS ABRAHAM

SCRIPTURE: Genesis 22:1-8

VERSE FOR TODAY: Abraham answered, "God himself will provide the lamb for the burnt offering, my son." And the two of them went on together (Genesis 22:8, *New International Version*).

HYMN FOR TODAY: "Channels Only"

Some members of our congregation have invited us to join them at a special prayer meeting scheduled for later this week at church. Many people will choose not to attend because they are simply too busy and are not able to squeeze in an hour for prayer. Others, who view prayer as some sort of spiritual exercise that certain religious people endure, won't bother coming if "all we are going to do is pray."

However, some may come because they think it is expected of them. Others will come because they know that God answers prayer. Jesus taught that if we believe, we will receive whatever we ask for in prayer (Matthew 21:22).

I wonder what Abraham thought as he walked out into the desert. Would God give him yet another son? Did he consider the possibility of resurrection?

I do know that Abraham totally trusted God. His life was a demonstration of that trust. God honors living faith.

PRAYER THOUGHTS: Father, teach us to trust You. Thank You for leading us in the way You have prepared. Forgive us when we go our own way. Help us today to follow where You lead. Use us to help someone who may need encouragement. May our lives bring blessing to others and to You. Amen.

July 12-18. **William E. Stauter** is chaplain at the Mount Healthy Christian Home in Cincinnati, Ohio. He and his wife, Geri, have four grown children and four grandchildren.

ABRAHAM PROVES HIS FAITH

SCRIPTURE: Genesis 22:9-14

VERSE FOR TODAY: Then he reached out his hand and took the knife to slay his son (Genesis 22:10, *New International Version*).

HYMN FOR TODAY: "I Surrender All"

Early this morning I looked out into the yard. The sky was just beginning to turn to the early gray of morning. I could identify objects in the yard, but I could not clearly see the sky. At first, the sky looked cloudy. Then, I realized the sun had not come up. In only a few minutes, the sun peeked over the eastern horizon. Suddenly, it was obvious. Yes, we were going to have a beautiful day. The sky was a brilliant blue, with wisps of white clouds.

Genesis gives no hint about the weather on the day when Abraham and Isaac walked toward the place of sacrifice. I try to imagine how Abraham must have felt. Did the day seem dreary, gray, and overcast?

Sometimes the burdens of the day weigh us down. There is no joy in what we do, yet we go on. Do we think of God? Do we ask for His help? Do we consider how He continually blesses us? Do we thank Him for His love?

Abraham had been called by God to do a special job. As he raised the knife, an angel called out his name! God is with you! He has been testing your faith. Because you have proven your faith, you are now ready to receive His special blessing. God has provided the lamb!

PRAYER THOUGHTS: Gracious God, thank You for walking beside us even when we feel alone. Help us to be aware of Your presence. Give us courage and wisdom so we will live well for You. Thank You for allowing us to serve in Your kingdom. In Jesus' name. Amen.

GOD BLESSES FAITH

SCRIPTURE: Genesis 22:15-19

VERSE FOR TODAY: I will surely bless you and make your descendants as numerous as the stars in the sky and as the sand on the seashore (Genesis 22:17, *New International Version*).

HYMN FOR TODAY: "Count Your Blessings"

After many years of city living, we moved to the country. Behind our house was a woods. I remember our first walk in those woods at night. We loved the sky. We were pleased that we had moved away from the polluted air and the bright lights which prevented us from really seeing the night sky.

I have a friend who loves the sky and has spent much of his life studying the stars. I love to walk out into the woods with him and listen to his description of the wonders of the heavens. I know a little about the stars, enough to point out the North star and the Big and Little Dippers. I know that navigators use the sky to direct their travels. I also know that scientists regularly discover stars they have not seen before. We are awed by the magnitude of the universe. How many stars are there? We could safely say they are beyond numbering.

Because of Abraham's faith, God promised that his descendants would be as numerous as the stars in the sky and the sand on the seashore. God did not just promise lots of descendants. He promise that all the nations on earth would be blessed by him. Today, you and I have the opportunity to be a blessing to others.

PRAYER THOUGHTS: Father, You have provided the world and all its wonders for us. May we understand the scope of Your love and be grateful that You continually give to us beyond measure. May we be willing to give of ourselves so others may know You. Amen.

GOD WILL RESCUE US

SCRIPTURE: Daniel 3:16-26

VERSE FOR TODAY: If we are thrown into the blazing furnace, the God we serve is able to save us from it, and he will rescue us from your hand, O king (Daniel 3:17, *New International Version*).

HYMN FOR TODAY: "Faith Is the Victory"

Shadrach, Meshach, and Abednego faced severe persecution because of their faith in God. They would not bow down and worship false gods. In a marvelous way, God rewarded their devotion by protecting them and reaching them.

As a boy, I used to worry about my faith. Jesus said that if anyone should deny him before men, he would deny that person before God (Matthew 10:33). If I ever faced a direr challenge, would I deny God? But I never faced such a trial.

The tests we face are less obvious if no less real. In the small town where I grew up, I used to walk to Sunday school on nice days. One morning, someone said something about my being a "preacher boy," carrying my Bible. I went another way after that so I would not meet anyone. Did I deny Jesus? Certainly my action was not a glowing testimony of my faith.

We have regular opportunities to confess Jesus. Romans 12:1 instructs us to offer our bodies as living sacrifices. Note that we are not to throw ourselves on a sacrificial altar, but we are to be a living testimony. This kind of confessing takes place at church, at home, and among our co-workers and neighbors. Are we living our testimony?

PRAYER THOUGHTS: All-powerful God, we thank You for Your strength and might. We confess our weaknesses and recognize our inadequacy. May we, today, entrust our lives fully to Your care. Protect us, Father, and allow us to live to please You. In Jesus' name, amen.

JESUS FACES DEATH

SCRIPTURE: Mark 14:32-42

VERSE FOR TODAY: "Abba, Father," he said, "everything is possible for you. Take this cup from me. Yet not what I will, but what you will" (Mark 14:36, *New International Version*).

HYMN FOR TODAY: "Jesus Paid It All"

My wife and I recently had our granddaughters for a two-week visit. We are used to a quiet house, so their visit required some adjustment on our part.

Our older granddaughter knows about sharing, but it doesn't come to her naturally. Her younger sister clearly believes she can get her own way if she makes a fuss.

I think I should be able to say to our older granddaughter something like, "Honey, don't fight with your younger sister over the toy. Let her have it for a while, then she will put it down and you can play with it." It sounds so simple to me.

She looks at me, wondering what planet I came from. Giving in to someone else is foreign to her thinking.

God surely understands. He created us with a free will. We can make our choices, but we aren't always right. Life would be so much smoother if we remembered to look for what God wants when we are making decisions.

Jesus knew He did not want to suffer on a cross. He also knew He had been sent for a purpose. So, after asking for some other solution that was more acceptable to Him, He submitted to God's will. May we follow His example.

PRAYER THOUGHTS: Almighty and all-wise God, help us to follow Your leading. We are stubborn and stiff-necked and often insist on having our own way. Forgive us when we put our wishes ahead of Yours. Teach us again to trust You, for we know Your ways are best for us. Amen.

TEMPTED IN EVERY WAY

SCRIPTURE: Hebrews 4:14–5:4

VERSE FOR TODAY: For we do not have a high priest who is unable to sympathize with our weaknesses, but we have one who has been tempted in every way, just as we are—yet was without sin (Hebrews 4:15, *New International Version*).

HYMN FOR TODAY: "No One Understands Like Jesus"

I spent my childhood years in a small church. Most of the ministers I remember were Bible college students. They were good, dedicated men, but they did not stay long with us.

One minister was older. He was married and had children. He came to us after having severe health problems. His doctor had suggested that he get away from the stresses of a ministry in a larger church. His time with us was good for him, his family, and our congregation. He was a great help to me in determining the direction of my life.

I remember one Saturday when we had a workday at the church building. Our preachers always came for workdays. This is a great way to get acquainted with the members. It also encourages others to lend a hand.

What impressed me and the others about our new minister was that he came ready to work. He brought along a well stocked tool box. He wore a pair of carpenter's overalls that had obviously seen some wear. Here was a man who knew what he was doing. Immediately, a bond was formed with the members of the church and our new minister.

In an even greater way, we can place our confidence in Jesus. He understands and cares about us.

PRAYER THOUGHTS: God, our heavenly Father, we thank You today for the experiences of life that were difficult and painful. Thank You that we have thus been strengthened. Help us now to help others. Amen.

LOVE NEVER FAILS

SCRIPTURE: 1 Corinthians 13:1-13

VERSE FOR TODAY: And now these three remain: faith, hope and love. But the greatest of these is love (1 Corinthians 13:13, *New International Version*).

HYMN FOR TODAY: "Love Led Him to Calvary"

The text above is often used in weddings. However, if we think of the love chapter only in the context of marriage, we miss much of its meaning. Jesus used marriage to illustrate His relationship with His bride, the church.

We are reminded of the responsibilities of a husband to his wife and family. He works hard to provide both the necessities of daily life and those extras which can bring great joy. He is concerned about the well-being of his family and will go to great lengths to care for them and to protect them. We should have this same level of concern for our church family.

The emphasis of this chapter is on "how" as much as "what." In our daily conversation, in our use of the Scriptures, in our giving to carry out the work of the church, and in everything else we do, we must be careful that what we do is done in a spirit of love.

If we pattern our behavior after Jesus, we will quickly see an improvement in our relationships. Jesus was concerned for others. When we put our loved ones first, we have learned the lesson of love. When we please others, we are blessed. When we care for others, we please God. May we live to serve God, His church, our family, and the others we touch.

PRAYER THOUGHTS: Father, thank You for giving us the capacity to love. Help us today to demonstrate Your love. We sometimes get so busy we forget that we represent You in all we do. Thanks for giving us special friends who love us. Thank You for loving us. Amen.

CHOSEN

SCRIPTURE: Genesis 25:19-26

VERSE FOR TODAY: And Isaac prayed to the Lord for his wife because she was barren; and the Lord granted his prayer (Genesis 25:21, *Revised Standard Version*).

HYMN FOR TODAY: "Give Them All to Jesus"

I love children. I often watch young mothers enjoy their children at play. After marriage, I longed for a child of my own. I prayed and asked God for a child, but year after year my prayers were not answered. My husband and I decided to adopt a child. We were so happy when our baby girl was born.

While she was being formed in the womb, God was creating her character. (For you created my inmost being; you knit me together in my mother's womb Psalm 139:13, *New International Version*). He knew all the time what she would be like. Maybe we had to wait so long for a child was because God knew we would need lots of patience. She was beautiful and strong willed, making parenting difficult at times.

When our daughter was a teenager she had a difficult time, and I was grasping for anything just to have her survive. I thought she would be happier with her natural mother, but our doctor discouraged it. Today, she is a loving daughter.

God always knows best. He had chosen her to be our child, and he had chosen us to be her parents.

PRAYER THOUGHTS: Father, forgive us when we question Your plan for our lives. Thank You for the children You have chosen for us and given us. What a blessing they are. In the name of Jesus. Amen.

July 19, 20. **B. J. Bassett** is a writer, teacher, and speaker who lives in Fortuna, California. She has four grown children.

MY BIRTHRIGHT

SCRIPTURE: Genesis 25:27-34

VERSE FOR TODAY: So he swore to him, and sold his birthright to Jacob (Genesis 25:33, *Revised Standard Version*).

HYMN FOR TODAY: "Lord, I Want to Be a Christian"

I can't imagine how anyone could be so careless as to sell his birthright. I don't believe I would do it. I don't care how famished Esau was for food—it was food that would only satisfy his hunger temporarily.

It means a great deal to me to come from a long line of hard-working, loving people. I have always been proud of my heritage—and of my birthright of being the firstborn. I am especially proud of my birthright as a Christian. I feel a responsibility to honor that name—to honor my Lord in my thoughts and actions.

I have often thought about how I would react if I were ever put in an extremely difficult situation where my faith was severely tested by someone who tried to get me to deny my faith in God. Would I stand the test? I feel I would be strong in a time of crisis; but how much could I take? I wonder. My constant prayer is, "Lord, may I always stand for You no matter what happens. May I be grateful that You have grafted me into Your family. Give me courage and wisdom to hold fast to You and Your ways. May I never sell my birthright as Your child—as a Christian."

PRAYER THOUGHTS: Dear Father, You know our concern to always be aware of Your sacrifice for us, to always be strong in our faith, to never dishonor You. Cover us with the blood of Christ that we may be counted worthy to be Your children. Amen.

LEAN, NOT SCHEME

SCRIPTURE: Genesis 27:1-17

VERSE FOR TODAY: "Then take it to your father to eat, so that he may give you his blessing before he dies" (Genesis 27:10, *New International Version*).

HYMN FOR TODAY: "Spirit of the Living God"

Isaac aimed to bless his eldest son. But, like with us today, Isaac planned well but things went wrong.

Though problems may seem to stem from the actions of others, we need to remember that the problem is often in our hands to remedy with the Lord's help. Like Isaac, I've planned to do certain things and found my plans have been thwarted by others. I've discovered 1 Peter 5:7 gives much comfort at such times: "Cast all your anxiety on him because he cares for you" (*New International Version*).

We must surely learn to lean on the Savior, knowing full well we have a decided advantage over Isaac, for we live in days beyond Calvary rather than days before Calvary. Before Jesus died, He told His disciples He would send another Helper. "These things have I spoken unto you, being yet present with you. But the Comforter, which is the Holy Ghost, whom the Father will send in my name, he shall teach you all things, and bring all things to your remembrance, whatsoever I have said unto you" (John 14:25, 26). A Helper who would guide us into all truth. Wisdom is available to us if only we will lean on the Helper who has been provided to guide us.

PRAYER THOUGHTS: Our Loving God, keep us from scheming, and please help us to lean heavily upon You this day. Help us to do this through the love of Jesus our loving Savior. Amen.

July 21-23. **David R. Nicholas** is a minister and writer who lives with his wife, Judith, in England.

TANGLED WEBS

SCRIPTURE: Genesis 27:18-29

VERSE FOR TODAY: He went to his father and said, "My father." "Yes, my son," he answered. "Who is it?" (Genesis 27:18, *New International Version*).

HYMN FOR TODAY: "Love Divine, All Loves Excelling"

Sir Walter Scott penned these famous words: "O, what a tangled web we weave, When first we practice to deceive."

Blessing was part of ancient Jewish life. Jacob was well aware of the procedure, and he allowed his mother Rebekah to lead him down the pathway of deception. The two plotted to deceive the aged Isaac. How sad. Lies led to hatred and running away, for Esau's anger was fanned into a flame, and he threatened to kill Jacob. Doubtless he was already angry because Jacob had robbed him of his birthright.

We could discuss at length Jacob's deception and the various tricks he used against Laban. The fact remains that God was with him and blessed him because he was the heir of His promise to Abraham.

And yet, deceit is the instrument of Satan, who is the "father of lies" (John 8:44). He has been using it since the temptation of Adam and Eve: "You will not surely die" (Genesis 3:4, 5). Jesus said, "Ye shall know the truth, and the truth shall make you free" (John 8:32). Jesus himself is the truth. As long as we cling to Him, we are holding onto the giver of all truth.

PRAYER THOUGHTS: Father in Heaven, please defend us from the "tricks of Jacob" so that we may live right in Your sight. When we are tempted to be deceptive, let us hold fast to You and to Your truth. Thank You for giving us power to overcome evil. In the name of Jesus. Amen.

SAFE ON THE HILLSIDE

SCRIPTURE: Genesis 27:30-40

VERSE FOR TODAY: Esau said to his father, "Do you have only one blessing, my father? Bless me too, my father!" Then Esau wept aloud (Genesis 27:38, *New International Version*).

HYMN FOR TODAY: "Blessed Assurance"

Disappointments are a part of life. Hardships can take their toll if we are not careful. Certainly we need to face them rather than try to hide.

William Gladstone, one-time leader of the British Parliament, was in Scotland. As he was climbing a hill, he saw some sheep walking up a hill, away from a valley. Gladstone said to himself, "Those sheep are silly—getting out of a sheltered valley and facing the storm on a hill." A little later Gladstone told a shepherd boy about the sheep. The boy said, "Those sheep have more sense than you think. If they stayed in the valley, they would be covered by snow drifts. They are safe on the hillside!"

Like Esau, we lift up our voice and weep at life's disappointments. He cried a great and bitter cry when he heard that his brother had now taken his blessing. Esau was so angry he was dangerous. His rage toward his brother caused him to want to do away with his brother. His disappointment and rage was so great that it was nearly his undoing. The lesson is that instead of staying in the valley of disappointment, we need to rise up the hill of faith and look to our Lord Jesus. Looking up, we need to ask Him to remind us of His rich promises to us.

PRAYER THOUGHTS: Keep us, Heavenly Father, on the hillside of life. When disappointments in life bring rage and frustration, help us to find safety and protection in Your ways. Let us not be overcome by life's daily disappointments. Let us live looking unto Jesus. In His name. Amen.

WISE AND RESOURCEFUL

SCRIPTURE: Luke 16:1-9

VERSE FOR TODAY: A kind man benefits himself, but a cruel man brings harm on himself (Proverbs 11:17, *New International Version***).**

HYMN FOR TODAY: "Take My Life, and Let It Be Consecrated"

Ants are the most dominant social insect in the world. In a September 1990 article on entomology, *Time* magazine reported that these creatures make up from ten percent to fifteen percent of the world's animal "biomass." If a leaf-cutting variety were grown to the size of a man, he could repeatedly run a four-minute mile while carrying 750 pounds of potato salad. It is the ant's work ethic, however, that draws the greatest attention. He always maximizes resources to obtain optimum results.

The steward in Jesus' story was dismissed for wasting his master's possessions. However, in spite of his mismanagement, he impressed his master with his plan to win friends through an unethical debt-reduction scheme.

Jesus never promoted dishonesty, but He admired people who knew how to make the most of their resources. He was often frustrated when His own followers refused to take advantage of their own faith and power.

Every day God provides opportunities for us to share His love with our world. Today, pray for insight into people and circumstances. Make the most of your resources and let God work through you to reach lost souls.

PRAYER THOUGHTS: Father, make us instruments of Your grace in our world. Help us to understand our strengths and learn to use them in our daily Christian witness. Amen.

July 24. **Larry Ray Jones** is the Senior Minster of the Northside Church of Christ in Newport News, Virginia. He and his wife, Jane have two children, Nathan and Laura.

CLIMBING THE HILL

SCRIPTURE: Psalm 24:1-6

VERSE FOR TODAY: Who may ascend the hill of the Lord? Who may stand in his holy place? He who has clean hands and a pure heart, who does not lift up his soul to an idol or swear by what is false (Psalm 24:3, 4, *New International Version***).**

HYMN FOR TODAY. "Redeeming Love"

I was sitting on my porch the other morning just as dawn was bursting forth, and I felt bathed in the peace and joy of God's creation. The birds were chattering away while the flowers were lazily opening their petals to another day. It felt good. However, it didn't last long. The duties, trials, and worries of my life soon crept in and that wonderful feeling of the presence of God floated away with the morning mist.

As I continued to sit on the porch I was reminded of today's Scripture in Psalms and how it proclaims that everything belongs to God the Creator. Can I ever enter the presence of the Lord? The answer is a resounding, "Yes!"

Everyone who claims God as Lord of life has the daily struggle of living a life of compassion, understanding, and patience in all that happens. One's faith must be strong and it must bring honor to God. It is not easy, for the ways of the world are different than God's ways. But if a believer can keep his hands clean and his heart pure he can climb the hill of the Lord and be in His presence.

PRAYER THOUGHTS: Almighty God, help me, a sinner, saved by Your grace, to live a life that is acceptable to You. Guide me in my daily walk that I might one day ascend Your hill and know Your complete presence. In the name of Jesus, I pray. Amen.

July 25. **G. William Zuspan** is Professor Emeritus in Engineering at Drexel University where he taught for thirty-seven years. He and his wife, Marilyn, have five children and thirteen grandchildren.

WHAT'S YOUR HURRY?

SCRIPTURE: Genesis 27:41-46

VERSE FOR TODAY: The end of a thing is better than its beginning; the patient in spirit is better than the proud in spirit (Ecclesiastes 7:8, *New King James Version*).

HYMN FOR TODAY: "In His Time"

Are you one who hurries? Always rushing? Impatient with waiting for the beginning of an expected event?

The Bible is full of people who couldn't seem to wait. People who wanted to hurry God. Jacob was a man who couldn't wait. He was an impatient man. He knew that God had said he (Jacob) would be stronger than his brother, Esau (Genesis 25:23). It was God's plan for Jacob to inherit the promise which had been given to Abraham and Isaac. But Jacob couldn't wait for God to work out the details. Jacob took things into his own hands and tricked Isaac into giving him the blessing that was for the family heir. Jacob's impatient action didn't change God's purpose, but it did make life a lot harder for Jacob. Because Jacob didn't wait, his brother was angry and wanted to kill him; Jacob had to leave his home and family and travel to a land that was strange to him.

It is important for each of us to be ready to become what God wants for us. But while we are waiting for God to fulfill His purpose, let's be the best we can be for God now. The timing of any opportunity is in God's hands. Be ready, be faithful, and be patient.

PRAYER THOUGHT: Lord, may we wait patiently and be watchful for the opportunities You give to us. Forgive our impatience. Amen.

July 26-31. **Nancy Hunt Sams** is a former editor at Standard Publishing Company. She and her husband, Don, have five grown children and live in Middletown, Ohio.

TREASURES FOR WISE CHILDREN

SCRIPTURE: Genesis 28:1-5

VERSE FOR TODAY: My son, hear the instruction of your father, and do not forsake the law of your mother; for they will be a graceful ornament on your head, and chains about your neck (Proverbs 1:8, 9, *New King James Version*).

HYMN FOR TODAY: "Faith of Our Fathers"

A recent survey of college students found that those who exhibited the greatest self-confidence, leadership, and well-defined goals were the children of loving, supportive parents. These students respected their parents and were motivated by a desire to be respected by their parents. The loving advice of godly parents is a treasured resource for wise children.

Jacob and Esau, twin sons of Isaac and Rebekah, took different directions for their lives. When Jacob left home to seek a wife who believed in God, he obeyed his father's command and his mother's wish. Therefore, Isaac renewed the blessing he had given to Jacob earlier. Esau, on the other hand, married women who worshipped idols and did not believe in God.

It is a happy young person who can enter upon life's journey carrying his or her parents' blessing. Obedient children are honored by those who know them, and they enjoy the favor of the Lord. "My son, if you receive my words, and treasure my commands within you, so that you incline your ear to wisdom and apply your heart to understanding; . . . Then you will understand the fear of the LORD, and find the knowledge of God" (Proverbs 2:1, 2, 5, *New King James Version*).

PRAYER THOUGHTS: Heavenly Father, thank You for the examples of obedience we find in Your Word. May we, both children and parents, be obedient to You. Help us to act in respectful ways toward each family member that You have given to us. In the name of Jesus Christ, amen.

CLIMB THAT LADDER

SCRIPTURE: Genesis 28:6-17

VERSE FOR TODAY: Be anxious for nothing, but in everything by prayer and supplication, with thanksgiving, let your requests be made known to God; (Philippians 4:6, *New King James Version*).

HYMN FOR TODAY: "We Are Climbing Jacob's Ladder"

Poor Jacob! He was the spoiled child of a protective mother. So confident, so bold, so unconcerned about the feelings of others. Now he is alone. His brother hates him, he has been forced to leave home, he has no friends. Jacob has reason to wonder if he has forfeited his place in God's promise. Will God now curse and reject him rather than bless him? His spirit is broken. Where will he turn? He wraps himself in his cloak and lies down on the ground. He falls asleep with his head pillowed on a rock. Jacob is at the lowest point in his life, but he is not alone! He is about to experience a high point.

Jacob dreams of a ladder that reaches up to Heaven. Angels are moving up and down the ladder and God is at the top. God has been with Jacob all the time. He has watched over Jacob and protected him. Now God himself gives Jacob the promise that He had given to Abraham and Isaac. God knows Jacob's heart. He assures the unhappy fugitive that He will keep Jacob in all his way, protect him, and supply his needs

God is also our loving, forgiving protector. He watches over us. He knows when we are sorry for being disobedient to Him. He wants to help us and protect us. He offers us a ladder that reaches into Heaven. That ladder is prayer.

PRAYER THOUGHTS: Loving Father, the knowledge of Your constant care for us gives comfort and security. Teach us to climb the ladder of prayer. In the name of our Savior, Jesus Christ, amen.

RECEIVE A PROMISE, GIVE A PROMISE

SCRIPTURE: Genesis 28:18-22

VERSE FOR TODAY: Where there is no vision, the people perish: but he that keepeth the law, happy is he (Proverbs 29:18).

HYMN FOR TODAY: "Follow, I Will Follow Thee"

Jacob had seen a vision! For the first time in his life he had a positive purpose. He had direction in his life. The God of his fathers had spoken to him. He had received the same promise that had been given to Abraham and to Isaac. Not only that, God promised to be with him, protect him, and return him to the land of his fathers. Jacob knew that a covenant with God required that he also offer a promise. Jacob promised to serve God and to return a tenth of all God would give to him. Jacob's faith had become personal.

God's promise to Abraham, to Isaac, and to Jacob had three parts: (1) That there should be a seed (or children), (2) that this seed should bless the world, and (3) that they should inherit the land. In the New Testament we learn how these promises also apply to the Christian.

Like Jacob, we have a vision of those things that are promised to us by God. We in return promise to serve God and to obey Him. We do not inherit our faith from our parents. We trust God's promises and are committed to serve Him because we know Him ourselves. We can walk with Him and talk to Him every day.

PRAYER THOUGHTS: Dear Father, joy fills our minds and hearts because we know You care for us. Help us to live a life of obedience to You. Forgive us when we do not act in a way that honors You. In the name of Jesus, we pray. Amen.

A HAPPY JOURNEY

SCRIPTURE: Genesis 29:1-14

VERSE FOR TODAY: Rejoice in the Lord always: and again I say, Rejoice (Philippians 4:4).

HYMN FOR TODAY: "Rejoice in the Lord Always"

Have you traveled when you were sad? Did the trip seem to take a long time? You didn't want to go. You were unhappy about everything!

On the other hand, have you started a trip when you felt good? You were happy and excited. You anticipate the adventure. Every view looked pleasant. The time seemed to fly.

Jacob knew about the effect on a trip of both of those attitudes. First, he felt sad and later happy while on the same trip. When he left home, he was very sad. His feet must have dragged as he turned his back on the only home he had ever known. He probably watched for Esau or one of Esau's sons to be waiting in ambush at every turn of the road. Then Jacob lay down to sleep at Bethel and the vision from God gave Jacob confidence that God loved him! Jacob woke up with joy in his heart, a happy spirit, eyes that saw a glorious new day, and he felt an attitude of anticipation for the trip ahead. The time seems to have passed quickly for Jacob. In a little while, he came to his destination. He asked about Laban's family and was told to look up and see Laban's daughter, Rachel, approaching. Jacob was not only in the right place, he was face to face with the right person. When we spend time with God, we, too, can know a happy, joyous spirit.

PRAYER THOUGHTS: Precious Lord, may our spirits be alert to Your presence. Forgive us for not seeking Your fellowship as often as we might. Thank You for the happiness You give to us. Amen.

MAKING THE BEST OF A BAD SITUATION

SCRIPTURE: Genesis 29:15-30

VERSE FOR TODAY: God is our refuge and strength, a very present help in trouble. Therefore we will not fear, (Psalm 46:1, 2, *New Kings James Version*).

HYMN FOR TODAY: "More Than Conquerors"

In today's Scripture, Jacob finds himself in a situation that was not of his own choosing. He had made a verbal contract with Laban. Jacob was commited to work seven years for the hand of Rachel, the younger daughter of Laban. If he could have had his way, he would have been committed to Rachel alone, all of his life. But Jacob was tricked by his father-in-law. He has been given the older daughter, Leah, for his seven years of labor. He had no choice; Jacob made the best of the situation. He must begin to work another seven years. The formerly impatient, selfish, inconsiderate Jacob we knew back in Canaan has changed. He has become a person who works to reach a goal, he is honest in his dealings, he works for peace, not strife. What made the change in Jacob? As we read the story, we can see the answer to this question—he came to know God personally. He desired to do God's will.

How can we find strength to face a difficult situation in life? The Word of God gives us the answer to this question. Like Jacob, we learn of God and choose to follow His leading.

PRAYER THOUGHTS: Lord God, You are the source of knowledge and good judgment. Forgive us when we have a bad attitude. Help us to appreciate all blessings, for we know that they come form You. Help us to see the good that You give to us each day. In the name of Jesus Christ, our Savior, we pray. Amen.

DEVOTIONS™

August

photo by Dr. Ward Patterson

August 1

AN HONEST WITNESS

SCRIPTURE: Deuteronomy 30:1-5

VERSE FOR TODAY: The LORD will again rejoice over you for good as He rejoiced over your fathers, "if you obey the voice of the LORD your God, to keep His commandments and His statutes which are written in this Book of the Law, and if you turn to the LORD your God with all your heart and with all your soul (Deuteronomy 30:9, 10, *New King James Version*).

HYMN FOR TODAY: "Great Is Thy Faithfulness"

God said to the nation of Israel, "You are my witnesses, . . . that I am God" (Isaiah 43:12, *New International Version*). It was the assignment of the nation of Israel to be witnesses to the world of who God is, of how He functions, of His faithfulness, His truth, His loyalty, His wrath at disobedience, and His great love to accept His repentant children into full blessing and forgiveness. God offered His grace and blessings to any who believed in Him and were obedient to His commands. God selected Israel as witnesses to receive the revelation of the coming Messiah and to preserve that revelation for all the world.

As Christians, we know that we can trust God's promises because Israel was a witness concerning God's faithfulness. Jesus, the Messiah, is in every way consistent with God's faithfulness. We are now the witnesses to the world that God is faithful in our lives.

PRAYER THOUGHTS: Thank You, heavenly Father, for the testimony of Your faithfulness. Thank You for the Bible. Help us to be believable witnesses for You today. In the name of Jesus, we pray. Amen.

August 1. **Nancy Hunt Sams** is a former editor at Standard Publishing Company. She and her husband, Don, have five grown children and live in Middletown, Ohio.

HIS WAYS ARE NOT OUR WAYS

SCRIPTURE: Genesis 32:3-8

VERSE FOR TODAY: In great fear and distress Jacob divided the people who were with him into two groups, and the flocks and herds and camels as well (Genesis 32:7, *New International Version*).

HYMN FOR TODAY: "O God, Our Help in Ages Past"

Murphy was part sheep dog—energetic, devoted, and lovable. He enjoyed being taken on walks. The leash was necessary, for while he loved people, he seemed to view cars as marauding lions. Whenever a car passed, Murphy would bark and try to chase it away from his family. Firm handling and a reassuring voice would sometimes convince him that it was safe to walk sedately and the cars would do us no harm. Indeed, on the leash with his master in control, he was a safe dog.

Jacob knew that God was with him. On his journey back to Canaan, just after Laban had left him, angels visited him. Twice, God himself had told Jacob to return and He would be with him (Genesis 31:3, 13), and yet Jacob was afraid of Esau and his four-hundred-strong army. Jacob worked out a means to save half of his possessions. He was not aware of what was happening in Esau's heart and life. Fear drove Jacob to take matters into his own hands.

When circumstances overwhelm us, deep prayer—a listening type of prayer—should precede our plans.

PRAYER THOUGHTS: Dear heavenly Father, it is sometimes difficult to know whether our actions are self-motivated or God-motivated. Please give us prayerful, listening hearts and the ability to stay close enough to You to hear Your voice. In the name of Jesus, our Savior, we pray. Amen.

August 2-8. **Elizabeth J. Margolis**, a native of England, is a freelance writer living in Dallas, Texas. She enjoys Bible study, gardening, travel, and people.

A PEACE OFFERING

SCRIPTURE: Genesis 32:9-21

VERSE FOR TODAY: For he thought, "I will pacify him with these gifts I am sending on ahead; later, when I see him, perhaps he will receive me" (Genesis 32:20, *New International Version*).

HYMN FOR TODAY: "Open My Eyes That I May See"

Mother wanted to celebrate the completion of her new home and had arranged a big party for everyone who had worked on the new house. Seventeen-year-old Emma refused to attend. Both parents expressed annoyance as she left the house on the night of the celebration, stealing their joy as she slammed the door. During the evening, Emma began to regret her actions. Guilt and the fear of repercussion drove her to a plan of action. She counted out the money left in her purse and visited the late night florist. She carefully chose a bouquet of flowers, making sure to include sweet-scented and expensive freesias, her mother's favorite.

Jacob must have felt great guilt and fear. Years earlier he had tricked his father into bestowing a blessing upon him instead of upon his brother. He had prospered, and it was probably not fear alone that prompted the peace offering he prepared. Perhaps he also felt an obligation to share with his brother some of the prosperity that came from being so blessed. Whatever his shortcomings, Jacob was a man of action. This time he did recognize his need of God and prayed for protection, but not without putting his own plans into action.

PRAYER THOUGHTS: Dear heavenly Father, please forgive us when we pray for help but do not keep alert for Your answer. Teach us to follow You and Your ways. In the name of Jesus, our Savior, we pray. Amen.

WHO'S THE BOSS?

SCRIPTURE: Genesis 32:22-32

VERSE FOR TODAY: When the man saw that he could not overpower him, he touched the socket of Jacob's hip so that his hip was wrenched (Genesis 32:25, *New International Version*).

HYMN FOR TODAY: "Trust and Obey"

"You bring the lemonade, and I'll buy the paper cups. There's a table in the garage, and we can set it up on my front lawn on Saturday." A smile flickered across Michael's face as he watched his fifth grader pace up and down the living room, portable phone to ear. Wait a minute . . . did Dan say Saturday? That was the day the men were coming to lop the two big trees at the front of the house. Daniel hung up the phone, and Michael grabbed hold of him playfully and wrestled him to the ground. As they struggled in mock fight, father first allowed son to gain ground before saying between gritted teeth, "So you think you can make arrangements without consulting me, do you? I'll show you," then he pinned him down on the ground and began to tickle him.

Like the boy in this illustration, Jacob had a good heart. He loved God and wanted to do right, but God needed Jacob to draw near to Him. He wanted Jacob to become a man of prayer as well as a man of action. Two-way communication was established. Limping with a disabled hip, Jacob would have a permanent reminder of his encounter with God.

PRAYER THOUGHTS: Heavenly Father, thank You for this passage of Scripture which reminds us that we are totally dependent upon You. Give us a pure heart, O Father, and help us to stay close to You today. In the name of Jesus, we pray. Amen.

RECONCILED

SCRIPTURE: Genesis 33:1-11

VERSE FOR TODAY: Blessed is he whose transgressions are forgiven, whose sins are covered (Psalm 32:1, *New International Version*).

HYMN FOR TODAY: "Crown Him with Many Crowns"

A long time ago, I attended a Bible study for new believers. Anna had been a regular participant in the class for more than three years, but had not yet accepted Jesus as her personal Savior. She seemed troubled by the Old Testament stories of God judging people and nations. She could not seem to grasp the merciful side of His character. Conversations proved that Anna felt unworthy to accept Christ's atoning death, and she tried desperately to get her life in order first. The Bible study leader said, "You're trying to put the cart before the horse, Anna! Jesus helps us to get our life in order. He forgives our past and helps us to take a new road—the road to Heaven."

Jacob, as well as fearing the wrath of his older brother, may well have felt unworthy to receive the forgiveness of his older brother. He wanted to offer something tangible to Esau. However, the only thing that mattered to Esau was that Jacob had finally returned home. We can imagine the weight that must have been lifted off Jacob's shoulders as Esau declared, "For to see your face is like seeing the face of God" (Genesis 33:10, *New International Version*).

PRAYER THOUGHTS: Heavenly Father, thank You that there is no need for us to prepare great gifts of work and service *before* we kneel at the foot of Jesus' cross to accept His gift of eternal life. You are already waiting with wide open arms. Help us to obey Your Word and accept Your gift of reconciliation. In the name of Jesus, we pray. Amen.

GOD'S PLAN OR JACOB'S PLAN?

SCRIPTURE: Genesis 33:12-17

VERSE FOR TODAY: Blessed is the nation whose God is the LORD, the people he chose for his inheritance (Psalm 33:12, *New International Version*).

HYMN FOR TODAY: "God Is Working His Purpose Out"

Some say that there are two kinds of drivers on the roadways: those who speed up when approaching a traffic light on orange (when the red light is changing to yellow) and those who slow down. Some claim to have a predisposition toward fast driving.

Jacob had a predisposition toward scheming and devising ways to get ahead, even though he knew God was in control. Jacob had wrestled with God. He had come face to face with his Creator. Jacob's intimate encounter and lesson left him with the disabling of his hip. However, Jacob would not suddenly change all of his ways. He was dishonest in his stated intention to follow Esau to Seir.

Jacob saw an area of land where he wanted to set up his home. God knew that Jacob intended to keep himself and his vast household to himself.

Isn't it wonderful that God does not wait until we are perfect to include us in His plans? Isn't it wonderful that God has chosen us for His inheritance?

PRAYER THOUGHTS: Dear heavenly Father, thank You that You look at our hearts rather than our actions and that even while You are transforming our minds, You are still carrying out Your sovereign purposes in our lives. Thank You for Jesus and His willingness to take our sins to the cross. Teach us, O God, to follow Your ways. Let us wait upon Your plan for our lives. In the name of our Savior, Jesus Christ. Amen.

INSIDE OUT

SCRIPTURE: Matthew 5:21-26

VERSE FOR TODAY: What a wretched man I am! Who will rescue me from this body of death? (Romans 7:24, *New International Version*).

HYMN FOR TODAY: "All Hail the Power of Jesus' Name"

One spring I planted two peach trees. The smaller one developed golf ball sized craters in its trunk from which it bled sap. I inquired of the garden center what the problem might be and was told that a boring insect from the soil had infested it . I was given a solution which smelled like gasoline and was told to scrub it into the damaged bark. Afterwards I was pleased to see that the weeping holes had dried up and scarred over. The following spring white blossoms appeared, and again I painted the tree with the pungent solution. Little green peaches developed, swelling and ripening in due season. In July I picked my first fruit. It was yellow and downy with a tinge of pink, and to my relief smelled like a peach, not gasoline. In anticipation I cut into it, but to my horror, it was full of worms! So it was with all the others. The infestation had gone deep into the core of the tree.

Sin in our lives is insidious. We may not commit murder, but we all carry within us anger and jealousy. Frustrated parents sometimes call their children demeaning names. This can have a lasting effect on the way their children perceive themselves in adulthood. The sin has done its insidious work just like the worms in the fruit tree.

PRAYER THOUGHTS: Thank You, dear Lord, that You are willing to deal with our sins quickly before we reach the judgment seat. In Christ, You have provided the complete solution. Amen.

ABSORBING THE PUNCHES

SCRIPTURE: Matthew 18:21-35

VERSE FOR TODAY: For if you forgive men when they sin against you, your heavenly Father will also forgive you (Matthew 6:14, *New International Version*).

HYMN FOR TODAY: "Dear Lord and Father of Mankind"

Have you ever watched a boxer practicing with a punching bag? The punching bag is firm yet yielding and absorbs the punches with very little change to its shape. The indentations soon smooth out again. If the boxer were to practice against a more unyielding surface, say a brick wall, he would be severely injured.

Our passage today focuses on God's requirement that Christians are to forgive one another. We are commanded to do so. There is more at stake here than the simple logic that if God forgives our sins against Him, then we, too, must forgive ourselves and others. We know that forgiveness comes from God. Therefore, refusing to forgive is sin. When we fail to forgive our fellow believers, we are joining the enemy's camp in his battle to destroy both them and us. Not forgiving hurts both parties. However, when we offer forgiveness, even in the face of injustice, we severely hinder the devil and his tactics. Our forgiveness is like a deep, soft cushion, able to absorb and melt away animosity. Instead of giving fuel to the devil, our accuser, we bring glory to God and allow righteousness to reproduce righteousness.

PRAYER THOUGHTS: O dear Father, the Scripture shows us the seriousness of being unforgiving. We neither want to perpetuate sin or suffer severe punishment, so we pray that You will change our unforgiving hearts. In Jesus' name we pray. Amen.

OH, YOU DREAMER

SCRIPTURE: Genesis 37:1-11

VERSE FOR TODAY: When he told his father as well as his brothers, his father rebuked him and said, "What is this dream you had?" (Genesis 37:10, *New International Version*).

HYMN FOR TODAY: "Turn Your Eyes Upon Jesus"

Dream—a series of thoughts, images, or emotions occurring during sleep. Yes, we do all dream—sometimes good things, sometimes bad things. Often dreams are highly motivating and sometimes puzzling. We ask, "Why did I dream that? What does it mean? Is it a message—maybe a word from the Lord?"

Apparently Joseph reacted with uncertainty. He thought his dream was important enough to tell his father. His father, Jacob, was both puzzled and angry about it and "rebuked" his son, but could not forget Joseph's dream. Jacob, too, thought it might be important—a message—and it was!

Does God speak to us in the largely unknown realm of the subconscious? Should we pay attention to our dreams?

But there is another kind of dreaming, and we can do something about it—daydreaming. Daydreaming can be important and motivating. It can be planning the use of our God-given bodies, minds, and spirits to maximize the most of the gifts God gives us!

PRAYER THOUGHTS: Loving Father who created us with capable minds, thank You for the ability to dream dreams in sleep and in wakefulness. Keep us focused on Your will and our Savior in whose name we pray. Amen.

August 9-14. **Bruce Miller** is a Senior Adult Pastor in Mesa, Arizona. **Onalee Grimes** is an elder at the Broadway Christian Church in Tucson, Arizona.

THE JEOPARDY OF JEALOUSY

SCRIPTURE: Genesis 37:12-24

VERSE FOR TODAY: His brothers were jealous of him (Genesis 37:11, *New International Version*).

HYMN FOR TODAY: "Our God Reigns"

We usually do not think of jealousy as an admirable trait. But God called himself jealous. "I, the LORD your God, am a jealous God" (Exodus 20:5, *New International Version*). He even said His name was "jealous" (Exodus 34:14, *New International Version*). Surely God meant that He would not allow or tolerate any rivalry or equality of His Lordship.

In the New Testament it is made clear that the human expression of jealousy is unbecoming and unacceptable in the Christian's life. The apostle Paul called it "worldly" (1 Corinthians 3:3, *New International Version*) and sinful (Galatians 5:20, *New International Version*).

In the Scripture for today we can see the evil, the jeopardy of jealousy, in the awful acts it prompted Jacob's sons to do to their own brother.

Doubtless all who read this can think of similar evil acts that jealousy has caused.

Is there any antidote to save us from the infection of this evil? Yes, in the beautiful words of God to King Solomon, "If my people . . . will humble themselves . . . and pray . . . I will forgive their sin . . . " (2 Chronicles 7:14, *New International Version*).

PRAYER THOUGHTS: O God, You know our hearts. Keep us from the sins of pride and envy. Forgive our foolish ways and keep us in Your everlasting love. In the name of Jesus, we pray. Amen.

SOLD !

SCRIPTURE: Genesis 37:25-28

VERSE FOR TODAY: God works for the good of those who love him, who have been called according to his purpose (Romans 8:28, *New International Version*).

HYMN FOR TODAY: "I Would Be True"

Sometimes we hear the statement, "We have to choose the lesser of two or more evils."

In the Scripture for today, when brothers made the choice in disposing of one of their own, it proved to be the salvation of a nation.

We, too, have to make similar choices in meeting the demands of home, family, job, church, and social relationships. It is not easy. How do we do it?

Rarely are the decisions we have to make clear and obvious choices between what is all right and what is all wrong. Mostly we have to choose what seems "best."

Then we make the best of the choice we have made. Our faith in God, our trust in divine order, our assurance that God works in all things for the good of those who love Him and seek to do His purpose (Romans 8:28, *New International Version*) is seen.

How do you suppose Joseph, a seventeen-year-old boy, felt when he was abused, sold, and abandoned by his brothers? That must have been an overwhelmingly devastating experience for him. But, judging by what history tells us, he trusted God to be his help and to work good out of that evil action.

Can we do that? Yes, we can.

PRAYER THOUGHTS: Father in Heaven, hear the groanings of our hearts as we try to discern the truth in our world. Help us to choose Your way in all things. We pray in the Savior's name. Amen.

NOT AS BAD AS HE THOUGHT

SCRIPTURE: Genesis 37:29-36

VERSE FOR TODAY: "Now I am ready to die, since I have seen for myself that you are still alive" (Genesis 46:30, *New International Version*).

HYMN FOR TODAY: "There Is a Balm in Gilead"

Probably most of us have said sometime, "That was not as bad as I thought" or "That was better than I expected."

Surely that was true in the incident of Joseph's sad experience at the hands of his brothers. Jacob, his father, must also have felt that way much later in Egypt when he found his lost son alive!

Last night I listened as a man told of the break-up of his 45-year marriage. My friend said he was struggling to overcome his hate and anger. He wanted to show forgiveness and love.

I visited a young woman with a terminal illness. She mentioned that her car was stolen while she was in the doctor's office being readied for her hospitalization. In her car was her purse with important cards and papers. Yet, when it came time to pray, she wanted to begin the prayer time, and she began by praying for others first.

In both of these incidents, there was the evidence that in their minds, God had something better for them because they loved and trusted Him.

God does work for good.

PRAYER THOUGHTS: Merciful God in Heaven, You know our fears and anxieties. We place our trust in You and feel the comfort of Your love. Remind us that many of our fears never are realized. Teach us to have confidence in You. Help us to live with the assurances that belong to all who follow Your leading. We pray in the name of Him who calmed the sea. Amen.

JEALOUSY AND/OR LOVE

SCRIPTURE: 1 Samuel 18:1-9

VERSE FOR TODAY: Jonathan made a covenant with David because he loved him as himself (1 Samuel 18:3, *New International Version*).

HYMN FOR TODAY: "Dear Lord and Father of Mankind"

The king was angry and jealous because a talented, lovable young man was more popular than he. The king's son, who would seem to be threatened by the popularity of a national hero, rather loved him and counted him as his closest friend.

Jealousy and love are such strong emotions that they cause strong and sometimes strange behavior. They surely did in the three-way interplay between Saul, David, and Jonathan.

Do those emotions do that to people today? Yes!

The newspapers, magazines, and TV programs tell of the actions of persons driven by their feelings of love and hate, jealousy and envy. These are feelings that all of us have at different times and in varying degrees. We need to be aware of these feelings and make an effort to control them. How?

Let us recognize that these emotions are ego-needs derived from that inherent drive for survival. Jesus recognized and identified the need but also taught us the necessity of bringing this human drive under control.

The Scottish poet Robert Burns urged us to see ourselves as others see us (from *To a Louse*). Jesus warned us that, "Everyone who exalts himself will be humbled, and he who humbles himself will be exalted" (Luke 14:11, *New International Version*).

PRAYER THOUGHTS: O God, our Father, forgive our foolish ways. Help us to diffuse anger with love and unforgiving thoughts with forgiveness. Your gift of grace cannot be measured. Thank You for the gift of Your Son in whose name we pray. Amen.

THE EVIL OF ENVY

SCRIPTURE: Matthew 20:1-16

VERSE FOR TODAY: Are you envious because I am generous? (Matthew 20:15, *New International Version*).

HYMN FOR TODAY: "Guide Me, O Thou Great Jehovah"

Envy can and does cause evil actions. Think how often you have heard or read about (or maybe even have been involved in) families being torn apart over settling estates. Someone thought someone else got better treatment or a better settlement. Someone felt he or she was given less recognition or attention than someone else.

Envy, jealousy, greed, and pride seem to be so closely related in their destructiveness to character that we need to be aware of, and on guard against, their intrusion into our attitude and behavior. All of us have all of these characteristics in varying degrees. Beware!

Perhaps if we knew how little those whom we envy enjoy the things we envy them for, there would be little to be envious about. Look at some of your own possessions. Remember how desperately you wanted them, how quickly they lost their appeal, and how little they satisfy now.

Have you ever moved? As you were packing your things and loading the truck, did you wonder where all that "stuff" came from and why you wanted it and got it?

My father's antidote to that urge of acquisition was, "Look at all the *stuff* I can get along without." He did, too. It was a lesson I never forgot.

PRAYER THOUGHTS: Loving God, give us the generosity of spirit to express joy for the good things that happen to other people. Remind us to give from our abundance. In the name of Jesus. Amen.

THE DISEASE OF ME

SCRIPTURE: Luke 14:7-11

VERSE FOR TODAY: "For everyone who exalts himself will be humbled, and he who humbles himself will be exalted" (Luke 14:11, *New International Version*).

HYMN FOR TODAY: "Humble Thyself"

In his book, *The Winner Within*, Pat Riley, who coached the Los Angeles Lakers to four NBA championships, writes about a malady that can destroy a once-successful team. He calls it the "disease of me." When the disease of me strikes a team, its members develop "an overpowering belief in their own importance." Jealousy, greed, and pride take root to divide and destroy even talented teams. Of their loss during the first playoff round of the year following their first championship, Riley writes, "Because of greed, pettiness, and resentment, we executed one of the fastest falls from grace in NBA history."

In our culture we have all sorts of ways of honoring the significant and successful. It is certainly appropriate for people to be honored by others for their accomplishments, but Jesus urges us to beware of seeking ways to honor ourselves.

Human nature has not changed a lot since the days of Jesus. We have a weakness for prominence, honor, and prestige. Jesus suggested that we take the lowest places, that we avoid the limelight, that we not worry that we are getting noticed and applauded. Rather, we are to humble ourselves and follow the example of Jesus himself (Philippians 2:3-11).

PRAYER THOUGHTS: O Father, forgive us when we seek our own glory. Help us to live our lives in love and humility as did Jesus. Amen.

August 15. **Dr. Ward Patterson** is Professor of Speech and Ministries at Cincinnati Bible College in Cincinnati, Ohio.

THE POWER OF SAYING NO

SCRIPTURE: Genesis 39:1-18

VERSE FOR TODAY: Submit yourselves therefore to God. Resist the devil, and he will flee from you (James 4:7).

HYMN FOR TODAY: "Yield Not to Temptation"

Do we always answer, *yes*, or can we sometimes say, *no*? Let's take a test.

1. A fellow Christian asks us to go to visit residents of a nursing home.

2. A neighbor asks us to help in preparing a food basket for a needy family.

3. A fellow worker asks us to join him after work for an alcoholic drink.

4. An acquaintance asks us to go to an X-rated movie.

How do we respond?

It is a serious problem when one does not understand when to say no. Often children say it when we want them to promptly obey. Adults sometimes say no when they are expected to accept responsibilities. Worst of all, people say it when they are urged to follow Jesus Christ.

Joseph learned the power of saying no at the right time. When he said it to Potiphar's wife, it caused him some trouble afterward. But in time God blessed him for that decision. God will bless us when we say no to temptation.

PRAYER THOUGHTS: Our Father in Heaven, please give us the wisdom to know when to say yes and when to say no. And then strengthen our resolve to make the wise response on every occasion. We pray in Jesus' name. Amen.

August 16-22. **Kenton Smith** is a Christian minister and writer. He and his wife, Eileen, are parents to four grown daughters.

MAKING THE MOST OF OUR PROBLEMS

SCRIPTURE: Genesis 39:19–40:8

VERSE FOR TODAY: For whatsoever is born of God overcometh the world: and this is the victory that overcometh the world, even our faith (1 John 5:4).

HYMN FOR TODAY: "Give of Your Best to the Master"

Someone has written a very clever and encouraging poem:
If somebody gives you a lemon,
Do not be dismayed.
Just take some sugar and water,
And make some lemonade.

A "lemon" in this case refers to something we obtain that turns out to be useless. When people buy a car, for example, and discover that it does not run, they call it a "lemon."

Joseph was given a "lemon." After arriving in Egypt as a captive, he became a slave in the house of Potiphar. He worked diligently there, but his good work proved useless.

Through no fault of his own, he was thrown into prison. There he immediately began "making lemonade." With God's help he turned his problems into fresh successes.

What kinds of "lemons" have we received recently? Has a job caused us frustration? Has a friend turned against us? Have we purchased a desired item, or received it as a gift, and then discovered it was not very useful?

God can help us "make lemonade." If we pray and seek His help, He can show us how to turn problems into mighty victories. What a challenge that is!

PRAYER THOUGHTS: Our dear Father, by faith we praise You for our problems. Help us to avoid the trap of merely complaining about them. Guide us in using them as stepping-stones to spiritual growth and fruitful service. We ask this in Jesus' name. Amen.

BEARERS OF GOOD NEWS AND BAD NEWS

SCRIPTURE: Genesis 40:9-23

VERSE FOR TODAY: As it is written, "How beautiful are the feet of those who bring good news!" (Romans 10:15, *New International Version*).

HYMN FOR TODAY: "Make Me a Blessing"

Whatever happened to Pharaoh's chief baker? Did the bad news that Joseph interpreted in the chief baker's dream come to pass? You say, "Yes, and that is the end of the story."

But what happened during those three days between Joseph's interpretation of the dream and its fulfillment? We do not know, but we wonder. Joseph was a man of God. How did he respond to the chief baker? Did he speak to him about God and life after death?

Occasionally we are all responsible for delivering bad news. Perhaps we must tell a fellow worker that he has lost his job. We may have to inform a neighbor that her home has been damaged. We may have to tell a loved one of an impending deadly illness. None of us is exempt from dealing with bad news. Even children sometimes must share sad news.

But if we must be a bearer of bad news, we can also proclaim good news. We can tell people that God cares about them and wants to help them with their problems. We can show this love and compassion by being willing to help those in need. Furthermore, we can announce to them that Jesus has the power to save them from sin and give them eternal life.

How wonderful that we can deliver such good news!

PRAYER THOUGHTS: Our Father, thank You for the privilege of communicating the good news of the gospel. Fill our hearts with eagerness for that day when all bad news will be swallowed up in the good news of Jesus' total victory. In His name, amen.

FOCUSING ON FORGOTTEN FAVORS

SCRIPTURE: Genesis 41:1-13

VERSE FOR TODAY: Remember that Jesus Christ of the seed of David was raised from the dead, according to my gospel: (2 Timothy 2:8).

HYMN FOR TODAY: "Lead Me to Calvary"

A string tied around a finger . . . a date encircled and starred on a calendar . . . a note fastened to the refrigerator or the bathroom mirror—these are common methods for combating forgetfulness.

Probably each of us must admit to being members of "the fellowship of the forgetful." We forget appointments, chores for which we are responsible, birthdays and other special days, and promises we have made. So we resort to the methods above in order to overcome our tendency to forget.

Would the chief cupbearer have done better if he had tied a string around his finger or pinned a note on his robe?

Perhaps so, but he should have remembered simply out of appreciation for what Joseph did for him.

Now is a good time for us to focus our attention on forgotten favors. Let us remember what human beings have done for us: assisting us in doing a job, helping us through a crisis, offering us needed words of comfort and encouragement. Let us remember and be appreciative.

Let us remember also what Jesus has done for us: dying on the cross and rising again to give us salvation and eternal life.

Let us remember and be appreciative.

PRAYER THOUGHTS: Our Father in Heaven, thank You for beautiful memories of human and divine blessings. Make us restless when we forget or take such blessings for granted. Stir up our sense of appreciation, and give us the words to express it. In Jesus' name, amen.

TELL ME YOUR PROBLEM!

SCRIPTURE: Genesis 41:14-24

VERSE FOR TODAY: Therefore, confess your sins to each other, and pray for each other so that you may be healed. The prayer of a righteous man is powerful and effective (James 5:16, *New International Version*).

HYMN FOR TODAY: "Blest Be the Tie That Binds"

One of the frequent scenes in Charles Schulz's *Peanuts* comic strip is Lucy's stand where she offers psychiatric help for a fee of five cents. Once when Charlie Brown came to her to discuss a problem, she announced he had come to the right place. Then she admitted, "Oh, this is the right place, all right—I need the money!"

Many people are willing to help with problems . . . for a price. They expect a favor in return. Of course, we know that some individuals make a living by counseling people with problems. Certainly they have a right to expect payment. But we have friends and neighbors who are ready to help on the basis of friendship or neighborliness.

What kind of helper are we? Do we give to others simply out of love for them or do we expect something in return? Do we assist other people simply because of God's love in our heart? Do we say, "Do you need me to listen? I'll be happy to make your problem an important part of my prayers to God"? What a privilege it is to *pray* for our families, our friends, and our neighbors.

PRAYER THOUGHTS: Dear Father, we thank You for Jesus' exhortation in Matthew 10:8: "Freely ye have received, freely give." We have received from You and Your people gifts of love and compassion. Help us to give freely of the same gifts to those in need. In the name of Jesus, our Lord and Savior. Amen.

THE PEOPLE WITH THE ANSWERS

SCRIPTURE: Genesis 41:25-45

VERSE FOR TODAY: Be ready always to give an answer to every man that asketh you a reason of the hope that is in you, with meekness and fear: (1 Peter 3:15).

HYMN FOR TODAY: "We've a Story to Tell to the Nations"

The popular television quiz program *Jeopardy* has one unusual feature. Host Alex Trebek does not ask questions to which the contestants respond with answers. Instead, Mr. Trebek gives the answers, and the contestants must respond with the questions.

Christ is the answer to life's most important questions. As Christians, we long for people to ask questions such as the following: "What is the meaning of life?" "How can I gain relief from guilt?" "Where can I find the power to live a better life?" "How can I gain eternal life?"

Perhaps the questions could be even more specific: What is the message of the Bible? Who is Jesus Christ? Why did He die on the cross? And then we hope they will ask the question the Philippian jailer asked Paul and Silas: "What must I do to be saved?" (Acts 16:30).

Pharaoh asked Joseph for help because of his troubling dreams. Joseph gave him God's answers. People today are troubled by fear, stress, loneliness, depression, and the prospect of death. Some are vaguely aware that sin is their basic problem. Oh, that they would ask for guidance! We want them to find God's answers.

PRAYER THOUGHTS: Our gracious Father, we thank You for giving answers to mankind's most insistent questions. Guide us in mastering these answers so that we can satisfy the needs of every questioner. Make us bold, but patient, in our responses. In Jesus' name, amen.

ENTERING THE SERVICE

SCRIPTURE: Genesis 41:46-57

VERSE FOR TODAY: Joseph was thirty years old when he entered the service of Pharaoh king of Egypt (Genesis 41:46, *New International Version***).**

HYMN FOR TODAY: "I Will Serve Thee"

The president of the United States is given his oath of office prior to beginning his duties. He swears to "preserve, protect, and defend the Constitution of the United States." At that point he enters into service as president—service that is meant to end only when he completes his term of office.

Did Joseph take an oath of office when he entered Pharaoh's service? Did he promise to "preserve, protect, and defend" the Pharaoh? We do not know. We do know, however, that he served his adopted country for the remainder of his life (See Genesis 50:22).

In a sense, our initial confession of faith in Jesus Christ is like an oath of office. He becomes our Savior, and He also becomes our Lord and our Master. We enter into His service, commencing a term of service that is to last a lifetime. It is our duty to preserve, protect, defend, and, yes, to proclaim His gospel.

What a privilege it is to enter the service of a King infinitely greater than Pharaoh. When we invest our intellect, energy, enthusiasm, and intensity into that service, we find true happiness. Our term of service will last for eternity.

PRAYER THOUGHTS: Dear Father, we praise You for the privilege of serving Your Son. Sometimes we lose sight of how wonderful a privilege it is. Open our eyes, stir our hearts, employ our hands and feet, lips and tongues in the glorious cause of the gospel. Let us know the true joy of serving You. In Jesus' name. Amen.

ON YOUR FEET!

SCRIPTURE: Genesis 42:1-17

VERSE FOR TODAY: And Jacob said to his sons, "Why are you staring at one another?" (Genesis 42:1, *New American Standard Bible*).

HYMN FOR TODAY: "Stand Up, Stand Up For Jesus"

The famine was two years old. The food stores were nearly gone. The family was rich, but of what use were riches when there was no food to buy? The eleven brothers, all heads of households, were discouraged and despondent. How were they to keep their families and livestock alive?

Perhaps they called a family council to seek an answer to the problem. Reuben, the oldest, may have spoken first, and then the others. They rejected every idea until there was none left. Their strategy meeting turned into a pity party. They sat and looked at one another, each seeing sheer desperation in the eyes of his brothers.

Their father entered the tent. Upon observation he said, "Why do you sit here staring at one another? . . . I have heard that there is grain to be had in Egypt; go down there and buy some for us, so that we may live and not die!" (Genesis 42:1, 2, *New American Standard Bible*).

Question: Do I want to focus on the negative, as the brothers did, and be paralyzed, or do I want to get on my feet and do what's necessary for life today?

PRAYER THOUGHTS: Heavenly Father, help us to resist focusing on the negative. Help us, rather, to be about Your work in spite of our circumstances. Amen.

August 23-29. **Edna Anne (Eddie) Baughman Smith** and her husband, Walter, serve as missionaries to Nigeria. They are parents to two grown children, Keith and Jerianne, who have blessed them with five grandchildren.

THE HONESTY TEST

SCRIPTURE: Genesis 42:18-38

VERSE FOR TODAY: Then they said to one another, "Truly we are guilty concerning our brother," (Genesis 42:21, *New American Standard Bible*).

HYMN FOR TODAY: "True-Hearted, Whole-Hearted"

What were Jacob's sons thinking as they journeyed toward Egypt? Was the hope of food for their families mixed with indignation at the thought of having to beg a foreigner for food? Did the thought of Egypt—those Ishmaelites twenty years ago were headed to Egypt—cause the first drop of guilt to land in the pail of conscience? *Plink!*

The ruler accused them of being spies, and they insisted they were honest men. Honest men? *Plink!* They spent three days in prison, finding no mercy in spite of their pleas. *Plink!*

Now, to pass the honesty test, they must abandon a brother to an Egyptian prison, go home, and return with their youngest brother. *Plunk!*

Maybe about here that familiar question entered their minds: What have we ever done to deserve all this? *Plink, plink, plink, plunk!* The pail, full now, overflows in a communal confession: "Truly we are guilty concerning our brother" (Genesis 42:21, *New American Standard Bible*).

The test, the honesty test, looms ahead. Will they pass it? Will conscience do its work? We shall see.

PRAYER THOUGHTS: Father, help us to be honest with You, with ourselves, and with others. Help us to train our consciences to know the truth we find in Your Word, and then to listen to it. Give us courage and strength to follow the leading of Your Son, Jesus, our Savior and Lord. In His name, we pray. Amen.

SEND THE SON AND TRUST THE LORD

SCRIPTURE: Genesis 43:1-15

VERSE FOR TODAY: "May God Almighty grant you compassion in the sight of the man," (Genesis 43:14, *New American Standard Bible*).

HYMN FOR TODAY: "Only Trust Him"

Jacob could not believe this was happening. The Lord had said his descendants were to be a multitude and a blessing to all peoples. But did his life show that kind of blessing?

True, he had been given many sons, but one by one he was losing them. Joseph, Jacob's favorite, to his knowledge had been devoured by wild beasts. Then, the famine had threatened to wipe out the whole family.

Jacob had taken heart as his sons left for Egypt to buy grain, but he had lost another son. Simeon was in prison in Egypt. The grain was finishing, and his sons refused to return to Egypt for more unless he allowed Benjamin to go along. But Benjamin was the only child remaining to him from his beloved Rachel, and he was not giving him up.

No father should have to make a decision like this! Perhaps at this point Jacob remembered the story of his father, Isaac, on the altar on Mount Moriah (Genesis 22). He decided to send Benjamin and trust the Lord to give all eleven sons back. He was not aware of the great and wonderful blessing awaiting him in Egypt. He would not just receive his eleven sons back, but he would receive all twelve!

Question: Might it be a good idea for *us* to trust God to work out His purposes in spite of our troubles, too?

PRAYER THOUGHTS: Father, help us to remember that understanding what You are doing in our lives is not nearly so important as trusting You, even when we cannot understand. In Your Son's name. Amen.

THE SUBSTITUTE

SCRIPTURE: Genesis 44:18-34

VERSE FOR TODAY: Please let your servant remain instead of the lad a slave to my lord, (Genesis 44:33, *New American Standard Bible*).

HYMN FOR TODAY: "Take My Life and Let It Be Consecrated"

The brothers must have looked a sorry lot as they stood before Joseph. All the joy they had felt outward bound from the city had turned to sorrow. Benjamin had been claimed as a slave. Judah, as spokesman, claimed no defense and offered all eleven as slaves. But Joseph said, "No. Just leave Benjamin and go on home to your father."

Once, even twice, they had gone home to Jacob and explained the absence of a brother. They could not do it again. Listen to Judah's impassioned pleading as he recounts their conversation with Jacob and the father's anguish over sending Benjamin, the youngest son.

Judah had offered himself as surety for Benjamin. He could not bear to go home now and see his father succumb in sorrow over his son. He knew that his father would surely die if he saw the brothers coming home without the father's beloved youngest son. He begged Joseph to allow him to remain as a slave in the place of his brother.

The last test had been passed, and through the line of this one who was willing to take his brother's place as a slave to pay the price of a supposed crime, came the One who willingly took our place on the cross to pay the price of our very real sin.

PRAYER THOUGHTS: Heavenly Father, Your Son, Jesus, showed the greatest love when He gave His life for us. May we love so much in return that we count our lives a small gift to give to You. In the name of Jesus, we pray. Amen.

GOD MEANT IT FOR GOOD

SCRIPTURE: Genesis 45:1-28

VERSE FOR TODAY: You intended to harm me, but God intended it for good to accomplish what is now being done, the saving of many lives (Genesis 50:20, *New International Version*).

HYMN FOR TODAY: "All Things Work Together"

The ten brothers were guilty of grievous sin. They hated their brother and allowed that hatred to grow to its natural conclusion. They got rid of him; sold their own brother as a slave into a pagan land.

Everything they did—the rough handling, stopping their ears against his cries for mercy, selling their own flesh and blood, lying to their father—was evil. But Joseph said though they meant it for evil, God meant it for good—for saving lives.

For Joseph to go to Egypt was in the best interest of Joseph, whom God raised to a position of prominence and power. It was in the best interest of Jacob and his family, whom God kept alive through the hand of Joseph. It was in the best interest of Egypt and the other nations God provided for through Joseph. And it was in our best interest, because it was God's means of saving the family through whom He would manifest Himself in the flesh.

The God who could bring about such good in spite of such evil intent can surely be trusted to deal with our problems, too. Let's trust Him!

PRAYER THOUGHTS: Father, the Joseph story shows us that You can bring good out of the worst circumstances. Give us a burning desire to read Your Word. We know that You have shown love to Your servants throughout history. May our trust in You grow day by day. Thank You that we can have assurance in Christ Jesus. In His name we pray. Amen.

"THEY ALSO SERVE"

SCRIPTURE: Exodus 2:1-10

VERSE FOR TODAY: And his sister stood afar off, to wit what would be done to him (Exodus 2:4).

HYMN FOR TODAY: "Give of Your Best"

Totally blind by age 43, the 17th-century Puritan poet, John Milton, wrote what would become a famous sonnet on his blindness. In it, he expressed his confusion over why his sight was taken away, even though he was trying to use his talent for God. He felt rather like the football player who is benched during the big game—useless, but ready to play if called on. He concluded the poem with the well-known line, "They also serve who only stand and wait."

Do you feel that circumstances have put you in a position in which you are simply standing and waiting? Think of Miriam. In the beginning she was not a major player in the drama of Moses. The baby, the mother, and Pharoah's daughter take center stage. Miriam stands aside to see what will happen. When opportunity strikes, she quickly responds. Had she not been willing to stay watchfully on the sidelines for awhile, would she have had the opportunity to serve?

During World War II, British prime minister Winston Churchill quoted Milton and declare that everyone—old or young, in any capacity—"could also serve." He said, in respect to the war effort, "From the highest to the humblest tasks, all are of equal honor; all have their part to play."

PRAYER THOUGHTS: Father, help us to know when to stand and wait and when to act. Teach us the importance of supporting roles. Amen.

August 30, 31. **Wanda Trawick** serves as Director of Christian Education for the Watauga Avenue Presbyterian Church in Johnson City, Tennessee.

August 31

MAN ON THE RUN

SCRIPTURE: Exodus 2:11-15

VERSE FOR TODAY: But Moses fled from the face of Pharoah, and dwelt in the land of Midian (Exodus 2:15).

HYMN FOR TODAY: "Abide with Me"

Today marks the anniversary of the death of Diana, Princess of Wales. She, along with three others, was in a speeding car at the time—fleeing photographers on motorcycles. Whatever our opinion of Diana and her fellow passengers might be, it is sad to think of a young, beautiful woman spending the last moments of her life trying hopelessly to outrun her pursuers.

Something about people running away fascinates us—perhaps because all of us have run at times. When I was a child, I ran from my mother when I had done something wrong. I knew she would punish me swiftly and severely. Now that I am old, fat, and arthritic, I don't run anymore. But we adults have our ways of fleeing, don't we? Sometimes we escape what's after us. Sometimes we don't.

Moses did escape. He was a man who saw an injustice but tried to correct it in the wrong way. He lost his temper with the Egyptian overseer just as the overseer had lost his temper with the Hebrew slave. A classic example of two wrongs not making a right. Moses escaped by running from Pharoah. He would find years later, much to his surprise, that he had not escaped from God—or from God's will for his life.

PRAYER THOUGHTS: When we are on the run from danger, we pray for God's protection. But when we are on the run from God, to whom can we pray? And for what can we ask? Lord, teach us when to stop, turn around, and face You. Amen.

DEVOTIONS™

September

photo by Ward Patterson

LIFE GOES ON

SCRIPTURE: Exodus 2:16-25

VERSE FOR TODAY: And Moses was content to dwell with the man; and he gave Moses Zipporah his daughter (Exodus 2:21).

HYMN FOR TODAY: "Day by Day"

"What did you do at school today?" "Nothing."

"How was work today?" "Same old thing."

"How did things go at home today?" "Okay, I suppose."

In other words, the school didn't catch on fire, and no one even threw up in class. No one was fired at work, and at home no evidence of termites was discovered, and no appliance broke down. Nor did money fall from the sky.

Much of life is the "same old, same old"—the times between moments of great joy and great sadness, between unbearable loss and ecstatic gains, between difficult challenges and unexpected windfalls.

Remember how, at the transfiguration of Christ (Mark 9:1-15), Peter wanted to stay on the mountain to hold on to that momentous time of revelation? But the everyday problems of everyday people waited below, and that's where Jesus took His three disciples—back to the everyday world.

Most days, life simply goes on without that rush of adrenaline we feel when faced with a crisis or a spiritual "high." How faithful are we during those "same old, same old" days? Do we "keep on keeping on" in what seems like the drudgery of everyday life? Or do we sit down and quit?

PRAYER THOUGHTS: O God, keep us faithful and obedient to You as we live life from day to day. May what we learn from You prepare us for the challenges of the day. In the name of Jesus, we pray. Amen.

September 1-5. **Wanda Trawick** writes from Johnson City, Tennessee.

"WHY" IS NOT A DIRTY WORD

SCRIPTURE: Exodus 3:1-10

VERSE FOR TODAY: And Moses said, I will now turn aside, and see this great sight, why the bush is not burnt (Exodus 3:3).

HYMN FOR TODAY: "Open My Eyes, That I May See"

Most of the girls in the Junior Sunday school class were yawning or staring out the window, but I was agog with interest and, prepared with a list of "whys?", I asked the first one. Miss Bessie's blue eyes wavered between a twinkle and a look of despair.

The thing that saved me from the reputation of "troublemaker" was that I hung on every word my teachers uttered. But eventually my "whys" began to trouble people, as though I were questioning God, the Bible, and the church. Not so. I simply wanted to understand. I still do. I don't always find the answer, but I learn a lot during the search.

Moses turned aside to see the burning bush up close for the same reason. He wanted to understand why the bush was burning, but not burnt. We can ask "why" for the wrong reasons, of course, when we are deliberately trying to discount the faith, at which times we really want to confuse and vanquish others rather than find the truth. But Moses approached the burning bush with curiosity and an open mind and found something more than he had bargained for when he approached the bush. We often find the same when we ask "why" for all the right reasons.

PRAYER THOUGHTS: Heavenly Father, as adults, give us patience and wisdom in answering the "whys" of our children. Have patience with us when we seek understanding, but deliver us from arrogance when our "whys" become confrontations rather than questions. Teach us Your ways. In the name of Jesus, we pray. Amen.

WHOM SHALL I SAY IS CALLING?

SCRIPTURE: Exodus 3:11-22

VERSE FOR TODAY: And God said unto Moses, I AM THAT I AM (Exodus 3:14).

HYMN FOR TODAY: "Holy, Holy, Holy"

When I first went to work as Director of Christian Education at our church, I sometimes answered the phone when the church secretary was out of the office. Very quickly I learned that I needed to ask, "Whom shall I say is calling?" when I didn't know the caller.

When someone calls on me to do something, I definitely want to know who is asking. So did Moses. And he knew the Israelites would want to know the same thing.

What a reply Moses got! What kind of name was that? I AM THAT I AM. The God who called Moses and who calls us today is simply I AM—not the sweet grandpa in the sky who can be manipulated by our wheedling. He isn't necessarily what we want Him to be, but simply who He is.

In a way, that's scary. Big words like "sovereignty" and "omnipotence" intimidate us. In another way, though, isn't it amazing that this I AM stoops to call us at all? Isn't it wonderful that He chooses us to be "laborers together" with Him in accomplishing what needs to be done? And that He willingly connects us to that power which is His alone—the power which belongs not to whom we wish Him to be, but to whom He is? Amazing and exhilarating!

PRAYER THOUGHTS: O Father, we are sometimes surprised and frightened when You call on us to accomplish something for You. Give us courage and the assurance that when You call us—although You stand so far above and beyond us—that You choose to call us and empower us. Thank You. In Jesus' name. Amen.

FROM ORDINARY TO EXTRAORDINARY

SCRIPTURE: Exodus 4:1-9

VERSE FOR TODAY: And the LORD said unto him, what is that in thine hand? And he said, A rod (Exodus 4:2).

HYMN FOR TODAY: "Here Am I, Send Me"

What is that in your hand? A dish rag? a math book? a cellular phone? a measuring cup? a hammer? ball-point pen? coloring book? hedge clippers?

Yesterday we looked at the story of the great I AM choosing to call a mere human to His service. Most of us would have been as terrified as Moses and would have backpedaled and made excuses like crazy. But the Almighty looked at a shepherd with a rod in his hand, and He touched that rod and transformed it.

There aren't many shepherds with rods around now, but there are many men, women, youth, and children with everyday objects in their hands, with bright new ideas in their heads, and "impossible" dreams in their hearts—all of which God can touch and transform. We all work or play with something every day that, with the touch of the Almighty, can become an instrument in His hands for changing His world. Maybe not the fate of a whole nation, as in the case of Moses, but our world. Perhaps it will impact our family, our neighborhood, or our church. It may change the world of medicine, art, or high finance—and anything in between.

What is that in your hand? In your head? In your heart? Do you dare to let God touch it? Are you willing to leave it or use it, whichever He wills—to change His world?

PRAYER THOUGHTS: Almighty God, when we seek to do Your will, help us not to overlook the ordinary that with Your touch can become extraordinary. Use us for Your glory. In the name of Jesus. Amen.

HELP ALONG THE WAY

SCRIPTURE: Exodus 4:10-20

VERSE FOR TODAY: I will be with thy mouth, and teach thee what thou shalt say (Exodus 4:12).

HYMN FOR TODAY: "Wherever He Leads I'll Go"

"Enjoy your baby," the obstetrician said as we prepared to take our firstborn home. At five o'clock the next morning, our baby daughter was crying, and we were not enjoying her. We had done everything we knew to do (which wasn't much) all to no avail. We needed help! And we would have help along the way—pediatricians, family members, and friends.

When our second child was born, our daughter was seven years old and not happy at losing her position as only child. Now she was a big sister, struggling with her new role. We taught her how to hold her baby brother, what to do when he spit up, and how to keep the cats from kneading on him, etc. She had help along the way and succeeded only too well. As an adolescent, little brother would exclaim with disgust, "It's like growing up with two mothers!"

Help along the way. God didn't give Moses and Aaron the help until they actually needed it. They had only His promise to be *with* them and to *teach* them along the way—learning as they went. So often we want to know everything and feel completely capable before we start out on what we believe is a call from God. It doesn't work that way. He teaches us and enables us along the way.

PRAYER THOUGHTS: Father, help us to overcome fear and self-consciousness. Give us confidence that, as we take our first faltering steps along the path You have set for us, to know that You are with us and will teach us what to say and do. In the name of Jesus, we pray. Amen.

WHAT'S WRONG WITH YEAST?

SCRIPTURE: Exodus 13:3-10

VERSE FOR TODAY: This day the LORD thy God hath commanded thee to do these statutes and judgments: thou shalt therefore keep and do them with all thine heart, and with all thy soul (Deuteronomy 26:16).

HYMN FOR TODAY: "Trust and Obey"

Let us think about a loaf of homemade bread. Now that should be a pleasant task. The aroma draws us to the kitchen, as the hot bread is taken from the oven. With butter melting over our slice or jam spread over its length and width, we have a taste treat that is difficult to match. Part of our enjoyment comes from the soft, cushiony texture of the bread. The yeast is responsible for that. Before the bread was placed in the oven, the yeast made little pockets of air to puff out the dough, making it rise, and thus softening the bread.

Moses, speaking for the Lord, told the Israelites to get rid of their leaven or yeast for seven days. They were to eat only unleavened bread during that period. If God said not to use it, then the Israelites simply had to obey.

God does not command us to stop using yeast. We are free to enjoy that soft bread. But He does command us to avoid other things: stealing, lying, adultery, disobedience to parents, and disobedience to the laws of our community. God knows what is best. It is wise for us to obey Him.

PRAYER THOUGHTS: Our heavenly Father, thank You for bread and all other good things You give us to enjoy. Help us to see Your wisdom and goodness in what You have commanded us not to do. May we learn to obey without complaining. In Jesus' name, amen.

September 6-12. **Kenton Smith** is a Christian minister and writer. He and his wife, Eileen, are parents to four grown daughters.

WHERE IS GOD LEADING US?

SCRIPTURE: Exodus 13:17-22

VERSE FOR TODAY: Lead me in thy truth, and teach me: for thou art the God of my salvation; on thee do I wait all the day (Psalm 25:5).

HYMN FOR TODAY: "He Leadeth Me"

The sky is filled with elephants, dinosaurs, and polar bears! Great cruise ships and submarines sail across it! But these objects are, of course, only clouds. In the cloud formations we see a resemblance to animals or ships or earthly scenes.

When the Israelites saw the pillar of cloud, what did it resemble? Did the children imagine it as a fluffy, moving mountain? Did it remind them of a camel carrying their goods? Did it remind them of Egypt's towering pyramids, only reaching higher into the heavens? One aspect of that cloudy pillar by day and fiery pillar by night was clear to all: it was God's way of leading and guiding the Israelites through the wilderness to the promised land.

If we had a pillar of cloud to lead us, where would it go? It would surely go before us to church on Sunday morning. At times it would direct us to a hospital or nursing home where someone needed our visit. And often it would lead us to the homes of neighbors or friends so that we could tell them about Jesus. And it would lead us to walk in kindness and love today.

But we do not need a pillar of cloud for that kind of guidance. We have the Bible, and God uses it to guide us where He wants us to go.

PRAYER THOUGHTS: Our gracious Father, we thank You for the blessed guidance we have in the Bible. Help us to use it in a very practical way in determining where You want us to go today and every day. In Jesus' name, amen.

GOD'S CHECKMATE

SCRIPTURE: Exodus 14:1-9

VERSE FOR TODAY: The wicked shall be turned into hell, and all the nations that forget God (Psalm 9:17).

HYMN FOR TODAY: "A Mighty Fortress"

A grandfather agreed to play chess with his seven-year-old grandson. The grandfather easily won the first two games. In game three he decided to dazzle his grandson with a mighty attack. Soon he surrounded the lad's king with a queen, a knight, and a couple of other pieces. He was one or two moves from ending the game and he was certain that victory was soon to be his.

The grandson examined the situation and then moved his queen the length of the board. He was not quite aware of what he had done. The man reluctantly pointed out to him that he had just placed his grandfather's king in checkmate. The grandfather was so intent on surrounding his grandson's king that he left his own king wide open to attack.

Pharaoh apparently thought he had the children of Israel hopelessly surrounded. However, he failed to take into account the wisdom and power of Israel's true and living God. In the end it was Pharaoh and Egypt who suffered defeat in the middle of the Red Sea.

And so it will be for any nation or person who dares to overlook the Almighty. God is capable of gaining His checkmate at any time.

PRAYER THOUGHTS: Our wise and mighty Father, we acknowledge how small and foolish in Your sight are the greatest of men. Teach us to humble ourselves before You and to put our complete confidence in Your power. Give us the wisdom to make the right moves in life. In Jesus' name, we pray, amen.

STAYING IN FORWARD GEAR

SCRIPTURE: Exodus 14:10-18

VERSE FOR TODAY: Forgetting those things which are behind, and reaching forth unto those things which are before, I press toward the mark for the prize of the high calling of God in Christ Jesus (Philippians 3:13, 14).

HYMN FOR TODAY: "I Am Resolved"

My daughters still laugh when they remember the car we had that would only go backward. It was a 1972 Buick LeSabre, which one afternoon lost its forward gears. To get it into our driveway I had to maneuver it around the block in reverse. Once it was in the driveway, it remained there until a tow-truck came for it.

Cars are meant to be able to go forward, and so are Christians. But some believers go in reverse. They return to habits and practices they should have left behind years ago. Some go back to using profane language or indulging in lies. Others resume old habits that are harmful to both the body and the soul.

Some Christians, like the Israelites at the Red Sea, are standing still when they should be moving forward. They are not improving their knowledge of God's Word. They are not growing in the effective use of prayer. And they are not developing skill in sharing their witness about Christ.

It is useful for the automobile to go forward. And it is fulfilling for a Christian to move forward in faith.

PRAYER THOUGHTS: We thank You, heavenly Father, that You have called us to move forward in the Christian life. Open our eyes to the tremendous challenges of spiritual growth and service that You have laid before us. In Jesus' name, amen.

WALKING BETWEEN WALLS OF WATER

SCRIPTURE: Exodus 14:19-25

VERSE FOR TODAY: For we walk by faith, not by sight. We make it our goal to please him, (2 Corinthians 5:7, 9, *New International Version*).

HYMN FOR TODAY: "I Know the Lord Has Made a Way"

Have you ever heard in a sermon or Bible lesson the following statement? "If the Lord tells you to jump through a wall, it is your job to jump, and it is the Lord's job to make a hole in the wall for you."

The Israelites marched toward the Red Sea at God's command, and He made an opening in the sea for them. What a long walk through the sea that must have been! According to Exodus 14:22, "the waters were a wall unto them on their right hand, and on their left." They must have trembled at those watery walls rising high above their heads on either side. They may have questioned whether or not those walls would remain in place. But by faith they marched on.

While we are not likely ever to walk between walls of water, we will face similar challenges. It takes faith to go on when we suffer a serious illness or struggle with the loss of a job or experience rejection because of our stand for Christ. It takes faith to continue to walk the path of holiness when those around us seem to be enjoying a life filled with worldliness. But, praise the Lord, He will respond to our faith and will make a way for us, as He did for the Israelites.

PRAYER THOUGHTS: Almighty God and Father, we are awed when we read in the Bible of Your powerful works. We realize we are not promised that waters will be parted for us, but open our eyes and help us to see the wonders You do perform for us every day. In Jesus' precious and wondrous name, amen.

WE CAN BE CONQUERORS!

SCRIPTURE: Exodus 14:26-31

VERSE FOR TODAY: But thanks be to God! He gives us the victory through our Lord Jesus Christ. Therefore, my dear brothers, stand firm. Let nothing move you (1 Corinthians 15:57, 58a, *New International Version*).

HYMN FOR TODAY: "Faith Is the Victory!"

Israel's problems with the Egyptians ended at the Red Sea. God's timing of the return of the waters of the Red Sea saved the Israelites and destroyed the Egyptians. But what would have happened if Pharaoh's army had not been destroyed by the returning waters?

Pharaoh's heart was so hardened against God that he would have kept on trying to defeat the Israelites. We can imagine him ordering his men into boats. We can picture him leading his troops in crossing the sea in those boats. And we can envision him commanding a fresh attack on the traveling Israelites.

But none of that occurred. God gave His people a decisive victory. As He had promised (Exodus 14:13), they would see the troublesome Egyptians no more. Their last look at them was of the charioteers and horsemen dead on the seashore. God fought for His children and all they needed to do was "to be still" (Exodus 14:4).

God wants to give us "the victory that overcometh the world, even our faith" (1 John 5:4). He aims for us to be "more than conquerors through him that loved us" (Romans 8:37). Are we ready to trust Him for such tremendous triumph?

PRAYER THOUGHTS: Our great God in Heaven, we praise You for the victories You have already enabled us to win. Guide us in waging spiritual warfare in the wisdom of Your Word and the power of Your Spirit. In Jesus' name, amen.

A CELEBRATION OF VICTORY

SCRIPTURE: Exodus 15:1-13

VERSE FOR TODAY: Thine, O LORD, is the greatness, and the power, and the glory, and the victory, and the majesty: (1 Chronicles 29:11).

HYMN FOR TODAY: "Come, Thou Almighty King"

It was once common at high school athletic contests to hear the cheering sections call out these words:

Victory! Victory is our cry!

V-I-C-T-O-R-Y!

That's the way you spell it,

Here's the way you yell it:

Victory! Victory! Victory!

That, in a sense, was what Moses and the Israelites did after God defeated the Egyptian army at the Red Sea. They celebrated the victory God had given. They anticipated future triumphs and said, "Fear and dread shall fall upon them" (*our enemies*); (read Exodus 15:14-16).

The book of Revelation contains some of the church's ultimate victory songs. Listen to the outcry found in Revelation 19:6, "Alleluia: for the Lord God omnipotent reigneth." Do you feel an irresistible urge to join with the heavenly choirs in the praise found in Revelation 4:11, "Thou art worthy, O Lord, to receive glory and honor and power?"

Our daily praise of the God almighty is getting us warmed up for that great victory celebration in Heaven in which we will participate. Alleluia!

PRAYER THOUGHTS: O God, our great Creator and Redeemer, we anticipate with joy the heavenly praises we shall raise to You and Your Son. Stir up in us even now a foretaste of that heavenly worship. In Jesus' name, amen.

ON EAGLES' WINGS

SCRIPTURE: Exodus 19:1-9

VERSE FOR TODAY: "You yourselves have seen what I did to Egypt, and how I carried you on eagles' wings and brought you to myself" (Exodus 19:4, *New International Version*).

HYMN FOR TODAY: "On Eagle's Wings"

One of the most remarkable behaviors in nature is the eagle's method of teaching its young to fly. Because eagles build their nests high in trees or on mountain cliffs, the eaglet must be able to fly to leave the nest, or it will tumble to a certain death. To encourage the eaglet to fly, the mother will take the youngster on her back and soar out of the nest. At a high enough altitude, the mother will flip the eaglet off her back, forcing it to fly. If it struggles, mother eagle will dive under it and catch the youngster, then resume the lesson. If the eaglet fails several times, the mother will know that it will never fly, and will allow it to fall to its death.

When God led the children of Israel out of the land of Egypt, He likened the Exodus to a mother eagle bearing her young on her wings. But, unlike an eagle, God never gave up on Israel, and He will never give up on us. We may desert His care, as the Israelites sometimes did, but if we are faithful, He will bear us through every trial until we soar with Him to heavenly heights.

PRAYER THOUGHTS: Father, we thank You for all Your loving care and daily guidance, leading us in the way we should go. Please lift us up when we grow weary, and teach us to soar, with Christ, above the cares of the world. Amen.

September 13-20. **Richard Koffarnus** is a college professor who lives in Moberly, Missouri and teaches at Central Christian College.

WARN THE PEOPLE!

SCRIPTURE: Exodus 19:16-25

VERSE FOR TODAY: And the LORD said to him, "Go down and warn the people so they do not force their way through to see the LORD and many of them perish" (Exodus 19:21, *New International Version*).

HYMN FOR TODAY: "Rescue the Perishing"

Late on April 18, 1775, Paul Revere and William Dawes left Boston for Lexington, Massachusetts, to warn John Hancock and Samuel Adams that British troops were marching to arrest the two patriots, as well as seize gunpowder and weapons stored at nearby Concord.

Revere rode into Lexington shortly after midnight. Dawes, who took a longer route, arrived thirty minutes later. After meeting with Hancock and Adams, Revere and Dawes rode on toward Concord.

They were captured before reaching the town, but other riders made it through. Because of the early warning, Hancock and Adams escaped, the British did not capture the stores at Concord, and the Minutemen turned out to chase the Regulars back to Boston.

One of the duties of the biblical prophets was to warn the people. Moses warned Israel not to come too close to God, and Ezekiel warned the people to repent, lest they die. Christians today have similar duties. We are called to warn our Christian brothers not to stray, and to warn the lost to repent and accept Christ lest they, too, die. As in the days of Paul Revere, a timely warning can mean the difference between victory and loss. Will you raise the call for Christ?

PRAYER THOUGHTS: O Lord, let us never forget our duty to warn the lost, so they can find salvation in Christ. In Jesus' name we pray. Amen.

NO OTHER GODS

SCRIPTURE: Exodus 20:1-11

VERSE FOR TODAY: "You shall have no other Gods before Me" (Exodus 20:3, *New International Version*).

HYMN FOR TODAY: "Holy, Holy, Holy"

Of all the great buildings of ancient Rome, including the Colosseum and the Hippodrome, the best-preserved major structure is the Pantheon. It is a huge cylinder with a great vaulted dome on top and a rectangular colonnaded porch in front. The dome is 142 feet in diameter, and the entire building is lighted through one opening, called an "oculus," in the center of the dome. This magnificent building was constructed by the Roman emperor Hadrian as a temple dedicated to all the Roman gods.

Why is the Pantheon still standing when all the other great Roman buildings are in ruins? Because in the early 7th century it was turned into a church, Santa Maria ad Martyres, and the Christians preserved the building.

When God delivered the first commandment to Israel, He was not simply saying that worshiping other gods is wrong; He was warning the people that pagan religions were worthless and guaranteed to bring about disaster. Isaiah 41:24 says of these gods, "You are less than nothing and your works are utterly worthless; he who chooses you is detestable." Like the Pantheon, the one who is dedicated to false gods is destined for ruin. Only Christ can save us from destruction.

PRAYER THOUGHTS: Heavenly Father, may we never forget the folly of worshiping false gods. Help us to keep our minds and hearts fixed on You, the true and living God. May we always be dedicated to You, alone. In the name of Jesus, our Savior, we pray. Amen.

SHAME, SHAME!

SCRIPTURE: Exodus 20:12-21

VERSE FOR TODAY: Moses said to the people, "Do not be afraid. God has come to test you, so that the fear of God will be with you to keep you from sinning" (Exodus 20:20, *New International Version*).

HYMN FOR TODAY: "Yield Not to Temptation"

Centuries ago, our forefathers made a spectacle of petty criminals by displaying them in stocks on the village green. The purpose was to shame the offender so he would not make the same mistake again, and to warn others what to expect if they broke the law.

Eventually shame was abandoned as a deterrent to crime. Today, there are judges who are returning to the disgrace of shame to teach first offenders a lesson. One judge made a shoplifter walk around town wearing a sign which described his offense. He hopes that public humiliation will make people afraid to commit future crimes.

When God appeared to Israel at Mount Sinai, the people were naturally frightened by His incredible display of supernatural power. Moses reassured them that fearing God was a healthy response because it would make them afraid to sin in the future, lest they fall under the Lord's terrible judgment.

Today we are accustomed to thinking of God as a loving Father. We sometimes forget that, although God does love us, He also has promised to punish unrepentant sinners at the judgment day. A healthy fear of God is still a good thing, if it deters us from sin.

PRAYER THOUGHTS: O God in Heaven, we tremble before Your power and we resolve to obey Your will to the best of our ability. Help us to follow in the footsteps of Your Son, Jesus. In His name, we pray. Amen.

SIMPLE ARITHMETIC

SCRIPTURE: Deuteronomy 4:1-8

VERSE FOR TODAY: Do not add to what I command you and do not subtract from it, but keep the commands of the LORD your God that I give you (Deuteronomy 4:2, *New International Version*).

HYMN FOR TODAY: "How Firm a Foundation"

I received a lesson in concrete mixing when a friend and I were pouring a foundation for a new deck on the back of our home. I learned that if you add too much water to the concrete, you get a mixture that is weak and cracks when it dries. And, if you don't add enough water, the concrete mix will be too dry, and the surface will crumble. However, if you get the concrete mix just right, you will have a durable foundation that will last for many years.

When God delivered His Law to the children of Israel at Mount Sinai, He was giving them a legal, moral, and religious foundation that would last indefinitely, if they would keep His commandments. But if they attempted to add to or subtract from the Law, they would cause the foundation to crack and the nation to crumble.

Today, Christians face similar risks if we add to or subtract from God's Word. The apostle Paul writes, "I want to remind you of the gospel I preached to you, which you received and on which you have taken your stand. By this gospel you are saved, if you hold firmly to the word. . . . " (1 Corinthians 15:1). Keep the foundation of your faith firm. Don't water down the gospel with man's traditions.

PRAYER THOUGHTS: Heavenly Father, help us to remember that Your Word is complete, and needs nothing added or deleted by us. May we always keep that foundation firm, because our salvation depends on it. In the name of Jesus, we pray. Amen.

TEACH YOUR CHILDREN WELL

SCRIPTURE: Deuteronomy 4:9-14

VERSE FOR TODAY: Only be careful, and watch yourselves closely so that you do not forget the things your eyes have seen or let them slip from your heart as long as you live. Teach them to your children and to their children after them (Deuteronomy 4:9, *New International Version*).

HYMN FOR TODAY: "A Christian Home"

As a college student, he joined a radical group called the "Young Hegelians," who opposed all organized religion. After he received his doctorate in philosophy, he became convinced that man had invented the idea of God. He called religion "the opiate of the people" and demanded its abolition. You know him as Karl Marx, the father of communism, but he was not always an enemy of God.

As a boy in Prussia, Karl was raised in a traditional Jewish home and worshipped regularly with his family in the local synagogue. After the family moved to a community with no synagogue, his father decided that the family should convert to Christianity, not because he believed the gospel, but because conversion would help his business. Karl was dutifully baptized, but, repulsed by his father's shallow faith, he soon became bitter and antagonistic toward all religion.

No wonder Moses counseled the Israelites to teach their children well the things of God. Imagine how the world might be different today if Heinrich Marx had taught his son to have a sincere faith in Christ.

PRAYER THOUGHTS: Heavenly Father, help us to live each day close to You and to Your Word. Let us be a godly example for our children. Give us wisdom to teach our children to be faithful to Your Word, loyal to Your Son, and devoted to Your kingdom. In Jesus' name, amen.

LIVE LONG AND PROSPER

SCRIPTURE: Deuteronomy 4:32-40

VERSE FOR TODAY: Keep his decrees and commands, which I am giving you today, so that it may go well with you and your children after you and that you may live long in the land of the LORD your God gives you for all time (Deuteronomy 4:40, *New International Version*).

HYMN FOR TODAY: "O That Will Be Glory"

In the old television series, *Star Trek*, Mr. Spock's favorite greeting was, "Live long and prosper." Long life and prosperity have always been viewed as important ingredients to human happiness. George Mason, a colonial American, wrote in Virginia's *Declaration of Rights*, in 1776, that all men have a natural right to "the enjoyment of life and liberty, with the means of acquiring and possessing property, and pursuing and obtaining happiness and safety." Thomas Jefferson compressed those thoughts, in the United States' *Declaration of Independence,* into the familiar phrase, "life, liberty, and the pursuit of happiness."

Long before Jefferson, God's Word already revealed the secret of a long and prosperous life: keep His decrees and commands. Now God never promised that believers would not have to face disappointment, disaster, and even death, but He did promise that those who trust in Him would have more than long life and prosperity; they would have eternal life and blessings. "Jesus said unto her, I am the resurrection, and the life: he that believeth in me, though he were dead, yet shall he live" (John 11:25). For Christians, a daily greeting should be, "Live eternally and be blessed!"

PRAYER THOUGHTS: Thank You, Lord, for granting us eternal life through Jesus. Truly, this is infinitely greater than all the world's riches combined. Amen.

YOU TOO CAN BE A PRIEST

SCRIPTURE: Exodus 40:1-15

VERSE FOR TODAY: And thou shalt put upon Aaron the holy garments, and anoint him, and sanctify him; that he may minister unto me in the priest's office (Exodus 40:13).

HYMN FOR TODAY: "More Holiness Give Me"

When Aaron was set aside for the priesthood, they took the blood of a ram and put it on the lobe of his right ear, and on the thumb of his right hand and on the great toe of his right foot (Leviticus 8:23). It symbolized the fact that he was to listen for the voice of God, do the work of God, and walk in the ways of God. Today, the priesthood of all believers is a fundamental doctrine of all Protestant churches (1 Peter 2:5; Revelation 1:6). A group of churches wanted to catch the attention of believers in the Roman Catholic Church. They printed a tract entitled, *You, Too, Can Be A Priest.*

We are to listen for the voice of God, and do the work of God, and walk in the ways of God. Those priests wore a garment of gold, blue, purple, and scarlet. On the front of their turbans, a golden plate was engraved with the words: "Holiness Unto the Lord." It was not meant for show. It was to remind people that holiness is more important than pomp or ceremony. So we today who are priests of the most High God must be holy. We wear no golden plate. We need none. Our lives proclaim it.

PRAYER THOUGHTS: Thank You, God, for being a holy and forgiving God. Help us as we try harder to reflect Your holiness. Through Christ our Lord, amen.

September 20-26. **Robert Shannon** has enjoyed a varied career as minister, missionary, and college professor. He is now enjoying retirement in Valle Crucis, North Carolina.

I'LL DO WHAT YOU WANT ME TO DO

SCRIPTURE: Exodus 40:16-20

VERSE FOR TODAY: Moses did everything just as the LORD commanded him (Exodus 40:16, *New International Version*).

HYMN FOR TODAY: "Trust and Obey"

The instructions that precede and follow verse 16 of Exodus 40 seem needlessly detailed. Why is God so concerned about little things? There may be many reasons. One is that everything was highly symbolic. Another reason is that it showed the willingness of Moses to obey God in all details.

Most of us are willing to follow God in general. It is when God gets specific that we have problems. "Love the Lord your God" seems reasonable enough, until we are asked to be faithful in worship, to give a tenth of our income, to be prepared to sacrifice and to suffer. "Love your neighbor" seems proper enough until we are told to lend, give, pray, and forgive. Then it seems burdensome. The problem is in the details. But God will not accept those who honor him in general but dishonor in specifics. We are, after all, first tempted to commit the little sins. Later on, after we've come to accept them as part of our lives, we'll be tempted to bigger sins. We are first tempted to omit the little virtues. Later on we'll be tempted to forget the cardinal virtues, too. Life and character often turn on very small hinges. Take care of the little things and you will be strong when you must face the big temptations, the big tasks, the big opportunities.

PRAYER THOUGHTS: O God, we thank You for being concerned about little things. We know that nothing is too small or too great to bring before You in prayer. Now give us a mind that mirrors Yours. Save us from little sins. In Jesus' name. Amen.

WHITER THAN SNOW

SCRIPTURE: Exodus 40:21-33

VERSE FOR TODAY: They washed whenever they entered the Tent of Meeting or approached the altar (Exodus 40:32, *New International Version***).**

HYMN FOR TODAY: "Are You Washed in the Blood"

It was a symbolic washing. Moses and Aaron and all the priests washed their hands and feet before they entered the place of worship. Surely it was meant to evoke in them a sense of reverence. Surely it was to impress those who watched with the sacredness of the place and the sacredness of worship. Still today, Moslem men wash their hands and feet before they enter the mosque. They do it even if their hands and feet are already clean. It is symbolic.

For us, this is an illustration in reverse. Ours is a spiritual washing. We find our cleansing in the very acts of worship. Often we sing about being "washed in the blood." Of course, that is a contradiction in purely physical terms. It is only in a spiritual, symbolic and metaphorical sense that blood cleanses. It is in this inward sense that we sing, "Wash me and I shall be whiter than snow." We understand that sin stains. We recognize, as David did, that one must come into the presence of a holy God with "clean hands and a pure heart" (Psalm 24:4). But for Christians, worship itself is a cleansing process. Faced with the holiness of God, and confessing all our sins, we are cleansed. How beautifully this is illustrated in today's text—even though it is an illustration in reverse.

PRAYER THOUGHTS: Dear Lord, forgive our pride. Forgive our failure to see our own sins. Show us where we need to repent, and as we repent, make us clean. For Jesus' sake. Amen.

COUNT YOUR BLESSINGS

SCRIPTURE: Leviticus 26:1-13

VERSE FOR TODAY: And I will walk among you, and will be your God, and ye shall be my people (Leviticus 26:12).

HYMN FOR TODAY: "In the Garden"

The Scripture for today begins with a prohibition against idols and ends with a promise of God's presence. The children of Israel are urged to count their blessings. It is appropriate that the rehearsal of God's blessings should follow a verse about idols. What has an idol ever done for anyone? The answer is, "Nothing." What has the living God done for us? The answer is, "Everything." God has given His people good weather and a full harvest. They have food to eat. They live in safety, in peace, and without fear. They have the respect of others and the opportunity to worship. The crowning blessing is that God will acknowledge them as His people and will walk among them and be their God. Often, when we count our blessings, we count only the physical, visible, tangible blessings. We forget the spiritual, invisible, and intangible blessings. Having counted our blessings, we conclude with the best of all blessings, expressed in the chorus of the hymn, "In the Garden."

> And He walks with me
> And He talks with me
> And He tells me I am His own
> —C. Austin Miles

PRAYER THOUGHTS: Oh Lord, forgive us when we have failed to thank You for the best of all blessings. You are our greatest blessing. Thank You for walking with us and calling us Your people. Help us to walk as Your children. In Jesus' name, we pray. Amen.

THE IMPORTANCE OF SMALL WORDS

SCRIPTURE: Leviticus 26:14-22

VERSE FOR TODAY: "**If after all this you will not listen to me, I will punish you**" (Leviticus 26:18, *New International Version*).

HYMN FOR TODAY: "Yield Not to Temptation"

The little word "if" keeps appearing in today's Scripture:
If you will not listen to me—verse 14;
If you reject my decrees—verse 15;
If after all this you will not listen—verse 18;
If you remain hostile toward me—verse 21.

The choice is ours. If we reject God and do not listen to Him then He will allow sin to run its awful course. If we listen and obey, He will intervene in the course of nature for our good. He will intervene in the affairs of men and nations for our good. God's promises are conditional. Thankfully, His warnings are also conditional.

The choice is ours. God would not be fair with us if He did not warn us ahead of time of the consequences of our choices. The problem with so many today is that they want to make choices and then avoid the natural and obvious consequences of those choices. That's impossible. It's impossible in the natural scheme of things, and a just God tells us it's impossible in the heavenly scheme of things. We need to learn, and teach our children, that all our deeds have consequences. We cannot blame God when we make the wrong choices and then suffer because of them.

PRAYER THOUGHTS: O Father, we see Your love in the guidance You give us. Bless us with the wisdom and strength to follow Your plan for living and not our own. In the name of Jesus, amen.

PHANTOM FEARS

SCRIPTURE: Leviticus 26:27-39

VERSE FOR TODAY: "If in spite of this you still do not listen to me but continue to be hostile toward me, then in my anger I will be hostile toward you" (Leviticus 26:27, 28).

HYMN FOR TODAY: "Gentle Shepherd"

If you remember your first lessons in geometry you will recall the word *axiom*. An *axiom* is a truth that does not need to be proven. It is a self-evident truth. It is an axiom of faith that God is just. If God is not just then there is no point in anybody trying to please Him. We must begin here. Therefore, any interpretation of Scripture that makes God appear to be unjust must be wrong. Sometimes God appears unjust because we do not have all of the facts. We know so little of situations far removed from us by both time and distance. If today's verses seem harsh, we must hold firm to the fundamental truth: the true and living God is just.

The closing verses, though, are plain enough. Disobedience brings fear, and it should. Some of the things we fear are reasonable. But we are also plagued by phantom fears. Some will flee and fall though no one is pursing them. We call these phantom fears *phobias*. If we rebel and are hostile toward God, we have reason to fear. If we listen to God, if we are not hostile toward him, then we need not be afraid. But over and over again the Bible says, "Fear not!" First John 4:18 says "perfect love casts out fear." Of course, our love is always imperfect. It is God's perfect love that casts out fear.

PRAYER THOUGHTS: Dear God, we thank You for both Your justice and Your love. Help us to fear the things we ought to fear, but deliver us from phantom fears. In Christ's name, amen.

THE GOD WHO REMEMBERS

SCRIPTURE: Leviticus 26:40-46

VERSE FOR TODAY: I will remember my covenant . . . and I will remember the land (Leviticus 26:42).

HYMN FOR TODAY: "Great is Thy Faithfulness"

Two words are important for us today. The first is *covenant*. When God makes a covenant with man, it is simply a contract. The second word is *remember*. We use the word *remember* in more than one way. So does the Bible. We say, "I will remember you in my will." We say, "Remember me to your parents." In neither case does remembering have anything to do with forgetting. That's the case with today's Scripture. God did not ever forget His covenant with His people. In fact the only thing the Bible says that God forgets is the forgiven sin. Hebrews 10:17 quotes Jeremiah 31:34, "Their sins and iniquities will I remember no more."

In today's verses, *remember* does not mean to recall, but to bear in mind or to keep in mind. It was God's covenant that He kept in mind. We must do the same. God made covenants with Noah, Abraham, Isaac, and Jacob. He kept every one. His final covenant with us was made through Jesus Christ. We call it the New Covenant. It can be called the New Testament, as in "Last Will and Testament." God will be faithful to keep His part of the covenant (contract). We must be faithful to keep our part of the covenant. If we fail to keep the covenant, we cannot expect to enjoy the blessings it was intended to bring.

PRAYER THOUGHTS: O Lord, we praise You for Your faithfulness. Give us grace to keep our part of the Covenant. Through Christ our Lord, amen.

FILLED WITH HIS PRESENCE

SCRIPTURE: Exodus 40:34-38

VERSE FOR TODAY: For we know that, if our earthly house of this tabernacle were dissolved, we have a building of God, an house not made with hands, eternal in the Heavens (2 Corinthians 5:1).

HYMN FOR TODAY: "Since Jesus Came Into My Heart"

God is so good to us! When He wants to teach a spiritual truth, He gets out His paintbrush and paints a word picture.

Moses had been busy for some time building a tabernacle or tent for God's dwelling place. In today's Scripture text the work is completed, but the building is standing dark and empty. What a picture of fallen man! He was created for fellowship with God, but he lost the light of God's presence when he fell into sin.

Until Jesus came, mankind was like that empty tent with no inner light to guide them, and no way to return to God. When He died and rose again, Jesus made it possible for God's Spirit to live in the hearts of men. Just as God's glory left the first man, Adam, when he sinned, so the glory of God left Jesus when He hung on that cross. There the Lord became sin for us. On the third day, the glory of God filled the person of the resurrected Christ.

When we receive Christ as our Savior, His glory fills the temple of our hearts giving us light in our souls.

PRAYER THOUGHTS: Heavenly Father, thank You for bringing us out of darkness into Your marvelous light. Help us to see the needs of others who are still in the bondage of sin. Touch our lips that we may share the good news of deliverance to them. In Jesus' name, amen.

September 27-30. **Bud Atkinson** restores vintage Mustangs and writes Southern Gospel Music. He and his wife of 38 years live in Conyers, Georgia.

FOLLOWING THE LEADER

SCRIPTURE: Numbers 9:15-23

VERSE FOR TODAY: Jesus saith unto him, I am the way, the truth, and the life: no man cometh unto the Father, but by me (John 14:6).

HYMN FOR TODAY: "He Leadeth Me"

Have you ever asked for directions to a certain destination, and the person simply says, "Just follow me; I'll take you there"? Remember how you kept your eyes riveted on his car? You were in strange territory, and you had to follow closely because without that person's leadership you would have been lost.

In today's Scripture passage, the children of Israel were traveling to the land of promise, but they didn't know the way. So they played a grown-up version of "Follow the Leader." Wherever God's presence went, they followed.

You and I are on a spiritual journey to Heaven, but, without Christ, we don't know the way. Today we don't have a visible cloud to follow. We walk by faith and not by sight. Still, God has not left us to make our own way through the wilderness of this world. He has given us Jesus to follow. He has given us His Word to show us the way.

Isn't it wonderful that God has chosen to dwell within us in the person of the Holy Spirit? We must stay close to Him and be ready to "go" or "stay" at His command. We are following our "Leader" into the land of promise.

PRAYER THOUGHTS: Heavenly Father, we are strangers on this earth and pilgrims traveling through a strange land. Help us to keep our eyes on the Lord today, and to let Him guide each step of our way. Help us to be attentive to His "still, small voice" for He alone knows the way home. Let us follow Jesus, our leader. In His holy name, we pray. Amen.

MOVING DAY!

SCRIPTURE: Numbers 10:29-36

VERSE FOR TODAY: Wherefore the law was our schoolmaster to bring us unto Christ, that we might be justified by faith (Galatians 3:24).

HYMN FOR TODAY: "On Jordan's Stormy Banks"

Moving day! The children of Israel were about to leave Sinai behind them. Moving day is a good time to stop and take an inventory. Are we sure we have everything we need for the journey? Are we carrying some unnecessary things that will weigh us down and hinder our progress?

Just as a person who is moving should take one last look around the house before leaving, perhaps we should take a last look at Sinai. Can we learn from the Israelites experience?

At some time in our life, we will all have to face our own Sinai. It is there we learn the awesome holiness of God. There we find the Ten Commandments—so pure, no honest person would dare say, "I have kept them all."

You may be shocked to find you can't keep the commandments, but it doesn't surprise God. You see, God gave the Law for that purpose; to show us ourselves. The Ten Commandments act as a mirror, revealing the "dirt" on our faces. Still, we shouldn't try to wash in a mirror. We need the water of the Word for that.

Moving day! Don't dare leave Sinai without Christ as your personal Savior!

PRAYER THOUGHTS: Holy God, we thank You for the words Jesus uttered as He was dying in our place on the cross. He cried out, "It is finished," and we know that You accepted His work on our behalf because You raised Him from the dead. We know that through Him we can have eternal life. Thank You that we are accepted in Him. In His holy name, we pray. Amen.

YOU PROMISED!

SCRIPTURE: Psalm 105:1-15

VERSE FOR TODAY: For ever, O LORD, thy word is settled in heaven (Psalm 119:89).

HYMN FOR TODAY: "Standing On The Promises"

"But Daddy, you promised!" Do those words sound familiar? You made a promise, and your child is not about to let you forget. At times we make promises we can't keep. Sometimes there's a legitimate reason—such as the time you said you would take your son fishing only to wake up to find it raining "cats and dogs."

God never breaks His promise! Years ago God made a covenant, or in modern terms, a promise, to a man named Abraham. It concerned a land called Canaan and a King who would be born of Abraham's seed. In today's lesson, God is reminding the descendants of Abraham that they are to inherit the land by faith.

God has also made some promises to us through His Son, Jesus Christ. He said, "I will never leave you nor forsake you" (Hebrews 13:5). He provided for the children of Israel in the wilderness, and He will provide for us. His Word says, "But my God shall supply all your need according to his riches in glory by Christ Jesus" (Philippians 4:19).

Since God's Word clearly tells us He will provide all our needs, we may go to Him whenever we are in want and say to Him respectfully, "But, Father, You promised!"

PRAYER THOUGHTS: We thank You, Father, for the exceeding great and precious promises of Your Word. Thank You for being our constant companion as we walk this pilgrim way. We are thankful that You always keep Your promises. Most of all we are grateful that Your Word is eternal. We pray this prayer in the name of Jesus. Amen.

My Prayer Notes

_____

_____

_____

_____

_____

_____

_____

_____

_____

_____

_____

_____

_____

_____

_____

_____

_____

_____

DEVOTIONS™

October

photo by Chuck Perry

October 1

A PRISONER, A PURPOSE, AND A PLAN

SCRIPTURE: Psalm 105:16-25

VERSE FOR TODAY: We know that all things work together for good to them that love God, to them who are the called according to His purpose (Romans 8:28).

HYMN FOR TODAY: "Where He Leads Me"

Joseph must have thought the Lord had forsaken him when he was sold into slavery. Still, he made the best of his situation until he was given a position in Potiphar's house.

Life was good until the day his convictions caused him to be tossed into prison. Now, how could being in prison in a strange land be the will of God? Hadn't he tried to live for the Lord? Poor Joseph! Look what trying to do right did for him!

Jacob and his sons must have wondered why God allowed such a severe famine in the land. After all, weren't they set apart for God? God had made such glowing promises to this family. What could His purpose be in allowing this tragedy?

Are you going through some trying times today? Have you reached the point of saying with Jacob, "All these things are against me" (Genesis 42:36)? Ah! If we could only see what God sees! You and I are looking at the individual events while God says, "All things work together for good" (Romans 3:28). He may use an unusual circumstance to provide for us. Trust Him; He knows what's best for us!

PRAYER THOUGHTS: Dear Father, we have only to look back at the many ways You've provided for us in times past to know You are faithful. Sometimes You weave some dark threads into the pattern of our lives. Help us to know that You do all things for our ultimate good. Amen.

October 1-3. **Bud Atkinson** restores vintage Mustangs and writes Southern Gospel Music. He and his wife of 38 years live in Conyers, Georgia.

WHEN GOD SAYS, "ENOUGH"

SCRIPTURE: Psalm 105:26-36

VERSE FOR TODAY: For the great day of his wrath is come; and who shall be able to stand? (Revelation 6:17).

HYMN FOR TODAY: "Work, for the Night Is Coming"

Everything was going wrong! God's children were in bondage. That was bad enough, but now it seems that Moses and Aaron had angered the king. As a result, the people were forced to work twice as hard as before. They were God's chosen people. They must have asked many times: "Why doesn't God do something?"

The Egyptians must have laughed at these so-called, "People of God." After all, God didn't seem to be doing much to help them out. The Egyptians had all the "good things" of this world while the children of Israel were a bunch of slaves!

Does this sound familiar? Sure it does! Things haven't changed all that much in the past few thousand years! Christians are often perplexed and sometimes in poverty while that worldly crowd seems to prosper.

Just as the Lord waited until the iniquity of the Egyptian nation was full, so He is waiting today. God's children will not always be in bondage. That worldly crowd will not always be in control. There will come a day when God will say to His Son, "It is enough; go and bring my people out of Egypt." The Lord will return, and the long night of our bondage will be over!

PRAYER THOUGHTS: Dear heavenly Father, help us to realize that the hour is late and soon the judgment of this world will begin. Show us the fields already white to harvest. Help us to do our part to warn people of the coming judgment. Help us to tell the world about Jesus, in whose name we pray. Amen.

ON THE WAY HOME

SCRIPTURE: Psalm 105:37-45

VERSE FOR TODAY: He brought forth his people with joy, and his chosen with gladness: . . . that they might observe his statutes, and keep his laws. Praise ye the Lord (Psalm 105:43, 45).

HYMN FOR TODAY: "We're Marching to Zion"

Moses was raised in Egypt by his biological Hebrew mother as the privileged son of the Pharaoh's daughter. He may have been in line for the throne of Egypt. However, as an adult, Moses had a choice to make. He had heard the clear call of God instructing him to lead the children of Israel out of Egyptian bondage. Moses tried to make excuses about his ability, and asked God, "Who am I that I should go unto Pharaoh, and that I should bring forth the children of Israel out of Egypt?" (Exodus 3:11). God gave Moses the answer—the same answer that He gives to us when we are asked to do His work. "I will be with you" (Exodus 3:12, *New International Version*). When God calls us, He is with us in the task He has assigned.

The world is plunged into spiritual darkness. People are blinded by Satan and are held captive by sin. All around us are people who need the love and salvation that comes only through Christ Jesus.

You and I who have heard the Gospel are on our way to the Promised Land called Heaven. What a blessed time to be alive when the whole world seems to be a mission field. Let's share the truth that will set them free.

PRAYER THOUGHTS: Holy Father, help us to see a world that is perishing without any hope. Help us to look with compassion as You did when You walked the earth, long ago. Give us boldness to speak of You. In the name of Jesus, we pray. Amen.

SEEING GOD

SCRIPTURE: Numbers 12:1-9

VERSE FOR TODAY: "He [Moses] beholds the form of the LORD" (**Numbers 12:8,** *New Revised Standard Version*).

HYMN FOR TODAY: "Battle Hymn of the Republic"

There is a small stream that runs through the farmlands near to where I used to live. It was a beautiful setting, especially in the spring and fall. It was quiet and peaceful. The running water made a gentle sound as it cascaded over a small rock dam. It was my special place to go when the world seemed a bit too much for me. It was a time to hear the Lord as He spoke through creation.

Many of us want to see God face to face. We want to hear a booming, heavenly voice but only a few people see God in person. Moses was special and God spoke to him face to face.

Too often as we struggle to follow God, we miss those wonderful opportunities the Almighty prepares for our listening enjoyment. We all need to have moments beside the still water as we open our hearts and souls to the Creator God. I find God in the spring as all nature bursts forth anew and again in the fall in the midst of a bountiful harvest. It is a precious time of communing with God. It is a time of renewal and spiritual awakening that can sustain a person through many of the trials of life.

PRAYER THOUGHTS: O most wonderful and magnificent God, may we walk this earth in union with Your creation. Help us to hear Your voice in the wind and see Your words spring forth in rustling leaves and the clouds in the sky. In the name of Your holy Son, Jesus. Amen.

October 4-9. **G. William Zuspan** is professor emeritus in Engineering at Drexel University where he taught for 37 years. He and his wife, Marilyn, have five children and 13 grandchildren.

PLEADING FOR MERCY

SCRIPTURE: Numbers 12:10-15

VERSE FOR TODAY: "Moses cried to the LORD, "O God, please heal her" (Numbers 12:13, *New Revised Standard Version*).

HYMN FOR TODAY: "God Will Take Care of You"

Several years ago I was called for jury duty. I really didn't want to go but my sense of duty prevailed. It was the first time I had been in a courtroom. I was nervous because I knew I would have to make a decision affecting someone's life.

The defendant was a young mother who had become involved in drugs and committed the crime of robbery. As her lawyer began to present the case it was obvious that the woman was not a hardened criminal but someone who had been trapped by circumstances. The lawyer ended with a plea for mercy. He was interceding on her behalf.

The judge on the bench that day called a meeting of the lawyers. He dismissed the jury and showed mercy. He placed the young woman on probation.

Miriam had sinned against God. She had spoken against Moses which angered God. Moses, feeling compassion, interceded with God on behalf of Miriam.

Each of us sins and has need of someone to intercede for us with God. Jesus does that for us. He presents our case to God and pleads for mercy. The true and living God is a merciful God, thus we are granted forgiveness of our sins.

PRAYER THOUGHTS: Awesome God, as we walk this life, may we be compassionate and plead for forgiveness for those who sin against us. May God's Spirit be with us always, giving us strength to go against the ways of the world. In the name of Jesus, we pray. Amen.

WALKING WITH GOD

SCRIPTURE: Numbers 13:1-16

VERSE FOR TODAY: "Obey my voice, and I will be your God, and you shall be my people; and walk only in the way that I command you" (Jeremiah 7:23, *New Revised Standard Version*).

HYMN FOR TODAY: "I'll Go Where You Want Me to Go"

Some years ago we had a dog in our home. He simply would not obey any command we gave him. It made life miserable for the whole family. When company came he nipped at their feet and at times tore at a person's pant leg. In desperation we took him to obedience school where both the dog and family members learned their role. Upon graduation we had a truly obedient dog. Life for all of us was much more pleasant. Even the dog seemed happier.

God's Word gives guidance. We are to learn His Law and obey. The psalmist says, "Commit your way to the Lord; trust in him and he will do this: He will make your righteousness shine like the dawn, (Psalm 37:5, 6, *New International Version*). When we live by God's commands, we experience an internal satisfaction that brings true joy to the soul.

An obedient dog is a delight to its master. A person who struggles to be obedient to God's commands will reap the benefits. Walking with God brings many benefits. Let's enjoy the blessing today!

PRAYER THOUGHTS: Most merciful and powerful almighty God, we admit that sometimes it is difficult to be obedient. Help us to be aware of our disobedience and give us the strength to obey You. Help us to walk in the ways that You command. We pray this prayer in the name of Jesus, our Savior. Amen.

BEING SENT

SCRIPTURE: Numbers 13:17-24

VERSE FOR TODAY: Moses sent them to spy out the land of Canaan (Numbers 13:17, *New Revised Standard Version*).

HYMN FOR TODAY: "So Send I You"

Being asked to go somewhere you've never been before is oftentimes frightening. My wife and I were asked to go to Haiti for a short-term mission project. We were to help start a feeding program at an already established school, and to develop a small business for the local people. We knew it was a good thing to do and felt called by God to go. However, our anxiety level was high for we knew nothing about the culture nor the language. There was little time for preparing ourselves for the unknown surroundings.

However, being sent is a wonderful spiritual experience. One has to depend on God for everything. In Haiti there were no hospitals, and the nearest doctor was a day's journey away. We learned that God does care for our needs.

God told Moses to send men into a country that was alien to them. In their journey they would encounter a culture that was new and strange to them. They would have to depend on God for their food and water. They had to have faith in God to protect them in these new surroundings.

Being involved in new adventures for the Lord is a faith experience unequaled by any other activity. It is when we go beyond our comfort zone that we then experience the power of our true and living God in life.

PRAYER THOUGHTS: Heavenly God, we seek Your voice. Help us to depend upon Your presence and power. In the name of Jesus, our Savior, we pray. Amen.

STUMBLING BLOCKS

SCRIPTURE: Numbers 13:25-33

VERSE FOR TODAY: So then, each of us will give an account of himself to God. Therefore let us stop passing judgment on one another. Instead, make up your mind not to put any stumbling block or obstacle in your brother's way (Romans 14:12, 13, *New International Version*).

HYMN FOR TODAY: "Are You Washed in the Blood?"

We lived in a two-story condominium when our oldest child, Johnny, was about four years old. He and his sister had many toys. Keeping them in order was always a chore. One day, Johnny was running down the stairs. At the bottom of the stairs were some blocks strewn around. He stumbled, fell, and hit his head on the edge of a table. This caused a large cut which bled profusely.

There are many occurrences in life that can be stumbling blocks to our spiritual growth. In the Scripture text for today, the men who had been sent out as spies to the land of Canaan were fearful of the new land and told lies about the land. This news sent panic among the people and they did not want to follow God's plan for them. Likewise our actions and our words can keep others from going forward in their faith walk. Paul points out that harsh judgment of others can turn them from the Lord. As we fellowship with believers, all our words and actions of encouragement help one another to grow stronger in faith.

PRAYER THOUGHTS: Almighty and everlasting God, we acknowledge that You are a most gracious and compassionate God. Teach us to have both compassion and understanding for those we meet today. Help us to live in such a way that we are not a stumbling block to others. Help us to show compassion and love to all we meet today. In the name of Jesus we pray. Amen.

NOT TO FEAR

SCRIPTURE: Numbers 14:1-12

VERSE FOR TODAY: Only, do not rebel against the LORD; and do not fear the people of the land (Numbers 14:9, *New Revised Standard Version*).

HYMN FOR TODAY: "Faith Is the Victory"

Situations arise in life where fear is a natural and expected reaction. In many instances it helps us deal with the danger. There are many accounts of people showing super-human strength during traumatic accidents.

Fear can also overcome us and cause us to freeze. We may become so anxious we are unable to think clearly. Several years ago, I entered the hospital for major surgery. Several months before the scheduled surgery, I began to feel fear creeping into my thoughts. As the day neared, the fear mounted and I was on the verge of canceling the surgery. Then I turned to the Bible for the wonderful Words of assurance that we are in God's hands. We have no reason to fear.

My fear calmed when I thought of words to Christian hymns. In the operating room, just before I was given the anesthetic, I was singing in my thoughts, "We are standing on holy ground, and I know that there are angels all around." I slipped off into sleep knowing that God was present and I had nothing to fear.

Moses sent his people out into the unknown to face people who might do them harm, but he reminded them that God would be with them and they should not fear.

PRAYER THOUGHTS: O Father, help us to feel Your presence. Give us courage and strength to face the future. May we be able to live our lives in service to You, knowing that You will provide our needs. We pray in the name of Jesus, our Savior. Amen.

WHEN THE ROAD GETS ROCKY

SCRIPTURE TEXT: Numbers 14:13-25

VERSE FOR TODAY: In accordance with your great love, forgive the sin of these people, just as you have pardoned them from the time they left Egypt until now (Numbers 14:19, *New International Version*).

HYMN FOR TODAY: "O For a Thousand Tongues"

As our bus rumbled out of Cairo toward Mount Sinai in the early morning hours, I looked intently out the window. Many in the bus dozed, but I wanted to miss nothing. For years I had wanted to see the Sinai peninsula, the "wilderness" through which the children of Israel wandered for forty years.

It is hard, cruel country. There is little water and much desert. Ragged hills are covered with loose, rough stones. Walking seems well nigh impossible.

That bus trip left me much more sympathetic toward the Israelites than I had been before. I began to understand why they longed for the fertile land of the Nile. I could almost hear their grumbling as they walked through this tortuous terrain.

As I read in Scripture of God's anger toward their rebellious and complaining attitudes, I wonder about His judgment on us. Though God has given us so much, we grumble about the weather, about the government, about what we have to eat, about the sins of others, about our taxes, about our jobs, and about things in the church. I even grumble about grumblers. Would that my mouth better reflected my trust in the providence of God.

PRAYER THOUGHTS: Father, we often lift our voices in complaint when they should be raised in adoration. Give us grateful and discerning hearts to trust You. In Jesus' name, amen.

October 10. **Dr. Ward Patterson** is a professor at Cincinnati Bible College in Cincinnati, Ohio.

PLEASE TAKE MY HAND

SCRIPTURE: Deuteronomy 1:1-8

VERSE FOR TODAY: Behold, I have set the land before you: go in and possess the land which the LORD sware unto your fathers, Abraham, Isaac, and Jacob, to give unto them and to their seed after them (Deuteronomy 1:8).

HYMN FOR TODAY: "Trust and Obey"

We often face challenges. As youth, we may be nervous before a big game. Will we play our best? Will we score? As adults, the first day on a new job may intimidate us. We may wonder what our coworkers will be like, whether the boss will like us or whether we'll be able to do the job. But if someone who has gone through the same experience pulls us aside and tells us what to expect, we are no longer so fearful. That person may remind us that even though we may have made mistakes in the past, we can do better this time. That person may remind us that God goes with us in our new experience.

That's what Moses did for the children of Israel when they were about to enter the Promised Land. He had a heart-to-heart talk with them about their past failures, and reminded them of their present opportunities. He told them to take courage. God had called them to this mission and God keeps His promises.

Just as Moses' words encouraged the Israelites, the words of Scripture encourage us today. They remind us that God forgives our mistakes.

PRAYER THOUGHTS: Dear Father, give us the courage to go wherever You call us to go. Thank You for being with us in each experience of life, both the good and the bad. In Jesus' name. Amen.

October 11-13, 15-17. **Shirley G. Brosius** serves on the faculty of the Evangelical School of Theology in Myerstown, Pennsylvania. She and her husband have two adult sons and one granddaughter.

WHO ARE YOU LEADING?

SCRIPTURE: Deuteronomy 1:9-18

VERSE FOR TODAY: Ye shall not respect persons in judgment; but ye shall hear the small as well as the great; ye shall not be afraid of the face of man; for the judgment is God's: and the cause that is too hard for you, bring it unto me, and I will hear it (Deuteronomy 1:17).

HYMN FOR TODAY: "I Would Be True"

A young Christian mother once told me that she did not try to teach her children about spiritual things at home because she was afraid she might not do a good job. She thought she should leave such important work to Sunday school teachers who were more qualified. I assured her that God calls us to teach and lead our families, and He blesses our efforts as we do the best we can. He helps us to fulfill the responsibilities He gives us—in the church and in the home.

Perhaps Moses had to reassure his young leaders too. Some may have been hesitant to accept such a lofty position because they didn't feel as wise as Moses or as spiritually mature. But Moses reassured them that he would support them in their work. God had called them and they could do the job.

All of us are called to serve as leaders at some time in our lives. At such times we can look to more mature Christians for advice. Just as Moses did, they will probably offer to support us and remind us to be fair to those whom we serve. By God's grace we can assume leadership responsibility with confidence because God goes with us.

PRAYER THOUGHTS: Heavenly Father, we know that being a Christian carries with it a responsibility to lead others in Your ways. Give us the confidence we need to do a good job whether we are called to lead in the school, the home, the workplace, or the church. We want to be role models to others. In Jesus' name. Amen.

WHAT DID YOU SAY?

SCRIPTURE: Deuteronomy 1:19-33

VERSE FOR TODAY: Notwithstanding ye would not go up, but rebelled against the commandment of the LORD your God: (Deuteronomy 1:26).

HYMN FOR TODAY: "Lord, Speak to Me"

From a distance, ear plugs and hearing aids can look very similar, but they are used for two entirely different purposes. Ear plugs protect our ears by shutting out loud noises, whereas hearing aids amplify sound. They help those who are hearing impaired to hear more clearly.

It seems as though the people of Israel were wearing ear plugs when they should have been wearing hearing aids. They knew God had sent them on a mission to conquer a new land. They had seen His Presence travel with them in the form of a cloud by day and a fire by night. But when the spies reported that giants lived in the new land, they were afraid. No matter what Moses said, they wouldn't listen. They shut their ears. They refused to obey God.

Sin and disobedience in our lives may block out God's nudgings just as ear plugs block sound. But the Word of God and the Holy Spirit work together and serve as a hearing aid. When we get rid of sin, read the Word of God and pray, He can amplify the whisperings of God's voice to our hearts. He nudges us to put our thoughts into action. He encourages us to respond to God's Word by depending on God's promises and obeying God's commands.

PRAYER THOUGHTS: Dear Father, forgive us for the times we may have shut out Your voice. Help us to recognize and respond to You. Perhaps even today You want us to speak to someone of You or to reach out to meet a need. Thank You for the Presence of Your Holy Spirit Who amplifies Your voice to our hearts and heads. Amen.

WHEN GOD TURNS A DEAF EAR

SCRIPTURE TEXT: Deuteronomy 1:34-45

VERSE FOR TODAY: You came back and wept before the Lord, but he paid no attention to your weeping and turned a deaf ear to you (Deuteronomy 1:45).

HYMN FOR TODAY: "I'll Go Where You Want Me to Go"

Fear! Have you ever faced real, uncontrollable fear? Have you ever felt that there was no way you could cope with your circumstances, that you were hopelessly beyond your depth, that the forces against you were insurmountable? If you have, you may be able to empathize with the children of Israel at Kadesh-barnea.

They feared defeat. The opponents who held the land they wanted to enter were like giants, so it was reported. The people of Israel refused to trust God to bring victory.

And God was angry with them. So they changed their minds and, against God's will, tried to conquer in their own strength. They returned, bloodied and battered by the Amorites.

God was forming a people unto Himself during their wilderness experience. He was teaching them to trust Him. The lessons were painful. God turned a deaf ear to them.

We are often very like those desert travelers. We are slow to do God's will, even when we know it clearly. We often want to substitute our own wisdom for God's instruction. To do so is to court failure, for God intends to be taken seriously.

PRAYER THOUGHTS: Merciful God, it's easy for us to be critical of others. You know how quick we are to think we know more about our realities than You do. Help us, our Father, to be willing to run some risks, in order that Your power may be clearly seen. In Jesus' name, amen.

October 14. **Dr. Ward Patterson** is a professor at Cincinnati Bible College in Cincinnati, Ohio.

October 15

THANK YOU FOR CARING

SCRIPTURE: Deuteronomy 1:46–2:13

VERSE FOR TODAY: For the LORD thy God hath blessed thee in all the works of thy hand: he knoweth thy walking through this great wilderness: these forty years the LORD thy God hath been with thee; thou hast lacked nothing (Deuteronomy 2:7).

HYMN FOR TODAY: "Our Great Savior"

When we videotape a television program and then watch it later, we fast forward through the commercials. We avoid what we consider to be the unpleasant part of TV watching.

The people of Israel probably wished they could have fast forwarded through their wilderness experience so they could get to the good part and possess the land God promised to them. But even though God kept them wandering for forty years, He taught them many wonderful truths during those trying times. They learned He was faithful and true to His promises. They learned to trust Him as He provided food to eat and water to drink. He even kept their clothes from wearing out. Although he was disciplining them for refusing to obey Him, He still cared for their every need, and they learned how much they needed His care.

We have a wonderful God Who loves us and cares for us. Even though we may disappoint Him from time to time, He not only cares for us physically but He loves us so much that He sent His Son to die for our sins. And what a gracious God He is to use times of testing to help us to grow spiritually.

PRAYER THOUGHTS: Thank You, Father, for giving us our daily bread. Thank You for providing for our physical needs and for forgiving our sins through Your Son Jesus. We thank You for walking closely with us through every experience of life, both the pleasant and the tiresome. You are a wonderful God, and we praise Your holy name. Amen.

GOD'S PROMISES ARE TRUE

SCRIPTURE: Deuteronomy 2:16-25

VERSE FOR TODAY: The space in which we came from Kadesh-barnea, until we were come over the brook Zered, was thirty and eight years; until all the generation of the men of war were wasted out from among the host, as the LORD sware unto them (Deuteronomy 2:14).

HYMN FOR TODAY: "Standing on the Promises"

God had told the people of Israel that a whole generation of men would not enter the Promised Land because they failed to obey Him. He was true to His Word. Each one of those men died during the wilderness journey. God is an omnipotent God Who carried out His promises to the people of Israel and Who is still true to His Word today.

George Muller was an ordinary man who lived in England during the 1800s, but he was extraordinary in the way he trusted God. He started a home for orphans, and then simply took God at His Word to provide for their daily needs. When food was lacking, Muller prayed. When finances were nonexistent, Muller prayed. And God remained true to His promises. He always provided for Muller and his many small charges, often in a most surprising way.

That same God stands ready to help us today. He is just as powerful as He was in the days of Moses and in the days of George Muller. We can trust His promise to meet our needs. And we can rejoice that even though our generation, too, will pass away, our names are written in the book of life because of Christ's death on the cross.

PRAYER THOUGHTS: Holy Father, thank You for Your promises to provide for our needs, to love us, to care for us. We praise You for being a powerful God. Teach us to hold fast to You in times of need. Help us to be true to You. In Jesus' name, we pray. Amen.

October 17

WE ARE WEAK BUT HE IS STRONG

SCRIPTURE: Deuteronomy 2:26-37

VERSE FOR TODAY: From Aroer, which is by the brink of the river of Amon, and from the city that is by the river, even unto Gilead, there was not one city too strong for us: the LORD our God delivered all unto us (Deuteronomy 2:36).

HYMN FOR TODAY: "How Great Thou Art"

The tiny computer chip has united the world in a way that brute force could never do. Through the Internet, people anywhere around the world can communicate instantaneously with one another. According to God's design, the secret of the power of a telecommunications system for our global village lies in the tiniest of particles rather than in the mightiest.

God's ways often confound man. The people of Israel were not such brilliant military strategists that they could conquer the land God gave them by their own might. But the Spirit of God went with them in every battle, therefore, no town was too strong for them. As long as they followed God's directions and obeyed His commands, they were victorious.

When we feel helpless, we can remember that God's power is there for us, too. He can help us face any giants in our lives. He can equip us to attack the hard tasks we face at school, work, or home. We need not be afraid of people. We need not fear circumstances. Our God is stronger than any earthly force. He is an awesome, powerful God. It is no secret that His might is greater than our plight.

PRAYER THOUGHTS: Heavenly Father, sometimes we feel helpless. Sometimes we worry about the problems we face. Thank You for reminding us in Your Word that You walk with us in every situation of life. You empower us to face the challenges of each day. Thank You for the peace that comes to us as we trust in Your care. Amen.

CONTINUED BLESSINGS

SCRIPTURE: Deuteronomy 6:1-9

VERSE FOR TODAY: Love the LORD your God with all your heart and with all your soul and with all your strength (Deuteronomy 6:5, *New International Version*).

HYMN FOR TODAY: "More Love to Thee, O Christ"

I paused before signing the check. I was a brand new Christian, a babe in Christ, and I was preparing to give my tithe. It was a new experience, a formidable challenge. Could I afford it? How would I make ends meet?

It wasn't long before those questions were replaced by others. Did I really believe what I had confessed just three days previously? Did I really trust God—no, did I really love Him with all my heart, soul, and strength?

The key to God's continued blessing was Israel's adherence to this greatest of commandments, "Love the LORD your God with all your heart and with all your soul and with all your strength" (Deuteronomy 6:5, *New International Version*).

Jesus often quoted from the book of Deuteronomy. He taught that all of the Law and Prophets hung upon these two greatest commandments (read Matthew 22:37-40). In other words, the rest of the commandments are simply extensions and explanations of how to love God whole-heartedly and how to love our neighbor as ourselves. And love for God results in the right actions toward our heavenly Father.

PRAYER THOUGHTS: Lord, You see the fruit of wholehearted love as reflected in acts of unhesitant obedience. Teach us to show love to all around us this day. Amen.

October 18-24. **Dan Nicksich** ministers with the First Christian Church in Somerset, Pennsylvania. He and his wife, Donna, have three sons, Denny, Andrew, and Derek.

THE TEST OF PROSPERITY

SCRIPTURE: Deuteronomy 6:10-15

VERSE FOR TODAY: Be careful that you do not forget the LORD your God, failing to observe his commands, his laws and his decrees that I am giving you this day (Deuteronomy 8:11, *New International Version*).

HYMN FOR TODAY: "Count Your Blessings"

We live in the age of the instant millionaire. Pick a few numbers, plop down a dollar, and you might be the next big winner. But most find they can't handle this sudden windfall. While adversity may well develop character, there's nothing like prosperity to test it.

Houses they did not build, vineyards they had never tended, olive groves they had neither planted nor pruned, and flowing wells they had not dug. All theirs for the taking. And all Israel needed to do was to remember their benefactor. God deserved their undivided loyalty.

The Proverb writer once gave a unique prayer: "Keep falsehood and lies far from me; give me neither poverty nor riches, but give me only my daily bread. Otherwise, I may have too much and disown you and say, 'Who is the LORD?' Or I may become poor and steal, and so dishonor the name of my God" (Proverbs 30:8, 9, *New International Version*). Here was a man who understood his weakness and who knew the difficulty of the test of prosperity! May it be that we exercise such wisdom by being sure to remember He who is the source of all our blessings!

PRAYER THOUGHTS: Heavenly Father, we are sometimes quick to call out to You when in need. May it be that we are as quick to thank You when we have plenty. Remind us that You are the source of all blessings and that our dependence on You should never end. In Jesus' name, we pray. Amen.

WORTH BRAGGING ABOUT

SCRIPTURE: Deuteronomy 6:16-25

VERSE FOR TODAY: But he brought us out from there to bring us in and give us the land that he promised on oath to our forefathers (Deuteronomy 6:23, *New International Version*).

HYMN FOR TODAY: "Tell Me the Story of Jesus"

A life of obedience and observance of the laws, decrees, and commands of God inevitably leads to the question, "Why?" Why observe them? What is the meaning? It's then that we can proudly say, "Let me tell you about my God."

The Bible tells us that while the people served God under Joshua and the elders who had seen the mighty acts of God, there came another generation who knew neither the Lord nor what He had done for Israel (Judges 2:7, 10). In the days of the Judges, the people were faithful only as long as the Judge remained alive (Judges 2:19). It would seem the admonitions given in the days of Moses were quickly forgotten.

Those who have experienced God's deliverance must always seize those teachable moments when the next generation asks, "Why do we obey the Lord?"

I came to the Lord during a time of crises in my life. I found myself eager to hear what the Lord had to say. Those I sought out were those who had consistently demonstrated lives of faith and obedience. Their lives had been saying all along, "Ask me about my God!"

I may have never asked this exact question, but now I was saying, "Why should I obey the Lord?"

PRAYER THOUGHTS: Heavenly Father, help us to recognize those teachable moments when someone asks, "Why?" Daily remind us to lift up others in prayer that they, too, might come to know of You and Your mighty acts. Amen.

TREASURED POSSESSIONS

SCRIPTURE: Deuteronomy 7:6-11

VERSE FOR TODAY: But you are a chosen people, a royal priesthood, a holy nation, a people belonging to God, that you may declare the praises of him who called you out of darkness into his wonderful light (1 Peter 2:9, *New International Version*).

HYMN FOR TODAY: "Redeemed"

No visible flame, but the smell of smoke was growing stronger. We had been roused out of our sleep by blaring smoke detectors and everyone was safely out of the house. I remember distinctly thinking that there were no treasured possessions in the house for which I needed to risk my life.

Israel was God's "treasured possession." What delight they must have brought when faithful, what dismay when they were not. What a surprise for Israel for they, who had always been the last and least among all peoples, was now first and foremost in the eyes of God!

We are God's treasured possession, chosen by His love and grace. We are "a chosen people, a royal priesthood, a holy nation, a people belonging to God" (1 Peter 2:9, *New International Version*). God has shown that we are worth the sacrifice of His Son! We are not just a possession that can easily be parted with in the face of impending disaster, for God has shown that we are worth dying for!

It is wonderful to know that our Creator values us so highly.

PRAYER THOUGHTS: Dear God, how humbling to reflect on the price with which You redeemed us. In Your sight, we are worth dying for! Help us to live appropriately—to bring delight to You as Your treasured possession! When the world suggests we are worthless, remind us of our true value in Christ. In Jesus' name, amen.

PRECIOUS REMINDERS

SCRIPTURE: Deuteronomy 10:12-22

VERSE FOR TODAY: He is your praise; he is your God, who performed for you those great and awesome wonders you saw with your own eyes (Deuteronomy 10:21, *New International Version*).

HYMN FOR TODAY: "Open My Eyes That I May See"

You saw it with your own eyes! It wasn't an illusion. You saw the plagues which singled out Egypt for destruction, you saw the splitting of the Red Sea.

Such reminders were necessary. Shortly after seeing God's miracles, the people's sin had so enraged Moses that God's hand-written tablets had been shattered in disgust. Fresh from receiving the second set (Deuteronomy 10:1-10), Moses challenges the people anew.

Reminders are necessary. We live in a world seething with injustice; where a man's word is no longer his bond. A world where benevolence is lacking and cruelty abounds. How easy it is to compromise our call to holiness.

We too must be reminded to return God's affection. How fitting that the Lord gave us a precious time of remembrance which we enjoy in the fellowship of other believers who face the same trials and hardships of this world. How fitting that we must reflect on a perfect example and perfect sacrifice each Lord's Day. More than fulfilling a command, our times of assembly help remind us to resist the ways of an unholy world.

PRAYER THOUGHTS: We have each experienced your goodness, almighty heavenly Father, our God and Creator. We have, with our own eyes, seen Your blessings; our ears have heard the stories of Your wonders. How precious are those times when we gather with fellow believers to be reminded of what precious things You have done for us. In the name of Jesus, we pray. Amen.

ORDINARY BLESSINGS

SCRIPTURE: Deuteronomy 11:8-12

VERSE FOR TODAY: But the land you are crossing the Jordan to take possession of is a land of mountains and valleys that drinks rain from heaven (Deuteronomy 11:11, *New International Version*).

HYMN FOR TODAY: "There Shall Be Showers of Blessing"

"Illuminae, illuminae!"

"That's Creole for electricity," our host explained. "The children are always quick to let us know the power is on."

Our short trip to Haiti confirmed that Americans live in a land flowing with milk and honey. In Haiti, we had an average of one hour of electricity each day. The lone television station eliminated any thought of channel surfing. One night we were treated to an NBA basketball game. Our excitement quickly faded when we realized it was a tape of a game from two seasons past.

It's hard to appreciate abundance unless you've experienced scarcity. A well-lit house never seemed so extraordinary as when we returned home. Yet, before long, it was easy to take for granted that for which we once longed.

Israel's Promised Land was blessed by God because it "drank rain from heaven" and would not require irrigation as in Egypt. The rain gauge functioned as the measuring rod of God's blessing!

When was the last time you gave thanks for such ordinary, everyday blessings as sunshine and rain, peace and prosperity?

PRAYER THOUGHTS: Heavenly Father, You once healed ten lepers yet only one returned to give thanks. Help us to appreciate our cleansing from sin and to be grateful people. May such ordinary occurrences as the rain falling from heaven cause us to lift our eyes and hearts in praise to You. In Jesus' name. Amen.

BELIEVERS AND SKEPTICS

SCRIPTURE: Deuteronomy 11:13-21

VERSE FOR TODAY: Teach them to your children, talking about them when you sit at home and when you walk along the road, when you lie down and when you get up (Deuteronomy 11:19, *New International Version*).

HYMN FOR TODAY: "Jesus Loves the Little Children"

Adults are great skeptics. Children, on the other hand, will believe in flying reindeer, that a bunny brings colored eggs, and that a mystical, nocturnal being is interested in collecting their teeth.

Jesus suggested that we who are grown, in some ways, need to be more like they who are not (Matthew 18:1-4). Their willingness to believe reminds us that children will believe the facts about God just as easily as they believe the myths of Christmas. They'll learn songs about the Bible, the church, and Jesus, just as easily as they'll learn one about a flying red-nosed reindeer.

Are the children near to you hearing the facts of the faith? Are you bringing them up in the "training and instruction of the Lord" as Ephesians 6:4 suggests? Let's remember that instruction is verbally teaching and training is being an example or model. A Christian parent is one who says, "You need both to do and to say as I do."

Let's seize the opportunity to teach as we walk along the road, as we lie down and as we get up. Let us show people that we believe facts of the faith just as much now as when we first learned them—perhaps when we were children.

PRAYER THOUGHTS: Holy Father, help us to approach You as little children—humbly, with the innocence of belief and the willingness to obey Your teaching. In Jesus' name, amen.

WHAT'S IN YOUR HEART

SCRIPTURE: Deuteronomy 8:1-10

VERSE FOR TODAY: Above all else, guard your heart, for it is the well-spring of life (Proverbs 4:23, *New International Version*).

HYMN FOR TODAY: "Search Me, O God"

My husband grew up in Florida where sugar cane grows. Every year, just before harvest-time, he saw miles of sugar cane fields burning. He saw smoke in the horizon long before he saw the fields. What a strange way to prepare for harvest! Yet, the power of this blaze only destroyed the underbrush, weeds, mosquitoes, snakes—anything which hindered the harvest process. The sugar cane remained erect, unharmed, ready to be cut. The soil's nutrients were also replenished with the ashes left by the fire.

In our Scripture text for today, Moses reminded the Israelites about their forty-year wilderness adventure. The purpose of the tests they experienced was to check their heart condition (verse 2). These spiritual fires also allowed the people to see God's heart of compassion, provision and protection toward them.

Tests of waiting, hunger, desire, weariness, and loneliness reveal a person's heart. May the daily needs, desires, and stresses in life help to create a servant heart.

PRAYER THOUGHTS: Dear heavenly Father, we want a heart that reflects Yours. As each test comes today, remind us of the true expression of love that comes from Your heart before we express ours. Thank You for revealing Your heart in the life and suffering of Jesus Christ, our Savior, in whose name we pray. Amen.

October 25-31. **Pam Eubanks** and her husband, Bryan, minister with the Deaf Institute in Cincinnati, Ohio. They are the parents of six children.

THE "WHYS" GOD DOES ANSWER

SCRIPTURE: Deuteronomy 8:11-20

VERSE FOR TODAY: And we know that in all things God works for the good of those who love him, who have been called according to his purpose (Romans 8:28, *New International Version*)

HYMN FOR TODAY: "I Know Whom I Have Believed"

"Why?" is the last question which normally develops in a child's vocabulary. Three years of age seems to be the time most begin asking, "Why?" Do they ever stop? I haven't noticed any of our children deleting that question from their daily conversation.

God doesn't always provide His children with answers to the whys in life. James Dobson, in his book, *When God Doesn't Make Sense*, deals with life scenarios which end with, "Why, God?"

Moses gives the Israelites reasons for two "why" questions they might be asking at this time. The desert experiences, with the manna meals, were provided to humble and test them, so the end results of their choices would be good (verse 16). God also gave the Israelites their ability to produce wealth to confirm His covenant with them (verse 18).

Situations often happen that cause us to ask "Why?" Let's remember that God is looking out for our best interests. When we are blessed with abilities to provide for our families and others, let's remember God gives us that ability to prove His faithfulness to His covenant with us.

PRAYER THOUGHTS: Thank You, God, for Your ability to keep our highest good in Your decision-making processes. We trust You with all our "whys?" today which don't seem to be answered. Help us recognize the physical and spiritual wealth You allow in our lives. Thank You for keeping Your promises to us. In the promised name of Jesus, amen.

HOW TO GET RID OF A STIFF NECK

SCRIPTURE: Deuteronomy 9:6-14

VERSE FOR TODAY: But when he, the Spirit of truth, comes, he will guide you into all truth. He will not speak on his own; he will speak only what he hears, and he will tell you what is yet to come (John 16:13, *New International Version***).**

HYMN FOR TODAY: "Guide Me, O Thou Great Jehovah"

When you awake in the morning with a stiff neck that causes a sharp pain as you try to turn your head, it seems to limit your movement for the rest of the day.

Both Moses and God describe the Israelites' spiritual condition as being "stiff-necked." God said, "They have turned away quickly from what I commanded them and have made a cast idol for themselves" (Deuteronomy 9:12, *New International Version*). This sounds like a spiritual whip-lash!

Proverbs 29:1 explains what happens to a man who remains stiff-necked after many rebukes: he will suddenly be destroyed—without remedy.

What is the remedy for a spiritual stiff-neck? In Stephen's speech to the Sanhedrin as recorded in Acts 7:51, he names the members of the Sanhedrin as "stiff-necked people" and says they always resist the Holy Spirit (Acts 7:51). The remedy for a spiritual stiff neck is following the Holy Spirit's guidance. Sometimes pain is involved in the healing process. Resisting the Holy Spirit will only bring lasting pain. Looking to the Holy Spirit's direction brings ultimate freedom in our daily activities.

PRAYER THOUGHTS: Almighty God, our Father, thank You for Your Holy Spirit. Thank You for the promise of His guidance in life. Help us to not ignore His prompting as we walk through today. Guide us into all truth. In Jesus' name, amen.

WHAT DO YOU DO WHILE YOU WAIT?

SCRIPTURE: Deuteronomy 9:15-21

VERSE FOR TODAY: I will remember the deeds of the LORD; yes, I will remember your miracles of long ago (Psalm 77:11, *New International Version*).

HYMN FOR TODAY: "Living for Jesus"

Moses left the Israelites at the base of the mountain and went to the mountain top in order to talk with God for forty days and nights. Comparatively, the span of time would be from today until December 7. While waiting, the Israelites chose to build an idol for worship.

What other choices would have been better? Could they have gathered around the fire to share memories instead of gold? Memories such as the following:

—how the Lord provided the escape route from Egypt;

—how the walls of water were held back long enough for them to pass through and then covered the Egyptian armies;

—or what about taking turns praying for Moses as he was up on the mountain?

We can learn from the past. The Israelites made wrong choices while waiting. What do we do with our waiting time?

In times of crisis, remembering can overcome discouragement and despair. Memories such as the following:

—remembering times in the past when God was faithful to family and friends;

—remembering when God used specific people to touch us.

Try it! It will make the time fly while you are waiting!

PRAYER THOUGHTS: Faithful Father, help us to remember Your faithfulness. Help us to obey You. In the unchanging name of Jesus. Amen.

PRAYING FOR OTHERS

SCRIPTURE: Deuteronomy 9:25-29

VERSE FOR TODAY: Therefore confess your sins to each other and pray for each other so that you may be healed. The prayer of a righteous man is powerful and effective (James 5:16, *New International Version*).

HYMN FOR TODAY: "I Am Praying for You"

Moses finished his first forty-days and -nights prayer and fasting vigil before God on behalf of the Israelites. When he saw their rebellion and idolatry, he began another forty days and nights vigil. What an intercessor!

Jesus prayed for Peter before he faced the temptation of denying Jesus. He told Peter what he prayed: "that your faith may not fail" (Luke 22:32).

When Paul wrote down his prayer for the Ephesians, he asked for the following:

1) for God to give them the Spirit of wisdom and revelation to know Him better;

2) for their hearts' eyes to be enlightened to know the hope of His calling, His glorious inheritance, and His incomparably great power for those who believe (Ephesians 1:15-23).

James, Jesus' brother, describes the powerful and effective results of a righteous person's prayers: "Whoever turns a sinner from the error of his way will save him from death and cover over a multitude of sins" (James 5:20).

The prayer of faith on behalf of another is powerful. Who is on your prayer list today?

PRAYER THOUGHTS: Heavenly Father, thank You for providing Jesus, who intercedes for us. Hear our prayers today for those who need to turn around and come back to You. Keep prodding our memories to pray for these people. In Jesus' powerful name, amen.

HOW TO PASS GOD'S TEST

SCRIPTURE: Deuteronomy 13:1-5

VERSE FOR TODAY: Love the Lord your God with all your heart and with all your soul and with all your strength (Deuteronomy 6:5, *New International Version*).

HYMN FOR TODAY: "Take Thou Our Minds, Dear Lord"

False prophets and fortune tellers are useful to God! How? He allows them to test our love for Him. God want us to love Him with our whole being and to follow only Him—the true and living God.

Where does He allow the test to take place? Three main areas: the heart, the soul, and the strength of His children. He even gives this outline before the testing begins.

When does the test begin? Does it begin this morning when you awake? As you go through today, the questions will show up in the decisions you face. Notice the situations you encounter with your children, spouse, parents, roommates, friends, and neighbors. Listen as you make choices in your home, at work, in school, on the phone, at the store.

The test results for today can be reviewed before bedtime. Look over today's schedule. Remember your activities. How did you use your strength? What poured out of your heart and onto your lips? Where did your feet lead you? Who was honored with your mind, will, and emotions today? What thoughts and activities displayed Your love for God?

PRAYER THOUGHTS: Dear heavenly Father, You are our God. Earnestly we seek You; Your love is better than life. We want to glorify Your name. We want to show our love for You today. Help us in our choices today to express our love for You with ALL our heart, with ALL our soul, and with ALL our strength. In Jesus' name, amen.

BEWARE!

SCRIPTURE: Deuteronomy 13:6-11

VERSE FOR TODAY: Put on the full armor of God so that you can take your stand against the devil's schemes (Ephesians 6:11, *New International Version*).

HYMN FOR TODAY: "I Would Be True"

Check your closest relationships. Is God in the daily plans and discussions you share together? Your evaluation system needs to be continually activated.

Ephesians 6:14-17 gives a list of spiritual clothing which can guard against the devil's sneakiest plans aimed at your relationships.

l) belt of TRUTH

2) breastplate of RIGHTEOUSNESS

3) shoes of the GOSPEL OF PEACE

4) shield of FAITH

5) helmet of SALVATION

6) sword of the SPIRIT, WORD OF GOD

List the people you know will be in your life today. Do you expect any of them to challenge your relationship with God? Will they try to entice you to go places that conflict with your sense of what is right or wrong? Is there someone on your list who throws darts of doubt at your faith or salvation? What kinds of things will these people offer you with the promise of peace? Grab God's Word and find Scriptures to guard your heart's relationships.

PRAYER THOUGHTS: Father, we thank You for the daily relationship we have with You. We have other close relationships which need Your wisdom and guidance. Bring to our minds those Scriptures which will resist the devil's schemes and build our relationships closer to You. In the name of Jesus, we pray. Amen.

DEVOTIONS™

November

photo by Ward Patterson

A NOTE FROM HOME

SCRIPTURE: Deuteronomy 31:1-6

VERSE FOR TODAY: Teaching them to obey everything I have commanded you. And surely I am with you always, to the very end of the age (Matthew 28:20, *New International Version***).**

HYMN FOR TODAY: "I Know Who Holds Tomorrow"

Jim began his first morning at college thinking, "What have I gotten myself into?" The university campus seemed huge and intimidating. Afraid of all the unknown things to come and worried about what would happen next, Jim grabbed his backpack and headed for the college cafeteria.

After getting his cereal and toast, Jim sat down and bowed his head for a silent prayer. "Lord," Jim asked, "I don't know what's going to happen today. Please help get me through it. And thanks for providing me the chance to go to college and for this food. Amen." Later, he found a note in his backpack from his mom written on her favorite stationary. "Jim," the note read, "I know you're miles away from home and from all of us, but remember God is with you and will take care of you wherever you are. Love, Mom."

The Lord answered Jim's prayer with a gentle reminder from home. He was reminded that God is always with him. The Scripture reading for today is also an age old reminder that God is with us. Today, let's start with a bright hope that no matter what we fear or what we face, the Lord is with us.

PRAYER THOUGHTS: Heavenly Father, the promise of Your presence gives us peace and reassurance. We give You all our fears and worries now and thank You for Your care. In Jesus' name. Amen.

November 1-7. **Greg Swinney** lives in Kearney, Nebraska, where he has served as campus minister at the University of Nebraska at Kearney for the past 14 years.

TAKING IT TO THE STREETS

SCRIPTURE: Deuteronomy 31:7-13

VERSE FOR TODAY: Until I come, devote yourself to the public reading of Scripture, to preaching and to teaching (1 Timothy 4:13, *New International Version*).

HYMN FOR TODAY: "Tell Me the Old, Old Story"

A few years ago, the week before Easter was an exciting one for many people in our midwestern city. Christians from a number of churches joined together in the downtown area to read through the entire Bible.

The week began with a sense of anticipation on the part of dozens of sincere Christians. "The people of our town need to hear God's Word and this is a great way to bring it to them," one participant said.

For one week, as people shopped and went to and from meetings in the offices of the heart of the city, they heard the Word of God being read. The week came to an end, the Bible reading was completed, then next came the Sunday morning celebration. The worship services on Easter Sunday throughout the city were filled with joy and a feeling of accomplishment for taking God's Word to the people.

Moses' words to Joshua commanded that God's Word be read to the people to remind them to obey God and "learn to fear the Lord." Paul commanded Timothy to devote himself to the public reading of Scripture. Let's all recommit to spend more time in reading the Word of God aloud.

PRAYER THOUGHTS: Father in Heaven, Your Word is precious. When we read the Scriptures we find a message of hope, help, and happiness. Forgive us for the times of neglecting the Bible. As we bow before You today, we commit our lives anew to make Your Word a priority and to share it with others around us. Amen.

MAKE MY LIFE A SONG

SCRIPTURE: Deuteronomy 31:14-23

VERSE FOR TODAY: Speak to one another with psalms, hymns and spiritual songs. Sing and make music in your heart to the Lord, always giving thanks to God the Father for everything, in the name of our Lord Jesus Christ (Ephesians 5:19, 20, *New International Version*).

HYMN FOR TODAY: "Wonderful Words of Life"

The word "song" appears seventy-nine times in the Bible. "Music" occurs ninety times. Throughout all of Scripture, God's people are found singing. They sing songs of joy, exaltation, and dependence on God. Without a doubt, our God is a God who "writes the songs."

Today's Bible story tells of God writing another song. Moses is told to write the song down, to teach it to the people of God, and sing it that they might be a witness of Him. The song Moses is told to record is a song of warning. Forgetting the One True God and turning to the false gods of the world—materialism, selfishness, and fame—constantly tempt the Lord's people. God wanted them to sing a song to help them remember the tragic results of turning away.

Music lifts our souls, convicts our hearts, and challenges our spirits. Let's let our lives be songs of joy and victory. The music of life is shown in conversation, in attitude, and in actions. Today, let's be filled with music . . . and let the Lord sing His song through us.

PRAYER THOUGHTS: Almighty God in Heaven, use our lives today to sing a song of love to the people around us. Let them hear words of grace, mercy, and truth through us. Today, Lord, we want to be Your instruments for You to play music to the praise of Your glory. Help us to be strong and courageous. Thank You for being with us. In the name of Jesus, we pray. Amen.

A STAMP OR A STATUTE?

SCRIPTURE: Deuteronomy 34:1-7

VERSE FOR TODAY: Remember your leaders, who spoke the word of God to you. Consider the outcome of their way of life and imitate their faith (Hebrews 13:7, *New International Version*).

HYMN FOR TODAY: "In Remembrance of Me"

How would you like to be remembered? Some people have city parks named in their honor while the faces of others can be found on a postage stamp. A large statute is in the center of our city commemorating a brave pioneer who helped settle this area. Street names, colleges, and even military ships are all named in honor of people.

Moses indeed was a great man of God. He is remembered because he obeyed God and led the people of Israel out of slavery and into freedom. How was this man of character and sacrifice remembered? Was there a park named after him? Did the people erect a statute to Moses' honor? Of course not! The Bible tells us that after his life of influence and leadership, Moses died at a hundred and twenty years old. To this day the location of his grave is unknown. Still, the life of Moses remains unforgotten.

God insures that people of character and commitment live on in the memories of those who loved and respected them.

The question then is not how do you want to be remembered, but for what do you want to be remembered?

PRAYER THOUGHTS: Dear heavenly Father, great men and women of the past inspire us today. Their righteous lives and lives of servanthood remind us of how You want us to live. May we be persons of righteousness and integrity. Let us have the dedication to You that we see in Your servant, Moses. Lead us today to live out our faith so that others see the character of Christ reflected in us. In the name of Jesus, we pray. Amen.

MIGHTY POWER, ORDINARY LIVES

SCRIPTURE: Deuteronomy 34:8-12

VERSE FOR TODAY: But he said to me, "My grace is sufficient for you, for my power is made perfect in weakness." Therefore I will boast all the more gladly about my weaknesses, so that Christ's power may rest on me (2 Corinthians 12:9, *New International Version*).

HYMN FOR TODAY: "His Strength is Perfect"

I have a friend with the debilitating disease of rheumatoid arthritis. Even though she is very young, her joints continue to degenerate as she goes to the hospital for one surgery after another. She laughingly jokes about becoming the bionic woman after so many surgeries and treatments. Members of her church family tell me that her attitude is inspirational. Her constant smile is a testimony of God's love for her and through her in spite of the nagging daily pain of arthritis. They say, "She is so joyful and content. How does she do it?"

Her faith in God is deeply rooted in His limitless grace. People remembered Moses as a heroic figure who showed God's great power to others. In reality, many of us are walking heroes, examples of God's power. Often, as in the case of my friend, His power is more evident through weakness than through strength. God has chosen to reveal His power through the lives of ordinary people; people just like you and me.

My friend walks with a limp after her recent hip replacement. To me, her limp is more like a dance. The smile on her face and encouragement in her words say, "My grace is sufficient for you for my power is made perfect in weakness."

PRAYER THOUGHTS: Father, thank You for bringing people into our lives who have extraordinary faith. They inspire us and motivate us to live a life of dedication. Help us to display Your wonder-working power. In the name of Jesus, we pray. Amen.

THE WINNING GAME PLAN

SCRIPTURE: Joshua 1:1-9

VERSE FOR TODAY: Oh, how I love your law! I meditate on it all day long (Psalm 119:97, *New International Version*).

HYMN FOR TODAY: "Victory in Jesus"

As our football team staggered to the sidelines after a tough beating during the first half of the game, our coach said, "Come on guys, let's get out there and win, score some points, get charged up. Go, go, go." His words were inspirational and commanding, but they weren't very specific. We knew we needed to "go," we just weren't sure which direction!

The phrase "be strong and courageous" is repeated three times in the Scripture text for today. God doesn't leave us wondering how we're going to manage this. He gives us the specifics. Meditation on God's Word is the key. Then, and only then, we will be strong and courageous.

Like a cloudy day, discouragement often comes and keeps us from remembering the countless blessings from the Lord. The refreshing Scriptures we meditate on have a powerful way of blowing the clouds away and letting the light of the Son shine anew on our lives.

Our football team won a few and lost a few. Certain victory in the spiritual sense means walking with Christ each day. The promise of peace and security is for all who will meditate on His Word throughout the day.

PRAYER THOUGHTS: Dear Father, thank You for not giving up on us when we haven't been disciplined enough to focus on Your Word throughout our day. Your Words are so uplifting, so encouraging, so practical. They are just what we need for direction and guidance. We want to be strong and courageous today so we trust Your promise to be with us throughout the day. In Jesus' name. Amen.

SEATING OR SENDING?

SCRIPTURE: Joshua 1:10-16

VERSE FOR TODAY: In Damascus there was a disciple named Ananias. The Lord called to him in a vision, "Ananias!" "Yes, Lord," he answered (Acts 9:10, *New International Version***).**

HYMN FOR TODAY: "I'll Go Where You Want Me to Go"

The local church bought a new building recently. The anticipation of relocating to a larger facility encouraged the congregation. Someone asked, "Well, just how many people will your new church seat?" One quick thinking member responded, "Oh, it's not important how many we seat. What's really important is how many we send."

The people of God in today's Scripture text say to Joshua, "wherever you send us we will go." They knew God would provide and guide. God's provision was evident to them, His leading was obvious. Let's learn to trust the Lord and always respond with a "Yes, Lord," and never a "why? Lord."

Moving across the city was a gigantic stretch of faith for the church family. They were comfortable and content where they were. Still, many sensed God's guiding hand leading them to a new place where more people could worship.

A bumper sticker from a few years ago said it well, "We're a going church for a coming Lord." Is today "moving day" for you? Is today the day you say, "Yes, Lord"?

PRAYER THOUGHTS: God in Heaven, Your leading is sometimes hard to discern in our lives. Help us to see the direction You are pointing and to say, "Yes, Lord." Help us to be more concerned with our obedience and less concerned about our comfort. Move us to a deeper relationship with You so we can go more faithfully to a world that desperately needs to know You. In Your Son's name. Amen.

JUSTIFIED THROUGH FAITH

SCRIPTURE: Joshua 2:1-7

VERSE FOR TODAY: Therefore, since we have been justified through faith, we have peace with God through our Lord Jesus Christ (Romans 5:1, *New International Version*).

HYMN FOR TODAY: "Just As I Am"

I remember the struggle I went through when I first considered volunteering as the Christian Education Leader. I had been a Sunday school teacher for seven years, but never considered myself a leader. As someone who had come from an unchurched background only ten years previously, I felt very "unqualified" for such an honorable position.

Yet, I loved being with the children and teaching people about Jesus. Through prayer, I felt God urging me to take the position. Still, I argued: "I'm not worthy of this, Lord!"

I felt His reply, "I will help you." I began to understand that He saw me not only for whom I was at the moment, but for whom I had the potential to become, with His guidance.

The same can be said about Rahab in our Scripture text for today. Rahab was a well known prostitute, a sinful woman. Did she not also lie to the king of Jericho? Yes. How then could such a person be saved? She was saved by faith, not by her own righteousness. God chose her to do His work, not because she was good, but that she might become so.

PRAYER THOUGHTS: Father, thank You for seeing us not only for whom we are at the moment, but for whom we have the potential to become as we grow in Your grace. Help us each day to keep our mind and heart open to what Your will for us might be. Amen.

November 8-14. **Linda Wurzbacher** is a freelance writer and Sunday school teacher who lives in Webster, New York.

KEEP TELLING THE STORY!

SCRIPTURE: Joshua 2:8-14

VERSE FOR TODAY: When we heard of it, our hearts melted and everyone's courage failed because of you, for the LORD your God is God in heaven above and on the earth below (Joshua 2:11, *New International Version*).

HYMN FOR TODAY: "I Love to Tell the Story"

One of the many reasons I have such a passion for being involved in the Christian education of children is because I never had the opportunity to attend Sunday school when I was a child. Sadly, my family never attended church. Many times I have reminded the students in my classes how fortunate they are to be learning so much about God at a young age. It truly is a privilege.

The Bible teaches us that others are brought to faith by hearing and obeying the Word of God. Jesus calls each one of us to "follow" Him and to "become His disciple." Part of a disciple's job is to share the "good news" of the gospel. We can be an instrument used to tell the story. One of the ways we do that is by sharing with others how God continues to work in our lives on a daily basis.

In the Scripture today, Rahab was one of those people who had "heard" about some of the mighty acts of God. Though she was a Canaanite, Rahab recognized that Yahweh, the God of Israel, is the God above all other gods. Upon hearing the testimony of others on what Yahweh had done, she changed and became a believer.

PRAYER THOUGHTS: God of power and might, melt our hearts and help us to keep on telling Your story, so that others may know of Your glory and of Jesus and His love. May we find ways each day to keep on telling those around us of Your great love. In Jesus' name. Amen.

FINDING COURAGE

SCRIPTURE: Joshua 2:15-24

VERSE FOR TODAY: "I have told you these things, so that in me you may have peace. In this world you will have trouble. But take heart! I have overcome the world" (John 16: 33, *New International Version*).

HYMN FOR TODAY: "Constantly Abiding"

Why do you think Rahab risked her life to help the two spies from Israel? Would you say she had great courage to do what she did, or was she simply reacting out of fear for her own life and that of her family's? I think it was probably both. Why does anyone need courage, if fear is not present?

Rahab not only believed that the God of Israel was the God above all other gods, but she put her faith in action by helping the spies to escape. This must have taken great courage. We can assume that if she had been caught, she probably would have been killed. Yet, it was in the risking of her life, that her life and the lives of her family were spared.

Cowards do not last long on their spiritual pilgrimages. It takes enormous courage to repent and become a Christian. It takes enormous courage to continually put our faith into action. Some days our courage may seem to melt. But the Bible tells us there is One who's courage will never fail. The same One who promises never to leave us, our Lord and Savior, Jesus Christ.

PRAYER THOUGHTS: Our dear heavenly Father, please give us the same kind of courage that Rahab demonstrated. When our courage fails, as it often does, help us to remember that we can lean on You, that Your power is over us. Teach us to find courage in Your Word. Help us to allow the Holy Spirit to work through us. May we live a life of peace through Christ Jesus, our Savior. In Jesus' name we pray. Amen.

THE LORD WILL LEAD!

SCRIPTURE: Joshua 3:1-6

VERSE FOR TODAY: When he has brought out all his own, he goes on ahead of them, and his sheep follow him because they know his voice (John 10:4, *New International Version*).

HYMN FOR TODAY: "All the Way My Savior Leads Me"

My husband sometimes gets frustrated with me because I make plans without consulting him first. After seventeen years of marriage, I think I have a pretty good idea of how he'll feel about certain situations. But there are times when I am wrong and have learned over the years that it's not right to try to speak for him or to take him for granted.

Think about how many times in our lives we have taken God for granted. We rush ahead in situations without first stopping to pray and seek His will. We think we know what's best, what the truth is and what decisions should be made. Many times we are wrong. It is too often in retrospect that we realize we never asked God to show us or help us.

The Israelites could not simply pack God in their suitcase and move Him around. They, instead, had to learn to follow God obediently as He chose to lead. The Israelites were about to cross a seething, swollen river that surely must have looked to them like the river of death. If ever they needed to follow and obey, it was now. We, too, often forget that God calls us not necessarily to be great leaders, but to be obedient in following Him!

PRAYER THOUGHTS: God of mercy and compassion, thank You that You are a God who leads His people. Forgive us for the times when we try to do things without first stopping to ask for Your guidance. Help us to always have a servant's heart, as did Your Son, Jesus Christ. In Whose name we pray. Amen.

GOD WITH US

SCRIPTURE: Joshua 3:7-13

VERSE FOR TODAY: See, the ark of the covenant of the Lord of all the earth will go into the Jordan ahead of you (Joshua 3:11, *New International Version***).**

HYMN FOR TODAY: "Abide with Me"

Joshua called the Israelites together and told them the words that God had spoken to him. The message was clear. God was with them. He was very much present and among them. By the miracle that was about to happen, God was to show His people beyond any doubt, that He was with Joshua (their leader), and that He was with them.

The ark of the covenant of the Lord of all the earth was the symbol of the presence of the living God. God never sends His people out unless He treads the pathway first. Where the ark of the covenant of the Lord is, the waters of death can never overflow.

Do you see the golden threads that are woven throughout the Bible? Remember the words spoken to Joseph by an angel of the Lord in Matthew 1:23; "The virgin will be with child and will give birth to a son, and they will call him Immanuel"—which means, "God with us" (*New International Version*).

Today, just as in Joshua's day, God wants us to know that He is with us! We are comforted to know that Jesus will be "God with us" even in death and in His glorious presence forever!

PRAYER THOUGHTS: Father, You have shown Your great love in the sending of Your Son who is "God with us." Thank You, Lord, that we know there is nothing in life we have to face, that Your Son hasn't already faced for us. In Jesus' name we pray. Amen.

GOD OF MIRACLES!

SCRIPTURE: Joshua 3:14—4:3

VERSE FOR TODAY: You are the God who performs miracles; you display your power among the peoples. With your mighty arm you redeemed your people, (Psalm 77:14, 15, *New International Version*).

HYMN FOR TODAY: "God Of Our Fathers"

Several years ago my friend, Jim, hurt his back. The doctors said it was the worst slipped disc they had ever seen. It would not heal without surgery, they said. Still, Jim wanted to give it some time and prayer.

About a month later, Jim was lying in bed praying when suddenly a warm breeze came through the window and he felt someone touch his back. Immediately, the pain left his body. He knew somehow that he'd been healed.

The first few times I heard him tell the story to friends, he gave God all the credit. "It was a miracle!" he'd say. But after a few months, I noticed how his story began to change. He was now telling people that he just turned a certain way and felt something "click" in his back. Hmmmm. What happened to the miracle? I wondered.

Scientists today seem to have lots of logical explanations for events that people of faith would call miracles. We, like Jim, struggle at times to believe the miracles in our own lives. We seek worldly explanations when what we really need to do is simply to give God the credit, and to say a prayer of thanksgiving. We know that all healing comes from God.

PRAYER THOUGHTS: O God, Heaven and earth are full of Your glory! Help us to use our vision of faith more often so that we may know You even more fully. Teach us to give way to You and to allow You to work in and through us. In Jesus' name. Amen.

WE MUST REMEMBER

SCRIPTURE: Joshua 4:4-14

VERSE FOR TODAY: Remember the wonders that He has done, his miracles, and the judgments he pronounced (1 Chronicles 16:12, *New International Version*).

HYMN FOR TODAY: "On Eagle's Wings"

Several years ago, I attended the memorial service of a teenage boy from our church who died tragically in a car accident. His mother is a good friend of mine who has taught Sunday school with me for years. I find myself meditating on the word "memorial" and am surprised to find it in our Scripture for today.

God wanted the Israelites to build a memorial. He wanted the stones to remind them of the miracle of not only what He had already done for them in the past, but of what He had yet promised He would do for them. He knew that hard times were still ahead for His people. Many wars were yet to be fought, loved ones to be lost, and hardships to be endured. In the hard times yet to come, it was extremely important that the Israelites remember the power and faithfulness of their all-powerful and loving God.

It's important that we, too, have memorial stones hidden in our hearts. Now, more than ever, my friend will need to remember the power of God. She will need to remember not only what God has done in the past, but of the promises of life everlasting, yet to come.

PRAYER THOUGHTS: Father, thank You for giving us memorial stones. Every time we partake of the cup and the bread we are reminded that Jesus Christ suffered and died on the cross for our sins. In His glorious resurrection, He has delivered us from the power and sting of death. In His holy name, we pray. Amen.

REMEMBER GOD'S DEEDS

SCRIPTURE: Joshua 5:10-15

VERSE FOR TODAY: Moses said unto the people, Remember this day, in which ye came out from Egypt, out of the house of bondage; for by strength of hand the LORD brought you out from this place: there shall no leavened bread be eaten (Exodus 13:3).

HYMN FOR TODAY: "Be Still, My Soul"

Do you remember your first day in a new school; first date; first time traveling alone; graduation; first day of college; first day on the job; your wedding day; first child's birth; the children's leaving home?

These events are milestones—transition points—in our lives, causing joy and fear. They mark our entry into new territory. We wonder, will God be with us in this new place?

Joshua and Israel faced such a milestone entering the Promised Land. Thanks to God's perfect timing, Israel arrived in Canaan in time for Passover.

When God had delivered Israel from the Death Angel, judgment, and Egyptian bondage, God initiated the Passover. God had told Israel to observe Passover yearly and to use the celebration to teach their children about God's mighty deeds.

Recounting God's former deeds and faithfulness during Passover observations was an effective way for Joshua to reassure the nation. God would continue to provide for them just as God had on their journey there.

PRAYER THOUGHTS: Dear loving and heavenly God, when we face new events, remind us that you never change. Help us to have confidence in Your unchanging love. Amen.

November 15-21. **Lucinda Norman** is a Christian writer, teacher, and leader of a Bible study group in Brookville, Pennsylvania, where she makes her home with her husband, Ron.

WHAT BARRIER?

SCRIPTURE: Joshua 6:1-7

VERSE FOR TODAY: For it is for this we labor and strive, because we have fixed our hope on the living God, who is the Savior of all men, especially of believers (1 Timothy 4:10, *New American Standard Bible*).

HYMN FOR TODAY: "Lead On, O King Eternal"

Archaeology shows that there were two walls around Jericho. The inner wall is said to have been 12-feet thick and 30-feet high. The walls were linked together by houses built across the top of them.

God said he'd already given this city, its king, and warriors to Joshua. It was as if these walls didn't exist. Yet, God required Joshua to do his part by following instructions given to him by God.

Why would Joshua comply? God had prepared him. Battles, victories, hardships, temptations, and miracles during the journey to Canaan had provided Joshua with needed skills and confidence in God.

God prepares us to meet our barriers, too. In hindsight, I can see that majoring in the English language at a Christian college, being assigned to teach high school composition classes, and teaching women's home Bible studies prepared me to be a Christian writer.

I had to do my part—study writing, write, submit manuscripts, fail, sometimes succeed, rewrite, resubmit.

Now, I face writing tasks with Joshua's attitude—what barrier? God prepared me for this task. With God's help, I'll do what's required to accomplish it.

PRAYER THOUGHTS: Dear Father, when obstacles intimidate us, let us see how you've prepared us to face them. Help us to trust You and to work confidently, step-by-step, toward the goal you've given us. Amen.

WHO COULD FIGURE IT?

SCRIPTURE: Joshua 6:8-14

VERSE FOR TODAY: For my thoughts are not your thoughts, neither are your ways my ways, saith the LORD (Isaiah 55:8).

HYMN FOR TODAY: "Trust and Obey"

"The boss discharged me tonight, two weeks before my trial period ended," our son said. "I didn't fit the company."

His voice shook with controlled sobs, then anger. "When they hired me, you said God blessed me. Some blessing."

Now, like him, I wondered, *What was God thinking?* Bolstering both of us, I said, "Even when events look senseless, God has reasons we can't see."

God's battle strategy at Jericho sounded senseless, too. How could a silent army and priests carrying the ark of the covenant and sounding ram's horn trumpets conquer such a fortified city simply by marching around it once a day for six days? What was God thinking?

Joshua followed God's instructions against all odds, despite the situation's appearance. On the seventh day, God rewarded his trust and obedience.

For our son, what appeared to be a set-back turned into a blessing. After a month of job hunting, he contacted a previous employer who re-hired him—with a pay increase! Three months later, government fraud investigations started against the company our son hadn't "fit."

Sometimes, what seems like foolishness to us can be God's salvation for us.

PRAYER THOUGHTS: Holy Father, when events in our lives seem senseless and we're disappointed with our surroundings and with You, help us to focus on Your omnipotence and omniscience. Lend us Your perspective. In the name of Jesus, we pray. Amen.

GO STRAIGHT AHEAD, TOGETHER

SCRIPTURE: Joshua 6:15-20

VERSE FOR TODAY: I press toward the mark for the prize of the high calling of God in Christ Jesus (Philippians 3:14).

HYMN FOR TODAY: "True-Hearted, Whole-Hearted"

Although God's invisible hosts fought with Israel (Joshua 5:13-15, 2 Kings 6:14-17), Israelite warriors and priests had to jointly obey God's instructions to accomplish victory.

From the church's birth, God called his followers to service. We share one goal—to glorify God.

The church is far more than its buildings and far larger than the number of people meeting together on Sundays. However, the church is essentially a volunteer lay organization. The church's minimal number of clergy can't possibly do all the work the church needs to do.

The church works everywhere a believer serves God. That's in workplaces, courthouses, resorts, schools, neighborhoods, and homes. The church's battles aren't physical ones like the battle at Jericho. However, as believers serve God, they fight spiritual battles in every sector of society and in their personal lives as well.

Joshua and his warriors didn't fight their battle alone. Neither does the church today. The church, like Joshua and his army, is a partnership. As in Joshua's time, accomplishing our goal and victory requires obedience to God and the efforts of us all.

PRAYER THOUGHTS: Almighty God in Heaven, when our activities dominate us, remind us that each believer, along with our ministers, is part of the church, Christ's army. We battle individually and jointly. Victory comes when we're individually and jointly obedient to God, our Captain. Amen.

INDIVIDUAL FAITH

SCRIPTURE: Joshua 6:22-25, 27

VERSE FOR TODAY: Her children arise up, and call her blessed; her husband also, and he praiseth her (Proverbs 31:28).

HYMN FOR TODAY: "Pass It On"

Rahab's faith in Israel's God (Joshua 2:9-11) provided safety and deliverance for her whole family.

At first glance, this passage could lead readers to think a parent's or spouse's faith can save them—that they don't need individual faith. This passage doesn't explain ceremonies Rahab and her family individually underwent later to join with God's chosen people.

Rahab and her family acknowledged Israel's God as their God (Exodus 20:3-5). Priests performed ceremonial cleansing of each member of Rahab's family.

Each male of Rahab's family complied with personal physical rites required by God's covenant with Abraham (Genesis 17:12-14). These rites were also stipulated by God's instructions at the first Passover (Exodus 12:48-49).

So even though Rahab's faith saved her family's lives, each member had to claim faith in God personally.

Rahab later married the Hebrew, Salmon (Matthew 1:5). Their son, Boaz, married another Gentile, God-fearing woman, Ruth. Boaz was the great grandfather of King David.

Rahab is one of only four women mentioned in Christ's genealogies (Matthew 1:5-6). Her story shows us how God can use one transformed person to influence the world.

PRAYER THOUGHTS: Dear Father, remind us that one family member's faith can influence generations. Let this motivate us to be Christlike not only in church and in public, but also in our homes. Amen.

WHY DO WE GO TO CHURCH?

SCRIPTURE: Joshua 8:30-35

VERSE FOR TODAY: Then Joshua built an altar unto the LORD God of Israel in mount Ebal . . . and they offered thereon burnt-offerings unto the LORD, and sacrificed peace-offerings (Joshua 8:30, 31).

HYMN FOR TODAY: "I Love Thy Kingdom, Lord"

"I don't want to go to church," our ten-year-old son complained. "Andy's mom doesn't make him go to church. Why do we have to go to church anyway?"

Why do we go to church?

Today's Scripture text shows the value of worshipping God together in public. The children of Israel have given us an example to follow.

The young nation of Israel conquered, and now inhabited, this new land where people worshipped many false gods. Their leader, Joshua, built an altar to Israel's true God, and priests performed two offerings. In the Old Testament, burnt-offerings symbolized dedicating oneself to God; peace-offerings signified one's friendship with God.

These religious rites helped Israel to focus on the true and living God. The sacrifices reminded them to give God credit for what God had accomplished for them, to rededicate themselves to God, and to reinforce friendship with Him. Being together as a group let the individuals know they weren't alone in their battles. Practicing these sacrifices also showed the Canaanites Whom Israel worshipped.

Public worship does the same thing for believers today.

PRAYER THOUGHTS: Dear Father, help us to remember the examples You provide for us in the Bible, especially when our children or neighbors question us about faith matters. Nudge us when we neglect to worship You publicly. Amen.

TELL YOUR CHILDREN

SCRIPTURE: Psalm 44:1-8

VERSE FOR TODAY: We have heard with our ears, O God, our fathers have told us, what work thou didst in their days, in the times of old (Psalm 44:1).

HYMN FOR TODAY: "Praise God, from Whom All Blessings Flow"

"I don't know if my father was a Christian," my seventy-year-old mother said with tears glossing her eyes as we looked through old photos. "I don't know if I'll ever see him again."

What could I say? I remember seeing Grandfather six times. I knew nothing about his faith.

I do know my parents' faith. Whenever we celebrate together, my parents recite the history of God's work in our family. Some stories are miraculous and awe-inspiring; some touching; others funny.

"Remember the time when we were out of money, and I needed eggs . . . " Mother starts.

Someone else finishes. "You prayed. That afternoon, our neighbor arrived with a dozen eggs, saying he had this silly urge to bring you eggs."

We all laugh, commenting how amazing that God was concerned about our egg supply. A visitor would think God was a member of our family.

As Christian parents, one of the greatest inheritances we leave our children is the story of our walk with God. When our children can see that we live holy lives, it provides security and hope for them.

PRAYER THOUGHTS: Dear God, remind us that expressing our faith in You is just as important to our children and grandchildren as it is to us and You. As the psalmist says, let us boast about and praise You—in the presence of our children. Amen.

DON'T FORGET!

SCRIPTURE: Joshua 23:1-5

VERSE FOR TODAY: I will remember the deeds of the LORD; yes, I will remember your miracles of long ago (Psalm 77:11, *New International Version*).

HYMN FOR TODAY: "O Worship the King"

When Joshua, the great servant of God, felt his life drawing to an end, he assembled other leaders together and reminded them not to forget the great and wonderful things that God had done for them. He warned them of the danger of departing from godly ways. Unless reminders are given, much of what happened might be forgotten.

A famous leader once wrote, "A well-trained memory is one that permits you to forget everything that isn't worth remembering." Sometimes it is difficult for us to remember the right things. We all too often remember the trivial and forget the important.

Joshua wanted the Israelites to remember the deeds of God. He wanted them to remember how God had really been their leader in the past and that it was important for them to keep Him as their leader in the days to come.

This practice of remembering important things is why Jesus instituted the Lord's Supper with the words, "Do this in remembrance of Me" (Luke 23:19, *New American Standard Version*).

PRAYER THOUGHTS: Dear God, keep our memories fresh about all that You have done, both in ancient history and in our own personal histories. Thank You for remembering us through Jesus Christ. Amen.

November 22-28. **Arthur O. Peterson, II**, and his wife, Janis, minister with the First Christian Church of Lake Butler, Florida.

GREATER IS HE

SCRIPTURE: Joshua 23:6-10

VERSE FOR TODAY: Greater is He who is in you than he who is in the world (1 John 4:4, *New American Standard Version*).

HYMN FOR TODAY: "Greater Is He That Is In Me"

In *The History of Charles X*, Voltaire recorded that whenever the Swedes were able to marshal a force to the proportion of their enemies of 20 to 100, they never despaired and always felt victorious. Joshua reminded the Israelites they had been victorious again and again when they were outnumbered a thousand to one: "One of you routs a thousand." He reminded them that, "No one has been able to withstand you" and "The LORD your God fights for you" (Joshua 23:9, 10, *New International Version*).

But even with God's help we are called upon to "Be very strong and careful to obey" (Joshua 23:6, *New International Version*). It is important for us to remember that we are co-workers with God. It is not for us to just sit back and watch God do it all. He wants to work through us and help us to be partners with Him.

Are you facing tough issues today? Is life getting difficult? Are there mountains in your way? We used to sing this chorus, "Got any rivers you think are uncrossable? Got any mountains you can't tunnel through? God specializes in things tho't impossible; He does the things others cannot do" (Oscar Eliason © 1945 by Singspiration, Inc.).

PRAYER THOUGHTS: Father, forgive us when we forget Your power and Your promises. Remind us today that through You we can be "more than conquerors." Help us to live in such a way that those around us will know that we are indeed partners with You. In the name of Jesus, we pray. Amen.

PROMISE KEEPER

SCRIPTURE: Joshua 23:11-16

VERSE FOR TODAY: You know with all your heart and soul that not one of all the good promises the LORD your God gave you has failed. Every promise has been fulfilled; not one has failed (Joshua 23:14, *New International Version*).

HYMN FOR TODAY: "Standing on the Promises"

Usually when we hear the word "promise" we think of it only in terms that are positive and encouraging. It is interesting that in the passage before us today that Joshua expresses his concern both positively and negatively. He reminds the people of God's great promises, all of which have been faithfully kept. Then, he tells them that just as God keeps promises in positive ways, even so, He keeps His Word when He warns of punishment for disobedience.

If only the Israelites and their children would have remembered such counsel. . . . Their forgetfulness of the miracles that God provided for them as they left Egypt and of Joshua's warnings cost them dearly when the Babylonians carried them into captivity.

God is the greatest "Promise Keeper." He faithfully honors His Word—always! He has promised us life everlasting through His Son, Jesus. He has promised us His daily provision and care. He has promised us guidance through His Word and by His Spirit. Peter wrote, "He has given us his very great and precious promises" (2 Peter 1:4).

PRAYER THOUGHTS: Heavenly Father, we claim Your precious promises of grace and guidance for this day. Help us to enjoy Your promises and to be true to the promises we make to You and to others. Help us to rely upon You. In Jesus' name. Amen.

HINDSIGHT

SCRIPTURE: Joshua 24:1-7

VERSE FOR TODAY: Lord, you have been our dwelling place through-out all generations (Psalm 90:1, *New International Version*).

HYMN FOR TODAY: "O God, Our Help in Ages Past"

These words have been quoted numerous times: "Those who cannot remember the past are condemned to repeat it." Someone quipped, "The worst thing about history is that every time it repeats itself the price goes up."

When Joshua assembled the people together, he began with a history lesson. Joshua wanted Israel to remember their past. He wanted them to remember from what humble beginnings they had come. Joshua began his speech with the identification of their forefathers. He began with Terah, the father of Abraham. He wanted to indelibly impress upon them the workings of the hand of God in their history. To forget their history would endanger their future.

We must also remember our history: what it was like before Christ entered our lives; how enslaved we were to sin; the darkness that pervaded our thinking; the selfishness that frustrated our quality of life; the despair that framed our view toward the future. We must also remember: the joy of new life in Christ; the peace that transformed our hearts; the thrill of forgiven sin; the excitement of God's promise of eternal life in Heaven.

Our future is clearer when we faithfully ponder our past!

PRAYER THOUGHTS: "O God, our help in ages past, Our hope for years to come, Be Thou our guard while life shall last, And our eternal home." (verse four, *"O God, Our Help in Ages Past"*). Thank You, dear Father, for the great saints of the past. Help us to learn from them. In the name of our Savior, Jesus Christ, we pray. Amen.

RESOLVE

SCRIPTURE: Joshua 24:14-18

VERSE FOR TODAY: But as for me and my household, we will serve the LORD (Joshua 24:15, *New International Version*).

HYMN FOR TODAY: "Happy the Home When God Is There"

Often we may want to shy away from some great words and concepts. Words such as commitment, resolve, determination, decision, and responsibility. People who incorporate these words into their living are generally well-focused and adequately prepared for whatever they may encounter. They look forward to carrying out life's responsibilities.

Joshua was such a man. He was a man of resolve. He knew the direction he and his family had to take in order to be pleasing to God. He was not ashamed to declare that the priority of his life was faithful service to his true and living God. And Joshua spoke on behalf of commitment of his entire family.

We note that there's a difference between interest and commitment. When we're interested in doing something, we do it when it's convenient. But when we're committed to something, we work for results. The apostle Paul wrote, "This one thing I do: press on toward the goal to win the prize for which God has called me . . . " (Philippians 3:13, 14). Let's not be afraid of the important words.

Let's be able to say with Joshua, "As for me and my household, we will serve the LORD."

PRAYER THOUGHTS: Dear God, help us to be people of resolve. Help us to determine to do Your will today and to lead our families to serve You with commitment, determination, and faithfulness. Help us to resolve in love to follow You. We pray this prayer in the name of our Savior. Amen.

November 27

NOT IN SMALL PRINT

SCRIPTURE: Joshua 24:19-24

VERSE FOR TODAY: And the people said to Joshua, "We will serve the LORD our God and obey him" (Joshua 24:24, *New International Version*).

HYMN FOR TODAY: "I Will Serve Thee"

Have you ever tried to read the fine print of an insurance policy? Better yet, have you taken the time to read the small print of a bank loan contract? It's almost as if they don't want one to read this information because of all the legal information that is included to cover the liability of the loaning company or the bank.

God doesn't put His terms in small print. He wants those who follow Him to know exactly what they're getting into when a covenant is made with Him. Joshua plainly tells Israel's leaders what is required of them to be in covenant with this holy and jealous God. He clearly tells them the consequences of breaking covenant with Him.

In the same way, Jesus put in bold print the terms of discipleship in the New Testament. Terms like denying oneself and taking up one's cross and following in His footsteps are part of the requirements for discipleship. One day Jesus asked His ambitious disciples if they were indeed able to follow Him completely. They responded, "We are able" (Matthew 20:22). It wasn't long before they experienced what Jesus had asked of them.

How about it? Are you able? Am I able?

PRAYER THOUGHTS: Almighty Creator and living God, help us to submit our stubborn wills to You today. Discipline us when we start making our own terms with You. Our desire is to serve and obey You. May Your Spirit enable us to do that. We pray in Jesus' name, amen.

FIND US FAITHFUL

SCRIPTURE: Joshua 24:25-33

VERSE FOR TODAY: Precious in the sight of the LORD is the death of his saints (Psalm 116:15, *New International Version*).

HYMN FOR TODAY: "Precious Lord, Take My Hand"

In the short space of two weeks during the late summer of 1997, several notable personalities died. Princess Diana died in a automobile accident. Mother Theresa died after a long illness. Old-time comedian Red Skelton died. Rich Mullins, contemporary Christian musician, died in an automobile accident. Different emotions were experienced with the news of each of these deaths. Even when loved ones die we are confronted with the reality of our own mortality.

The last verses of the Book of Joshua contain the obituaries of Joshua, the courageous leader of God's people and Eleazar, the priest. There is mention of the faithful service of Joshua as well as his influence on succeeding generations to serve the Lord. Eleazar's death is mentioned almost without comment.

What influence will we have on others at the time of our exit from this life? Are we living in such a way as to leave some positive mark on the people that are close to us? What legacy do we pass on to others? Will our life of service be a motivation to others to continue in their service?

Through Christ we have much to look forward to beyond this life, but we also need to be faithful to Him between now and the time we are called home. "May all who come behind us find us faithful."

PRAYER THOUGHTS: Dear God, thank You for sending Your Son who had victory over death and the grave. Thank You for the promise and hope of eternal life that You have made available through Him. In His name, we pray. Amen.

SENT TO PREPARE THE PATH FOR THE KING

SCRIPTURE: Matthew 3:1-6

VERSE FOR TODAY: In those days came John the Baptist, preaching in the wilderness of Judea, and saying, Repent ye: for the kingdom of heaven is at hand (Matthew 3:1).

HYMN FOR TODAY: "Take My Life and Let It Be Consecrated"

Isaiah not only prophesied the coming of the King, but he also told of "The voice of him that crieth in the wilderness, Prepare ye the way of the LORD, make straight in the desert a highway for our God" (Isaiah 40:3). The fulfillment of this prophecy is recorded in Matthew 3:1-6 where we learn "the voice" is that of John the Baptist.

John's message was one of repentance. It was a cry in the wilderness of sin for people to confess their sins, to acknowledge their need for a Savior, and to prepare themselves to receive the greatest and most important promise there could ever be, the coming of the Messiah. Yes, The Messiah, Jesus Christ, who came to save people from sin, was about to be identified and introduced by John. But, without a heart of repentance, the people who had come to hear this powerful preacher could not receive the Savior.

God still allows the cry for repentance and preparation to be heard. Yet, we cannot accept the Lord Jesus until we acknowledge our sinful condition, our need for salvation, and obey Jesus Christ our Lord and Savior.

PRAYER THOUGHTS: Precious Father, thank You for sending Your Son, Jesus Christ, to die for our sins. We accept Your Son as our Lord and Savior. Amen.

November 29, 30. **Sallie J. Breaux** ministers with the radio and television ministries of the Hope of Glory Ministries in Lafayette, Louisiana.

REPENT, FOR HE IS COMING!

SCRIPTURE: Matthew 3:7-12

VERSE FOR TODAY: Bring forth therefore fruits meet for repentance: (Matthew 3:8).

HYMN FOR TODAY: "I Surrender All"

God is not interested in our performing rituals or any outward show of religiosity without true repentance. That was John's message to the Pharisees and Sadducees as he proclaimed the coming of Jesus Christ.

Some persons today who profess Christianity have the same attitude as the Pharisees and Sadducees. They have been good church members all their lives, their parents are Christians, perhaps their father, mother or even grandparents were ministers of the gospel. Yet, they have never truly repented and developed a relationship with Jesus Christ for themselves. Many persons boast in their church affiliation, involvement in ministry, or about their much giving of finances to a ministry, thinking somehow these things make them righteous. However, God is looking for purity of heart in people who will admit they are not who God designed His people to be and will admit the need for Jesus Christ to make the change in their lives.

Why not repent with a sincere heart, submit to the sovereignty of God, and allow Jesus Christ to be truly Lord of your life? He stands today with His arms wide open to forgive us and totally change our life for His glory. We need only to accept and obey His will.

PRAYER THOUGHTS: Dear God, we repent now of all our sins and of everything in our lives that is not pleasing to You. We accept Your forgiveness and trust You to take control of our lives today. In the name of Jesus, we pray. Amen.

My Prayer Notes

DEVOTIONS™

December

photo by Ward Patterson

December 1

JESUS' BAPTISM PLEASED THE FATHER

SCRIPTURE: Matthew 3:13-17

VERSE FOR TODAY: And Jesus answering said unto him, Suffer it to be so now: for thus it becometh us to fulfil all righteousness. Then he suffered him (Matthew 3:15).

HYMN FOR TODAY: "Have Thine Own Way, Lord"

John was preaching repentance and baptizing in the Jordan River. The Bible records in verse 17 of the Scripture text for today that God was pleased because His Son was baptized in water by John the Baptist.

Jesus came to John and asked to be baptized. John was very reluctant to do so for He recognized Jesus as the "Lamb of God." Jesus was sinless; why should He need baptism? John quickly responded to Jesus that it was Jesus Who should be baptizing him, not John baptizing Jesus.

We see in verse 15 of the Scripture text, Jesus' response to John. He insisted that John baptize Him, leaving such a profound word and example for us: " . . . for thus it becometh us to fulfil all righteousness." As we follow Jesus Christ, we do what is righteous and by faith we walk in obedience. Just as Heaven opened, the Spirit of God descended, and God spoke of His being pleased with Jesus because of His being baptized, God will witness His pleasure in our obedience to His Word. Let us seek to please God!

PRAYER THOUGHTS: Almighty God, we want to be pleasing to You in all we do. Help us, Father, to obey You even in the things You have designed for our lives that we do not understand. In the name of Your Son, Jesus, we pray. Amen.

December 1. **Sallie J. Breaux** ministers with the radio and television ministries of the Hope of Glory Ministries in Lafayette, Louisiana.

ARE YOU THE ONE?

SCRIPTURE: Matthew 11:2-6

VERSE FOR TODAY: Jesus replied, "Go back and report to John what you hear and see: The blind receive sight, the lame walk, those who have leprosy are cured, the deaf hear, the dead are raised, and the good news is preached to the poor" (Matthew 11:4 5, *New International Version*).

HYMN FOR TODAY: "Teach Me Thy Way, O Lord"

The Scriptures are honest in their portrayal of human history. The apostle John records that John the Baptist had a very clear idea of who Jesus was and of his own relationship with Him (John 3:27-30).

Yet, there came a time when John sent disciples to Jesus to ask, "Are you the one who was to come, or should we expect someone else?" It seems a strange question for one so resolute and committed to Jesus as was John.

Some suggest that the question was asked so the disciples could hear Jesus' messiahship affirmed. Others suggest that John, in prison, may have been impatient to see Jesus usher in His kingdom or that John longed for the reassurance that only Jesus could provide.

Whatever John's motivation, Jesus showed no impatience with him. Jesus instructed the disciple to return to tell John what they heard and saw, the miracles that He performed and the good news He was preaching to the poor. Like John, we today are assured of Jesus' divinity by His Words and actions.

Jesus was authenticated both by what He said and did.

PRAYER THOUGHTS: Eternal God, be with us in our moments of doubt. Strengthen us by Your Spirit to trust what You have made known to us. In the name of our Savior, Jesus Christ, we pray. Amen.

December 2-6. **Dr. Ward Patterson** is a professor at Cincinnati Bible College in Cincinnati, Ohio.

GREATNESS

SCRIPTURE: Matthew 11:7-11

VERSE FOR TODAY: I tell you the truth: Among those born of women there has not risen anyone greater than John the Baptist; yet he who is least in the kingdom of heaven is greater than he (Matthew 11:11, *New International Version*).

HYMN FOR TODAY: "Ye Servants of God"

I like the story about a boy who was playing baseball all by himself. "I'm the greatest hitter in the world," he called out. Then he threw the ball up in the air and took a hefty swing. When he missed, he called out, "Strike one!"

He again called out, "I'm the greatest hitter in the world," and threw the ball. "Strike two!"

He took a good look at his bat and examined the ball. Then he shouted, "I'm the greatest hitter who ever lived." He swung with all his might, but he missed once again.

"Wow," he said. "Strike three! I'm the greatest pitcher in the world."

It is a characteristic of human beings to strive after greatness. Jesus called John the Baptist great and it is not difficult to identify his traits of greatness. Jesus, however, did not stop here. He went on to say, "He who is least in the kingdom of heaven is greater than he" (Matthew 11:11).

Do we realize that we are judged great by Jesus? God has seen fit to make known to us in Christ what the prophets longed to see come to pass. We are a privileged and distinguished people indeed. Let us live up to our greatness.

PRAYER THOUGHTS: O God, we aspire to great things, but often we settle for mediocrity. Help us to realize that you have conferred on us the mantle of greatness by initiating us into Your kingdom. For this we are humbly thankful. Amen.

GREAT IN THE EYES OF THE LORD

SCRIPTURE: Matthew 11:12-19

VERSE FOR TODAY: For all the Prophets and the Law prophesied until John (Matthew 11:13, *New International Version*).

HYMN FOR TODAY: "In His Time"

Some people play pivotal roles in history. They come to prominence at a time when they are needed and they respond to the situation in heroic ways. Abraham Lincoln and Winston Churchill were such men in the history of their nations. The debate goes on as to whether they would have been great in any circumstances or whether it was the circumstances that made them great.

John the Baptist was a great man who served a pivotal role in the plan of God. Jesus said that John was the culmination of all the prophets and the law. He was the one coming in the spirit and power of Elijah (Luke 1:17) and the one of whom Malachi wrote in the closing verses of his great book. The angel said to his father, Zachariah, that John would be great in the eyes of the Lord and he would bring many to the Lord their God.

Yet, all people were not pleased with him or with Jesus. John was criticized for his austere life. Jesus was criticized for not being austere enough.

Godly people often endure criticism and ridicule from the mouths of the ungodly. If it is happening in your life, you are in good company—the company of John and Jesus.

PRAYER THOUGHTS: Sovereign God, help us to do Your will in the circumstances of our lives. Help us not to be discouraged by the ridicule of those who are not in tune with Your purposes in this world. Our trust is in You, O Father. Amen.

December 5

TO TELL THE TRUTH

SCRIPTURE: Matthew 14:1-12

VERSE FOR TODAY: The king was distressed, but because of his oaths and his dinner guests, he ordered that her request be granted and had John beheaded in the prison (Matthew 14:9, 10, *New International Version*).

HYMN FOR TODAY: "Once to Every Man and Nation"

A few years ago, a member of a political family was accidentally killed. He had separated from his wife and been embroiled in a sex scandal. An acquaintance commented that he hoped the world would not dwell on the man's private life but on his professional work. Such sentiments are frequent today—that we ought not to hold public people accountable for private behavior.

John the Baptist, however, would not have agreed. He went to prison and to his death because he told the truth about the sins of people in high places.

Herod Antipas, the powerful ruler of the region, ran away with his own brother's wife, Herodias. John condemned them in no uncertain terms. Herodias was furious and manipulated her daughter and Herod to bring about the death of the righteous prophet of God. Herod and his wife brought an end to John's life, but they did not bring an end to his influence.

Jesus spoke of the greatness of John (Matthew 11:11) and also the greatness of those in the kingdom of Heaven. Would that we of the kingdom were as resolute in our proclamation of truth as was John.

PRAYER THOUGHTS: God in Heaven, we sometimes are surprised when good people suffer and die. Yet, we know that it is because of their righteousness that many good people are persecuted. Help us to stand for truth and holy living in spite of what befalls us. Amen.

WORSHIP GOD

SCRIPTURE: Matthew 4:1-11

VERSE FOR TODAY: Jesus said to him, "Away from me, Satan! For it is written: 'Worship the Lord your God, and serve him only'" (Matthew 4:10, *New International Version*).

HYMN FOR TODAY: "Praise to the Lord, the Almighty"

Scripture tells us that Jesus was tempted in every way, as we are, but was without sin (Hebrews 4:15). He is, therefore, able to sympathize with our weaknesses. He knows what it is like to be tempted, so He is able to help those who are being tempted (Hebrews 2:18).

It is interesting to note that while the devil was certainly involved in the temptations of Jesus, it was the Holy Spirit that led Him into the desert to confront the evil one. Jesus' ministry began in combat with the distortions of the deceiver.

Satan's strategy bears close similarity to his approach to Eve in the Garden of Eden (Genesis 3:6). He sought to divert Jesus from unswerving obedience to God.

Jesus' answer, in every case, began with, "It is written. . . ."

Jesus knew Scripture and it served as His defense against the devil. Let's remember this as we deal with temptations.

Matthew's account of the temptations of Jesus closes with a note that the angels came to attend to Jesus. And Luke notes that the devil "left him until an opportune time" (Luke 4:13). Though defeated here, Satan continued to look for an opportune time to discredit Jesus.

PRAYER THOUGHTS: Dear heavenly Father, may we be strong in Your Word and may we be continually diligent in recognizing Satan's lies. We pray in the name of the victorious One, Jesus Christ. Amen.

December 7

COURAGE TO SPEAK THE TRUTH

SCRIPTURE: Matthew 4:12-17

VERSE FOR TODAY: From that time Jesus began to preach, and to say, Repent: for the kingdom of heaven is at hand (Matthew 4:17).

HYMN FOR TODAY: "The Old Rugged Cross"

"This is good," I said to friends as I read their manuscripts. I saw glaring grammatical errors and misspelled words, but I didn't tell them. I didn't want to hurt their feelings.

Then my daughter's friend gave me an article her father had written. "Be honest," he said to me earlier on the phone.

I cringed as my eyes scanned the page: incomplete sentences, misplaced punctuation, long paragraphs. What could I tell him? After a quick prayer, I returned it with a note saying, "You need to take a basic English course."

He called and said, "Thank you. My friends told me how good the article was, so I sent it out, but publishers sent it back. Thank you for speaking the truth."

The people of Jesus' time wanted a Messiah, but they didn't want someone to point out their sins. They wanted a Deliverer, but they didn't want someone to tell them to change their way of living. They wanted a Savior, but they didn't want to be told to take up a cross. They wanted a soft message, but Christ preached truth.

What message do we want to hear today?

PRAYER THOUGHTS: O God, You loved us enough to send us Your only Son. Help us to be willing to take up the cross and follow Him, no matter what price we have to pay. In the name of our Savior, Jesus Christ, we pray. Amen.

December 7-12. **Donna Clark Goodrich** is a freelance writer, proofreader, and seminar leader. She and her husband have three children and two grandchildren.

THE SECRET OF A SUCCESSFUL MINISTRY

SCRIPTURE: Luke 4:14-19

VERSE FOR TODAY: And when he had opened the book, he found the place where it was written, (Luke 4:17).

HYMN FOR TODAY: "Wonderful Words of Life"

"Swords up! Charge!"

I can still hear the rustling of the pages as the boys and girls in junior church raced to be the first to find the verse and stand to their feet to read it. I remember also how upset some of them were with me for using my father's Bible with tabs along the side.

Can you remember as a child memorizing verses, along with their "addresses?" It's important to teach our children the books of the Bible—through a song, a poem, or whatever method works. We need to be able to "give a reason for the hope that lies within us," and to know where to locate these truths in the Scriptures.

This is especially important for people in ministry. It's not enough to just know the verses, but can we "open the book" and find "the place where it [is] written"?

Jesus had an effective ministry. Why? Because He took time to open the book.

We're opening many books today: books by well-known Christian writers, books on the *New York Times* best seller list, the *TV Guide*. But how often are we opening The Book? Let's not neglect the Word of God.

PRAYER THOUGHTS: Father, so often we say we don't take the time to read the Bible. Yet we take time for television, crossword puzzles, or to play games. Help us to realize that we will have no power as Christians unless we read Your Word. Help us to know that there is no substitute for Your Word. In Jesus' name, we pray. Amen.

FROM PRAISE TO WRATH

SCRIPTURE: Luke 4:20-30

VERSE FOR TODAY: And all they in the synagogue, when they heard these things, were filled with wrath (Luke 4:28).

HYMN FOR TODAY: "Who Is on the Lord's Side?"

Today's text is an interesting passage of Scripture. In verse 15, when Jesus returned to Galilee, it says, "Everyone praised him" (*New International Version*). Later it says, "All spoke well of him" (v. 22, *New International Version*).

Jesus was a popular speaker. Crowds followed Him. So what events happened between verses 22 and 29 that they were filled with anger, that they "rose up, and thrust him out of the city . . . that they might cast him down"?

His message was safe up to this point. He was simply reading from Isaiah and sharing with His listeners what He felt His mission was to be. Nothing threatening in these words. Then His message changed. "I'm not even accepted in my home town," He told them, "because of your lack of faith."

What happened? He went from quoting the prophet to pointing out their sins. He went from sharing His mission to hitting them where they lived. He went from a safe message to acknowledging their need for change. And they became angry! Angry enough to want to take him out of the city and throw Him over a cliff.

How do we react today when we are faced with the truth? We must make a decision: What will we do with Jesus?

PRAYER THOUGHTS: O Father, it's so easy for us to listen when our minister tells us of God's love. Help us not to tune him out when he brings us God's message of repentance and shows us the life we should live. May we all "choose this day whom [we] will serve." We want to follow Jesus, our Lord. Amen.

JESUS CHANGES LIVES

SCRIPTURE: Luke 4:31-37

VERSE FOR TODAY: And they were all amazed, and spake among themselves, saying, What a word is this! for with authority and power he commandeth the unclean spirits, and they come out (Luke 4:36).

HYMN FOR TODAY: "Since Jesus Came into My Heart"

Not many of us have ever seen a demon-possessed person so we may not understand the full impact of this story. We know many, however, who have unclean spirits. Anyone who has not accepted Christ as Savior is saying in essence, "Let me alone. What have I to do with thee?"

For fifty years my friend's husband brought her to church and picked her up when the worship service was over. Eventually he began staying for the church service because "gas was too high to make two trips."

Later she wrote me, "Dale has stopped smoking. He says it costs too much, but I know it's because God is speaking to him." Each time she wrote, he had quit another habit, giving the cost as the reason.

At the age of eighty, he went forward one morning when the invitation was given and accepted Jesus as his Lord and Master. Later he said, "It's so nice to be on the inside instead of on the outside looking in." For years he had said to God, "Let me alone. What have I to do with thee?" Now the unclean spirit had been removed and he had been set free.

PRAYER THOUGHTS: "I stand amazed in the presence / Of Jesus the Nazarene, / And wonder how He could love me, / A sinner, condemned, unclean." (from *I Stand Amazed* by Charles H. Gabriel). Lord, we thank You today for Your love that sent You to the cross, and for freedom from our sin. Help us to give way to Jesus that we may become pure and clean in You. Amen.

THE GREATER HEALING

SCRIPTURE: Luke 4:38-44

VERSE FOR TODAY: At daybreak Jesus went out to a solitary place. The people were looking for him and when they came to where he was, they tried to keep him from leaving them. But he said, "I must preach . . . because that is why I was sent" (Luke 4:42, 43, *New International Version*).

HYMN FOR TODAY: "The Son of God Goes Forth to War"

We all want miracles. Sometimes a doctor will say, "I can't do anything here—only a miracle will change the situation." I saw a father carry his five-year-old daughter to the front of a church where we prayed for her because only a miracle could help her to walk. Before an operation, I went in for a final test. My doctor found a lump had disappeared, leading to a less extensive surgery than I had anticipated. And through a series of several people "accidentally" meeting one another, a medicine was found that healed my nephew of a life-threatening, painful disease he had endured for nineteen years.

We know Christ can heal today, even as He did in this passage in Luke. However, that was not the primary reason His Father sent Him to earth. Rather, it was to "preach the good news of the kingdom of God." When He healed the paralyzed man in Luke 5, He first said, "Friend, your sins are forgiven" (v. 20, *New International Version*), then in verse 24, He added, ". . . get up, take your mat and go home." He wanted to emphasize that healing of the soul is far more important than healing of the body.

PRAYER THOUGHTS: Dear Father, these people did not want Your Son to leave because of the miracles He performed on their physical bodies. But we know that only Christ can heal our broken and sinful hearts. Heal us today, Lord. Amen.

STRENGTH IN A LONELY PLACE

SCRIPTURE: Luke 5:12-16

VERSE FOR TODAY: Jesus often withdrew to lonely places and prayed (Luke 5:16, *New International Version*).

HYMN FOR TODAY: "Take Time to Be Holy"

It has been said, "A man can *give* nothing unless he first *receive* it, and no man can be successful in the ministry who does not constantly depend on God."

At the beginning of this chapter, Jesus was standing by the lake with the people crowding around Him. Later He healed the leper and the crowds followed Him all the more. He performed miracles, yet He was human and He became tired. He needed to withdraw into a secret place where He could receive a new touch from His Father.

God's people need to set aside some time each day to meet with God. A friend who has three teens scheduled one hour a day for them to be alone—no TV, no stereo, no homework—just to read, meditate or pray.

John Wesley is said to have prayed for an hour every morning, but if he knew he was going to have an unusually hectic day, he prayed for two hours.

What particular problem are you facing right now? Why not withdraw into a "lonely place" to pray. You'll find it won't be lonely very long because God will meet you there. There is strength in meeting God in prayer.

PRAYER THOUGHTS: Dear Father, we live in such a busy world. Our "to do" list contains too many items. We have many meetings to attend and church work to accomplish. Let the first thing on our list be time alone with You. Without that, we'll have no strength. Help us to find comfort in the quiet meetings with You. In the name of Jesus, we pray. Amen.

December 13

THE BEST POSSIBLE PEDIGREE

SCRIPTURE: Matthew 1:1-11

VERSE FOR TODAY: He predestined us to be adopted as his sons through Jesus Christ, in accordance with his pleasure and will (Ephesians 1:5, *New International Version*).

HYMN FOR TODAY "God of Our Fathers"

Many people enjoy studying their ancestors. Some libraries have genealogical sections, and there are professionals who will do your genealogy for you—for a fee. The study of genealogy has become a big business, but there is a real value there. Knowing who one's ancestors are gives one a sense of place in history. People easily identify with their ancestors once they are discovered, and people take a view of themselves based, at least partly, on who their ancestors are.

The Jews of Jesus' day identified themselves with Abraham in the same manner, and Jesus, too, was a descendant of Abraham.

But in Scripture, it is clear that Jesus saw God as His Father. His spiritual lineage took precedence over His physical background. His sense of identity was more with God than it was with Abraham, as He said in John 8:58, "before Abraham was born, I am" (*New International Version*).

We may get a certain pleasure from knowing who our ancestors are, but it is much more valuable to know who our spiritual father is. Because of Christ we are children of God.

PRAYER THOUGHTS: Heavenly Father, thank You for adopting us into Your family. We will praise Your name because our acceptance in Your sight is not based on what we have done, but on what Christ has done. Help us to realize that our true identity is in Christ. Amen.

December 13-19. **James Jordan** is a newspaper reporter from West Columbia, South Carolina.

THE PROMISE OF DELIVERANCE

SCRIPTURE: Matthew 1:12-17

VERSE FOR TODAY: Thus there were fourteen generations in all from Abraham to David, fourteen from David to the exile to Babylon, and fourteen from the exile to the Christ (Matthew 1:17, *New International Version*).

HYMN FOR TODAY: "Great Is Thy Faithfulness"

The exile to Babylon was a very bleak time in Israel's history. They were exiled because of repeated sin. They were taken from the promised land to which God had led them because they worshipped other gods. Even so, they were aware of the promise of God to bless all people through Abraham (Genesis 12:2). After the exile the people returned home, but they remained under the rule of foreigners.

Even through the darkest time, their hope was in the Messiah who would someday come. The genealogy attempts to show how Jesus came from Abraham and is the long awaited Messiah. The Jews thought the Messiah would deliver them from Roman oppression, but He came to deliver them from their original oppression, which was sin. The Jews did not recognize Jesus at least in part because they did not realize who their oppressor really was.

In our lives we may have very bleak times as well. It may be caused by sin, or by any number of things that can add difficulty to our lives.

We may seek relief from a physical situation, but God wants to relieve us of a deeper bondage—bondage to sin.

PRAYER THOUGHTS: Dear Father, help us recognize what our needs are and realize that our outward need may not be our deepest need. Thank You that as the divine healer, You know what our deepest needs are and You are able to meet them through Your Son, Jesus. Amen.

PRESSING ONWARD

SCRIPTURE: Matthew 1:18-25

VERSE FOR TODAY: But after he had considered this, an angel of the LORD appeared to him in a dream and said, "Joseph son of David, do not be afraid to take Mary home as your wife, because what is conceived in her is from the Holy Spirit" (Matthew 1:20, *New International Version*).

HYMN FOR TODAY: "We've a Story to Tell to the Nations"

In 1793, William Carey set sail from England to become a missionary to India. It was just a year after he wrote an essay that rocked the church, raising the question of why there were no missions to foreign lands at the time. At the time, many Christians believed the Great Commission had expired. Carey faced opposition even from the church, but because he believed God was behind his vision, he persisted. Carey expected great things from God, and attempted great things for God. The result of his essay and his attempts is the modern day mission movement.

Others followed in his footsteps, and today Christians from all over the earth are evangelizing and reaching the final people groups who have not yet heard the gospel message.

Carey was convinced of his vision and of what the Holy Spirit was up to in his life. He saw no fear of failure and would not be stopped by the world around him.

Today, with the power of the Holy Spirit, we can reach out to the lost whether they be around the world, at the workplace, or just down the street. We can overcome our fears by having faith in the One Who has sent us.

PRAYER THOUGHTS: O God, help us to not give in to fear or to be intimidated by the obstacles the world lays in our paths. Thank You that You are able to accomplish in our lives the things that You have given us the desire to attempt in Your name. Amen.

TICKET TO HEAVEN

SCRIPTURE: John 1:1-14

VERSE FOR TODAY: Yet to all who received him, to those who believed in his name, he gave the right to become children of God (John 1:12, *New International Version*).

HYMN FOR TODAY: "Blessed Assurance"

Reporters covering college or professional sporting events get special treatment to make the job as convenient and easy as possible. This should result in better reporting since obstacles are removed. Reporters have access to the game in ways that very few fans ever see. They may receive a parking pass which allows them to park near the press box. Food and drink are provided, as well as a large amount of statistical and background information. Once the game begins, statistics and other information are constantly being updated. After the game has been played, reporters go to the locker rooms to talk with athletes. Some stadiums even provide computers and telephones.

In a spiritual sense, we have this kind of access to God through Jesus. Because we believe in Jesus and have accepted Him as our personal Savior, we have total access to the Father. Not because of anything we have done, but because of what Jesus has done for us. He died on the cross, therefore we are given the privilege of being called children of God. An added bonus is that the Father, because of Christ, will give us everything we need to accomplish His purpose in our lives.

PRAYER THOUGHTS: Heavenly Father, we praise Your name for the things You have given us. Thank You for allowing us to be called Your children, which is something we could never have earned on our own if it were not for the sacrifice of Christ. Thank You for the assurance of salvation and a home with You in Heaven. In the name of Jesus. Amen.

BEING A WILLING VESSEL

SCRIPTURE: Luke 1:26-38

VERSE FOR TODAY: "I am the Lord's servant," Mary answered. "May it be to me as you have said." Then the angel left her (Luke 1:38, *New International Version*).

HYMN FOR TODAY: "Take My Life and Let it Be Consecrated"

There is no limit to what God can accomplish through us if we make ourselves available to Him.

Mary was perhaps just a normal young lady who believed in God. When the angel appeared to her she may or may not have realized the magnitude of what was happening. She simply trusted God and obeyed. Her response was a simple, "may it be so." She may have realized the dangers and obstacles, but her eyes were on God, and she must have had faith that God could handle whatever situation arose. Her top priority was obeying the true and living God.

Even in Mary's obedience, there is no indication that she realized what all would happen as a result. She probably did not realize that her son, Jesus, would be the most influential person this world has ever known.

It could perhaps be the same with us. We may not realize what God is doing in our lives, or the significance of things that happen. But if we have faith, and keep our eyes on God and not on the obstacles or opposition, we may just surprise ourselves at what is accomplished as we make ourselves available to God.

PRAYER THOUGHTS: Dear heavenly Father, please forgive us for seeing problems and not realizing they are opportunities for You to do great things through us. Father, thank You for loving us and using us to accomplish Your purposes. Help us to be faithful to the calling you have given us. Amen.

EVERYBODY NEEDS SOMEBODY SOMETIME

SCRIPTURE: Luke 1:39-45

VERSE FOR TODAY: As soon as the sound of your greeting reached my ears, the baby in my womb leaped for joy (Luke 1:44, *New International Version*).

HYMN FOR TODAY: "Blest Be the Tie"

Everyone has felt discouragement at one time or another. When the weight or pressure seems too much, we may want to give in to despair. However, if we get encouragement from a trusted friend, we regain our strength and are better able to stand the problems we face. Everyone needs both to have a friend they can count on, and to be a friend that someone else can count on for encouragement.

As an unmarried, though engaged, young woman, Mary was probably the scandal of her small community of Nazareth. Even though she has seen the angel and heard the message, she was also probably hearing the whispers as she walked in the market or around her community. This would be enough to weigh down even the strongest soul, and at that time she needed someone to lean on.

She packed her bags and fled to Elizabeth, a trusted friend, who was a great encouragement to her. After Elizabeth's encouragement, Mary sang a wonderful song in worship to God. Obviously her soul was lifted by Elizabeth.

In our lives we need such friends, and need to be such friends to others, so we can share our burdens with each other.

PRAYER THOUGHTS: Holy Father, we thank You that You have created other people that we can lean on in time of need. Thank You for giving us friends we can count on, and allow us to be a friend to someone when they need a friend to lean upon. Show us how to be a better friend to someone today. In the name of Jesus. Amen.

MARY'S SONG

SCRIPTURE: Luke 1:46-56

VERSE FOR TODAY: His name shall be called Wonderful, Counselor, The mighty God, The everlasting Father, The Prince of Peace (Isaiah 9:6).

HYMN FOR TODAY: "There's a Song in the Air"

In her humility, Mary's heart exploded in praise. Her words echoed language from the Old Testament prayers of praise.

Mary's song, the *Magnificat*, proclaimed words of hope for the hopeless. God in His mercy "scattered the proud," "put down the mighty," "exalted the lowly," "filled the hungry," and "sent the rich away empty."

Her exaltation defined her worship: "Holy is His name," "His mercy is on those who fear Him," "He has shown strength," "He has helped Israel," and "in mercy He spoke to our fathers."

And Mary's heart spilled over in personal gratitude: "My soul magnifies the Lord," "My spirit rejoices in Him," "He has regarded my lowly state," "All generations will call me blessed," and "He has done great things for me." How wonderful it must have been for Mary to be used by her Creator!

George Frederick Handel composed the oratorio, *Messiah*, in 24 days. A servant came in while he was writing the "Hallelujah Chorus" and found the composer weeping. When he could speak, he told the servant, "I think I did see all Heaven before me and the great God himself."

PRAYER THOUGHTS: Our Father, we praise and worship You. Fill our hearts with awe and gratitude for Your great work of creation and redemption. In Jesus' name, amen.

December 19. **Dorothy Snyder** lives with her husband, Wilbert, in Boulder, Colorado.

NO MISTAKE

SCRIPTURE: Luke 2:1-7

VERSE FOR TODAY: "For my thoughts are not your thoughts, neither are your ways my ways" declares the LORD (Isaiah 55:8, *New International Version*).

HYMN FOR TODAY: "O Little Town of Bethlehem"

When was the last time something happened to you that made little or no sense? Life is full of circumstances and events that leave us confused and perplexed. We ask ourselves, and God, "Why?"

Mary and Joseph must have wondered why God would have them make the rugged journey to Bethlehem right at the very time when the baby was to be born. From a common sense standpoint, it would be very uncomfortable and possibly dangerous for Mary and for the baby. When Mary and Joseph arrived in Bethlehem and found no room for them at the inn, I wonder if they again asked, "Why?" Surely, if this was God's plan, then He would see that everything was in place for Jesus' birth, including a room!

Life is full of events that seem to make no sense to us. Jobs are lost. People become ill. Loved ones die.

Jesus came into this world, not as we would have expected, but just as God planned. He lived a life guided, not by His common sense, but by His Father. God has a plan for us, too. When our circumstances don't make sense, let us not become discouraged. God knows what He is doing! Let's trust Him!

PRAYER THOUGHTS: Dear Father, life often seems unfair. Please help us to look only to You for our answers. In Jesus' name. Amen.

December 20-25. **Susan Petropolus** is a wife, mother, and freelance writer who serves her home congregation in Cranberry Township, Pennsylvania, as financial assistant.

December 21

PEACE AT WORK

SCRIPTURE: Luke 2:8-20

VERSE FOR TODAY: There were shepherds living out in the fields nearby, keeping watch over their flocks at night (Luke 2:8, *New International Version*).

HYMN FOR TODAY: "While Shepherds Watched Their Flocks"

The end of the year is looming and the work at the office is staggering. In addition to the everyday chores, there are presents to wrap, decorations to hang, and the inevitable last minute shopping. Life is busy all year long, but it is busier than ever at Christmas!

Did you ever think that the shepherds were also busy men? Even late at night, they were still on the job. Night was the most dangerous time for the sheep. The shepherds stood guard to watch for thieves, wolves, or other predators as well as the occasional sheep who might wander away. When the angels came to proclaim the news of Christ's birth, the shepherds were keeping watch of their flocks. They were working. The angels did not choose to appear to a group at the synagogue or the Pharisees during prayer. The good news broke into the normal workday of common shepherds.

Jesus longs to break into our everyday lives, just as He did the shepherds. Yet often we leave very little room in our hectic schedule for Jesus. We are stressed and hurried and often, anything but peaceful. Just as the angels declared to the shepherds, "A Savior has been born to you," Jesus came to bring peace into our lives. Will we make room for Him today?

PRAYER THOUGHTS: Almighty heavenly Father, forgive us for allowing busyness to rule our lives. Give us peace and help us to know You, really know You. We come before You this day in the name of our Savior, Jesus, our Lord and Friend. Amen.

REFLECTED GLORY

SCRIPTURE: Luke 2:21-27

VERSE FOR TODAY: "Do not think that I have come to abolish the Law or the Prophets; I have not come to abolish them but to fulfill them" (Matthew 5:17, *New International Version*).

HYMN FOR TODAY: "O Come, O Come, Emmanuel"

Have you ever caught a glimpse of yourself in the mirror and been surprised at what you saw? A stray hair, an ugly blemish, or extra pounds that can quickly dispel any illusions we might have about the way we look. Whether we like it or not, our reflection in the mirror is the truth about our external appearance.

God gave His people a mirror to show them how they look in relation to a Holy God. He calls it His Law. The requirements are precise. No matter how hard we try, by ourselves we will never be able to meet the requirements and reflect perfect holiness. Just as a mirror reflects our physical appearance, God's Law shows us our sin. For that very reason, God sent mankind a gift that only He could give. Only Jesus, the Son of God, can fulfill all the Law's requirements. Only He can stand before the mirror of God's holiness and reflect that holiness, perfectly! Only Jesus!

Are there areas in your life where you do not feel fulfilled? Are there places that do not reflect the Savior? Remember that our Savior came to fulfill all things. He came to fulfill you and me. Let's ask Him for His reflection in our lives today.

PRAYER THOUGHTS: Heavenly Father, thank You for sending Jesus to stand in our place in Your mirror of holiness. Please help us to reflect His holiness as we live our lives today. Give to us a burning desire to live godly lives. In Jesus' holy name we pray. Amen.

WHAT ARE YOU EXPECTING?

SCRIPTURE: Luke 2:28-38

VERSE FOR TODAY: "Therefore keep watch, because you do not know on what day your Lord will come" (Matthew 24:42, *New International Version*).

HYMN FOR TODAY: "Come, Thou Long Expected Jesus"

Have you ever totally missed an opportunity, just because you weren't paying attention? Life is full of opportunities to help others, to share our faith, to offer encouragement, or to speak a kind word. We often miss chances to touch another life because we are too busy or are easily distracted.

What if Simeon and Anna had not been at the temple when Mary and Joseph brought Jesus to be consecrated? They would have missed the most important opportunity of their lives. What if Simeon had business or family matters to attend? Suppose Anna had stayed home to clean or to prepare dinner. We have to assume that they had the same everyday responsibilities as we do. However, Simeon and Anna were looking for something out of the ordinary. They were looking for Someone who is much more important than any meal or deal or appointment. Simeon and Anna were looking for Jesus.

Our lives today are busy and distracted. We have many things to do and little time in which to do them. Could it be that today is the time to slow down and begin to pay attention? Jesus is coming again. Let's not miss any more opportunities. Let's not miss Jesus!

PRAYER THOUGHTS: Dear heavenly Father, help us to see every encounter of life as an opportunity to reflect Your love. Help us to see the places in our lives where we need to pay more attention. Help us to reflect on Your Word. Let us reflect Your love to those around us. In the name of Jesus, we pray. Amen.

THE GUIDING LIGHT

SCRIPTURE: Matthew 2:1-6

VERSE FOR TODAY: "Where is the one who has been born king of the Jews? We saw his star in the east and have come to worship him" (Matthew 2:2, *New International Version*).

HYMN FOR TODAY: "We Three Kings of Orient Are"

The sunlight was fading and my husband had no idea which direction he should go. He had wandered through the woods for most of the day, and now he was lost. Night came and with it the stars. The North star shone brightly. By following its lead, my husband was able to find his way to a road and back to the hunting camp.

It is easy to become lost. One wrong turn or missed intersection can cause us to veer far from our intended route. Life can often feel like an uncharted forest. It looms around us and we aren't sure which way to turn. We are bombarded with ideas and opinions, with theories and beliefs. We wonder which way we should go, whom should we believe. Without a guide, it is very easy to get lost.

From the very beginning, man has needed a guide. Today, Jesus gives us a light to follow. Just as the Magi followed the star to find Him, He wants to be our star. He wants to lead us through the maze of opinions, ideas and doctrines thrown at us every day. Wise men have always followed Jesus. Wise men always will!

PRAYER THOUGHTS: Almighty Heavenly Father, thank You for Your guidance in our lives. Please forgive us for not always watching You. Help us to keep Your light ever before us as we walk Your path. On this Christmas eve, let us, as the wise men from the east, follow the star that leads us to the Savior of the world, Jesus Christ. In His holy name, we pray. Amen.

December 25

GOD'S PERFECT GIFT

SCRIPTURE: Matthew 2:7-1 2

VERSE FOR TODAY: On coming to the house, they saw the child with his mother Mary, and they bowed down and worshiped him. Then they opened their treasures and presented him with gifts of gold and of incense and of myrrh (Matthew 2:11, *New International Version*).

HYMN FOR TODAY: "Joy to the World!"

It was just before Christmas and the excitement was almost unbearable. All the eight-year-olds in my second grade class anxiously waited for the Christmas gift exchange at my school. As I watched, each child opened a gift chosen by one of their classmates. Just when I was sure that I was forgotten, the teacher walked over to my desk and placed a beautifully wrapped box in front of me. I hurriedly opened it, expecting a game, a puzzle or a doll just as the other children had received. Instead, there before me sat a lovely hand painted china cup and saucer. It was beautiful, but to my eight-year-old eyes, it was totally useless. I'm sure my disappointment showed.

I have not totally outgrown that tendency to be disappointed when I don't receive just what I want. Sometimes I feel useless and unimportant because I am not gifted in the ways I would like to be.

The gifts the wise men brought to the Christ Child were not useful for a baby; they were gifts useful for a king. Do you need a new perspective on your gifts? Give them to Jesus. Forget yourself and worship Him!

PRAYER THOUGHTS: Precious heavenly Father, how good You have been to us. Thank You for the gifts, talents, and abilities You have given to us. Help us to use them to honor You. Let us not think too highly of ourselves, but let us worship the perfect gift to all mankind, Jesus, our Lord and Savior. He alone is the perfect gift. Amen.

GOD'S PLAN UNFOLDS

SCRIPTURE: Matthew 2:13-18

VERSE FOR TODAY: And so was fulfilled what the Lord had said through the prophet: "Out of Egypt I called my son" (Matthew 2:15, *New International Version*).

HYMN FOR TODAY: "God Will Take Care of You"

Sometimes, with the emphasis on the New Testament, Christians miss the connections between the Old Testament and the New Testament. Writing with a Jewish audience in mind, Matthew emphasized that God was the author of both testaments. God spoke through the prophet, Hosea, Matthew declared. While Hosea's reference was primarily God's calling of the children of Israel out of the bondage of Egypt (Hosea 11:1), Matthew saw in it a parallel with the life of Jesus.

God was very much involved in these first years of Jesus' life. The angel of the Lord appeared in a dream to Joseph, warning him to escape into Egypt for the protection of his small child. And it was an angel of the Lord that told Joseph when it was time to return to his own land.

Just as God led the people of Israel into and from the land of Egypt with His providential care, He led Jesus and Mary and Joseph into and out of that fabled land.

Scripture sketches only briefly what Mary and Joseph experienced during Jesus' early years, but it is very evident that the baby in their arms changed their lives. And He has changed the lives of countless people since.

PRAYER THOUGHTS: Our Father, we thank You for Your providential care. We know that You protect those who trust in You. Amen.

December 26. **Dr. Ward Patterson** is a Professor Cincinnati Bible College in Cincinnati, Ohio.

December 27

JESUS' INVITATION: FOLLOW ME

SCRIPTURE: Matthew 4:18-22

VERSE FOR TODAY: Then He said to them, "Follow Me, and I will make you fishers of men" (Matthew 4:19, *The New King James Version*).

HYMN FOR TODAY: "He Leadeth Me, O Blessed Thought"

What was it about this Man who could stroll along the lake shore and speak words of such magnetism and authority that four fisherman "immediately left their nets and followed Him?" (Matthew 4:20, *New King James Version*).

Jesus doubtless recognized the strength, training, and perseverance that molded these successful fishermen. But the four—Andrew, Peter, James, and John—were distinct individuals, not the bravest, perhaps, but they seemed willing to learn and change. Andrew was homespun and supportive; Peter was impulsive and headstrong. James and John were ambitious and competitive—Sons of Thunder.

The rabbis chose potential scholars for training, but Jesus called four trainees for discipleship; individuals who could learn from association with their Master.

Jesus still needs followers. His "Follow Me" continues to be a test of trust, loyalty, and commitment. If He should call us specifically to follow Him, would we be able to make a clear-cut decision?

PRAYER THOUGHTS: Our Father God, we love to read about how You chose certain people to be Your disciples. And what's even more interesting is how You trained them to teach other people about You and Your message of salvation. Will You use me? Teach me. In Jesus' name, amen.

December 27-31. **Dorothy Snyder** lives with her husband, Wilbert, in Boulder, Colorado, where she writes an inspirational column, *Reflections*, for the church newsletter.

MATTHEW'S INVITATION: CELEBRATE!

SCRIPTURE: Matthew 9:9-13

VERSE FOR TODAY: Levi made him a great feast in his own house: and there was a great company of publicans and of others that sat down with them (Luke 5:29).

HYMN FOR TODAY: "Where He Leads Me"

Matthew (Levi) wasn't a very popular person with his townspeople. He was a tax collector, being paid by a foreign government.

When Jesus passed by and said, "'Follow me" (Luke 5:27), Matthew arose and followed Him.

There was nothing secretive about his great decision. He rounded up his friends, tax collectors, and sinners and invited Jesus to the party.

This is "friendship evangelism." Entry to other people enlarges the opportunity to meet Jesus. He still hunts out the sinners. But He also appeals to the outcasts, the down-casts, and those whose potential has been overlooked.

The great sculptor, Michelangelo, also specialized in rejects. In his youth he was too poor to buy marble for his sculpting. But picking his way among the discarded stones, he found the marble from which he carved the renowned *Pieta*, which depicts Mary enfolding Jesus as He was taken from the cross.

The eye of the Master still discerns the potential of people who search for life with meaning. Aren't we happy that He chose Matthew, the tax collector who was capable of recording his first-hand experiences of his changed life with Him after he responded to Jesus', "Follow Me?"

PRAYER THOUGHTS: Thank You, heavenly Father, that You allow us to know Your Son, Jesus. Help us this day to focus on the salvation that You give. Let us celebrate. In the name of our Savior we pray. Amen.

...TION FOR CHOOSING THE TWELVE

...E: Matthew 10:1-4

...RSES FOR TODAY: And it came to pass in those days, that he went out into a mountain to pray, and continued all night in prayer to God. And when it was day, he called unto him his disciples (Luke 6:12, 13).

HYMN FOR TODAY: "Jesus Calls Us"

After spending the night alone on the mountain, praying, Jesus called His followers to Him and chose twelve to be His disciples. What a wonderful way to prepare for such an important decision!

Choosing twelve disciples reminds us of the Old Testament twelve tribes of Israel. But this was to be a new covenant, and these men were to help make God's message permanent in world history.

Prefaced by prayer which is subject to God's will, Jesus chose twelve men of radical differences, modest means, and limited schooling to come and learn.

Living with Jesus for three years, they discovered how to love God with the whole person and also how to love their neighbors. He taught them by parables—using simple earthly stories with heavenly meanings. But He didn't limit His teaching to words only. Jesus showed them that God extends His love to all—children, the poor, the sick, the needy, and society's discards.

The chosen twelve wondered about His power to heal the sick, to still the waves, and cast out demons. They also noticed He spent time alone with His heavenly Father. So they asked Him to teach them to pray. And He did.

PRAYER THOUGHTS: Our Father in Heaven, we love to read of Your relationship with Your Son, Jesus, and His disciples. Help us always to remember that we can talk to You in prayer. In Jesus' name, amen.